Postmodernism and Japan

**Post-Contemporary
Interventions**

SERIES EDITORS:
STANLEY FISH AND
FREDRIC JAMESON

Postmodernism and Japan

**Edited by
Masao Miyoshi
and H. D. Harootunian**

Duke University Press
Durham and London

© 1989 Duke University Press
All rights reserved
Printed in the United States of America
on acid-free paper ∞
Second printing, 1991
Library of Congress Cataloging-in-Publication
Data appear on the last printed page of this book.

The majority of this text was originally
published in Japanese in *Gendai shiso: revue de
la pénsee d'aujourd'hui*, Volume 15, December
1987 by Seitosha Publishing as "Problems of
Postmodernity." It was subsequently published
in English as Volume 87, Number 3 (Summer
1988) of *The South Atlantic Quarterly*. Articles
by Isozaki Arata and Ōe Kenzaburō, as well as
the index, have been added.

Contents

**Masao Miyoshi and
H. D. Harootunian**

Introduction

Postmodernism is bound to be retrospective. By placing itself after an event, it punctuates its past. Interiority, subject/object binarism, centrality, universalism, logocentricity, masculine neutrality—all such hegemonic traits that have ranged over the whole paradigm of the Enlightenment are bracketed. The West—for postmodernism is a Western event—thus sees a fracture which gapes wide as if unbridgeable. Playfulness, gaming, spectacle, tentativeness, alterity, reproduction, and pastiche are offered to guide the new age. Such terms are intent on dispersal, maintaining a sensitive aversion for any form of concentration. But denial is always contaminated by affirmation. Serious playfulness is no longer playful; the Other remains the Other only when looked at from the opposite side of the boundary; inconclusiveness is conclusive after all, once it becomes an identifiable consciousness. Likewise, as postmodernism empties itself of historicity, it is haunted by the memory of the erased past and anxious about the unarrived future. The present is as elusive as ever, and in the face of it looms the obtrusively substantial mirage of modernity.

The most problematized of all the absences in postmodernism is a relation with politics. As the agent of action is dispersed, so is the possibility of voluntary intervention, hence politics; postmodernism of course knows that the absence of politics is political, and (sometimes) fears the consequences of aloofness. The black hole that is formed by the rejection of modernism is also apt to obliterate the trace of historical Western expansionism that was at least cofunctional, if not instrumental, in producing epistemological hegemonism. Thus a paradox: as postmodernism seeks to remedy the modernist error of Western, male, bourgeois domination, it simultaneously vacates the ground on which alone the contours of modernism can be clearly seen. Furthermore, colonialism and imperialism are ongoing enterprises, and in distinguishing late post-industrial capitalism from earlier liberal capitalism and by tolerating the former while condemning the latter, postmodernism ends up by consenting to the first world economic domination that persists in exploiting the wretched of the earth.

By now everyone knows that at the end of the nineteenth century over 80 percent of the world was ruled or dominated by the Western powers. Fewer understand, however, how abruptly and completely the history and geography of the dominated were fissured by their first encounter with the West. National—or, more usually, regional —histories and geographies had to be broken off at the contact, and the stories of their whole past had to be retold in the new light of the "world" (i.e., Western) context. It is as if the pre-contact time had been wrenched off and replaced by an unfamiliar temporal system that would efficiently dissolve the residual old. Peoples were also displaced from their sundry geographic centralities to the peripheral positions assigned by the Western metropolis: thus appellations like the Middle East and the Far East—the fragmentation of regions into colonies/nation-states. New history and new geography combined to produce the magical peripheries of the primitive, in which the natives were enticed to participate as their proper residents. Always and everywhere the West is at the highest in evolution, at the normative center, and is seen as the newest in development and the oldest in tradition. Thus the West has been the utopian fulfillment, from which the non-Westerners are scrupulously excluded. No non-Western region is free from this exercise in rewriting, and, more importantly, no non-Western nation has yet to recover from the shock of the contact with the West even in these twilight years of the twentieth century: certainly not Japan, a third world copycat, the all-time economic wonderchild, that now threatens to become the hegemon of the twenty-first century.

Enter Japan and postmodernism.

Much of the news about Japan has been ominous of late. In the United States and Europe, we see an increasing number of reports on Japan's "agenda for world domination," which, according to a recent book by Michael Montgomery, have survived intact since the imperialist prewar years. Japan doesn't buy, and the Western manufacturers and politicians are outraged; Japan buys, and the media buzz loudly about the nouveau riche stealing off the treasures of the West. The *Wall Street Journal* prints an article about the American Japanologists turning into Japan-apologists bought off by the munificence of Japan-related foundations; William Safire of the *New York Times* complains about the discomforts of being in Tokyo, a city of knocked-down capitalism. The Japanese tourists are despised wherever they go for indecorous groupiness, although their spending is eagerly sought after. The bashing goes on unabated as if the outcry of the Yellow Peril a few generations ago was justifiable after all.

There might be some truth in some of this, but the overall perspective of such hocus-pocus is that of the same old Western hegemonism. It looks far more legitimate this time around, simply because the threat of Japan's economic power is now perceived to be real. Against such fearful self-projections, however, there is other news from Japan that indeed raises rather serious questions concerning the condition of Japanese society.

As the world marvels at Japan's dramatic growth in technology and production, its political and intellectual situations display many signs of stress and strain. Most educated Japanese, however, seem to be quite unconcerned with this development. There are extremely few oppositionists, and those few are scarcely heard anymore. The political intellectual arena itself, which was once—for generations before and after the Pacific War—central to the country's cultural vigor, has been disturbingly quiet and vacant. Academia and journalism have remained uninvolved for years in issues that are urgent to many outside of Japan: Japan's role in the East-West confrontation; the gradual return of nationalism and Japanism; Japan's contributions to the third world, and the lack thereof; racism, emperorism, consumerism, stupefying anti-intellectualism, governmental depoliticization of culture, institutional defanging of criticism, diffusing of environmental programs, tattering of information and analysis, unmistakable tryouts in rewriting world history and geography with the first world *and* Japan as the joint master-narrators. Japan, in short, is feeling its own economic muscles and seems complacent at present, readying for its future move.

The talk of premodernism, modernism, non-modernism, and antimodernism has been going on in Japan ever since the mid-nineteenth century. Like all the other non-Western nations for which the encounter with the West has been disastrous and traumatic, Japan had to face up to the chronopolitical condition as an urgent national thematic. Of course, there never was a unanimity, but the constant practice of locating the insular society on the international map of progress has at least provided it with a scheme of disagreements. They knew the extremes of ultranationalism and Westernizationism, and they were well acquainted with all the problematics of modernism. Many traits of postmodernism described by Lyotard, Baudrillard, Deleuze, and Guattari among others, have been at least glimpsed in Japan, though not certainly in the *post*modern terms. When the news of Habermas-Lyotard controversy traveled to Japan, in short, there had already been a trained audience there who felt sufficiently *déjà vu* about the whole range of opinions. It is this near colonial encounter with the West that had offered to the Japanese a privileged position distant enough from modernism but close enough to it to be in the know.

Japan's economy plays an indispensable role in shaping the discourse. Whether its productive mode is late-stage capitalist or premodern capitalist, the group dynamics of Japanese social and economic formation has obviously worked to enable a highly efficient system to emerge. Of a sudden, a chronopolitical situation looks insignificant to them in view of such an enormously conspicuous success: who cares whether it is *pre*modern or *post*modern, as long as people are well-fed, clothed, healthy, thoroughly socialized and strategically informed? Even critical consciousness appears immaterial in their view before such a visible and tangible success. Thus the nation's critical and intellectual space is now painlessly absorbed into its productive space, calming the discontented and silencing all the dissenters.

The clue to Japan's success in trade and exchange may not be found in a miracle at all. One readily recalls its long and repeated exposures to the superior outside civilizations before its encounter with the West: first Korea, then China and India, and then in the sixteenth century Portugal and Spain. Japan had opened and closed its ports to such external forces often enough to know how to connect its own temporality with different axes of time, progress, and power. Indeed Japan may never gain sufficient confidence to develop interiority and autonomy, to become the mover of its own fate, so far remaining decisive only in relation to the other more self-determined subjectivities. Japan's history is suffused with the sense of the dominant Other and its own marginality. And it has been forced to rewrite its history repeatedly. In the process it has somehow managed to represent itself, however imperfectly, to its own people in its own terms so that they might survive one more encounter. In a sense, the twentieth century's global integration has shown to Japan the culminating limits for accommodations, beyond which it needed to go no further. It may not have replicated modernism—despite the advice from enlightened historians such as Maruyama Masao. In the meantime, however, the West is becoming acutely aware of the shortcomings of modernity. And in this self-diagnosis of the West, Japan may have at last found its ghostly double.

Still, to confuse Japan's non-modernity with the West's "postmodernism" is perhaps a serious error. The two versions are differently foregrounded in history. Further, Japan's identification of itself with the first world might be a repeat performance of the archetypal colonial gesture, lusting after the coveted membership in the utopian sanctuary. Japan has lived through this process before in the mid-nineteenth century. Does it need to repeat it? Such a posture will result in justifiable suspicion and resentment in the rest of Asia. In this respect, the multivalence and uncertainty of postmodern gaming will ill serve Japan's equanimity. All the gibberish gushing from advertising copywriters and store designers (heroized appropriately enough in the crazed world of Tokyo consumerism) and their supposed apologists, such as Kurimoto Shinichiro or Tanaka Yasuo, is too tedious to be taken straight—except as a reminder that Japan's "postmodernism" seems indeed to totter at the very brink of lunacy and dissolving intelligence. Are we to follow/misread Deleuze and Guattari's prescription to a literal end?

Despite the doubts surrounding the "authenticity" of Japan's putative postmodernity, it should come as no surprise that the most successful latecomer to economic and social transformation, which literally incorporated the aporias of modernity as a condition for transformation, now signifies a "scene" or "space" that Lyotard has described as "that which in the modern poses the unpresentable in the presentation itself . . . that which is concerned with new presentations, not purely for the pleasure of it, but the better to insist that the unpresentable exists." Whether or not the several papers presented in this collection attest to the installation of Lyotard's vision in contemporary Japan and adequately account for and describe the performative dimensions of consumer culture, as described by Norma Field's reading of the novel, *Somehow, Crystal*, is, perhaps, less important than that they recognize the generally held conviction that Japan offers the occasion, in a way that may very well resist representation and narrativization, to examine the scene of this new imaginary.

   In a certain sense, the decision to confront the scene of Japan's postmodernity represents a delayed reaction to the opportunity provided three decades ago by Alexandre Kojève in a footnote to the revised edition of his *Introduction to the Reading of Hegel*, delivered first as a series of lectures in France between 1933 and 1939 at the Ecole des Hautes Etudes. Kojève observed after a trip to Japan (1959) that while Hegel's *Phenomenology of Spirit* had in fact revealed the fundamental structures of life that make history possible, Japan seemed to offer the spectacle of a society that had for nearly three centuries "experienced life at the 'end of History.' " To live in the time of post-history—a condition Kojève believed to be as universal as the structure of desire, recognition, and action (work) that propelled history everywhere—meant acknowledging the abdication of philosophy's claim to offer new truths about the human condition. "No doubt," he wrote, "there were no longer in Japan any Religion, Morals or Politics in the 'European' or 'historical' sense of the word. But *Snobbery* in its pure form created disciplines negating the 'natural' or 'animal' given which in effectiveness far surpassed those that arose, in Japan or elsewhere, from 'historical' Action, that is, from the warlike and revolutionary Fights or from forced Work." In a forecast currently shared by Japanese and foreign admirers of Japan's postmodernity, especially those who see the scene as a more complete and perfected version of the model of modernization, Kojève announced that the interaction between the West and Japan, inaugurated first by the former in the form of imperial expansion, will result not in a "vulgarization" of the Japanese but rather in the "Japanization" of the West. The importance of this observation lies in Kojève's willingness to imagine a universal condition of post-historical society reached first and most successfully by the Japanese. Yet he could be reassured, as are the epigoni who celebrate Japan as Number One, that the social order Japanese have evolved—the new age of culture heralded by the Japanese bureaucracy—is not only a universal condition to be followed by all societies but, more importantly, merely the last stage of a social model envisaged first by the modern West. Here, perhaps, is an "inversion" of the aborted project of modernity conceptualized by Takeuchi Yoshimi, as Naoki Sakai proposes, and the real meaning of his dim estimate announcing that "Japan is nothing." For in this sense, Japanese society is simply a more complete version of the Western model which critics like Takeuchi feared would sustain the role played by Japan and the Orient as "suppliers" of recognition so necessary for Western identity.

Echoes of Kojève's conception of Japan's post-historic incarnation are audible throughout all of those efforts which signify the elimination of guarantees to secure stable meaning and which, therefore, compensate for the loss of grounding by appealing to the indeterminate, the undecidable, and the unmasking of all master codes and narratives as fictions seeking to present what is invariably unrepresentable. To think beyond what is thinkable, and to live in a scene that must resist being represented, may qualify as the sign of the sublime but it also risks inviting the most dangerous forms of political inaction and abdicating even the possibility of resistance.

A number of the papers in this collection explore the status of resistance in the critique of modernity and its inevitable disappearance in the postmodern scene. Tetsuo Najita raises the question that a culture controlled by technology not only removes the principles of certainty that had guided people to embark upon meaningful and purposive political action but will result in the "possibility of mechanical reproduction, or the continuous reconstitution of things as they are, only more or less." Alan Wolfe discerns in suicide the ultimate form of resistance still capable of escaping reification and co-optation. Marilyn Ivy, in her discussion of how critical texts in Japan are consumed by an insatiable consumer public the moment they are produced, entertains the possibility claimed by postmodern spokesmen like Yoshimoto Takaaki that consumption might be employed as a form of critical intervention, that deconstruction, even in late capitalist commodity cultures like Japan, might still reveal "new critical extremes in deconstructing hegemonic modernism—what Hal Foster has called a 'postmodernism of resistance.'" Yet Norma Field's reading of the consumerist novel about consumption, *Somehow, Crystal*, demonstrates that even the language used to discuss exchange and consumption forecloses the possibility of resistance in favor of passive acceptance. Ivy and Brett de Bary both show that deconstructionist texts of writers like Karatani Kōjin and Asada Akira, the most serious voices among postmodernist critics in Japan, risk being reduced to exceptionalist dimensions precisely because they will be consumed by Japanese consumers and thereby forfeit whatever critical possibility they may have promised. And Karatani himself concedes that his criticism of modern literature (presented by de Bary in her reading of Karatani's *Kindai bungaku no kigen*), paralleling the work of younger writers such as Nakagami Kenji and Shimada Masahiko who seek to fashion new possibilities for literature, lost its "subversiveness" as "it spread and merged with the popular discourse of a full-blown consumer discourse"—that is, an endless consumption of literary and critical artifacts. "It may be said," Karatani contends, "that the paradise of idiots has been revived, so to speak."

This "paradise of idiots" is the precinct of all of those critics of modernity in Japan who, now occupying the site of an entirely new space (what Karatani calls a "new phase of capitalism" and others the "scene of the postmodern"), continue to aim their critique against modernity on the mistaken belief that they have, like their predecessors before the war, overcome the modern. But these critics invariably recuperate and re-present the views of conservative nationalists to deliberately affirm the claims of the status quo, which must be read in the figure of Japan as Number One. What concerns Karatani most, as it did Takeuchi, is the contemporary Japanese penchant for eliminating the Other altogether and suppressing all signs of the heterogeneous or different for a new "science of the same," called "Discussions on Being Japanese" (*Nihonjinron*). Yet he quickly warns against a formal wordplay that privileges difference over identity within the terms of a philosophic discourse that avoids considering genuine exteriority or otherness which remains beyond the formal reading of the text. By referring to an otherness beyond the immediate boundaries of discourse, Karatani returns to the promise of the modern discourse on the social which marked the Japanese effort to steer a course between the "poetry of the past" and the "poetry of the future." One practitioner who might fit such specifications is Isozaki Arata who in "Of City, Nation, and Style" retraces the problematics posed by the Tsukuba Science City project. In so doing, he redefines the ideological terms and architectural expectations that have been drastically revised as a result of the new economic and political conditions of Japanese society.

The postmodern "scene" that emerges in these essays is not to be grasped simply as a permanent refusal which escapes received narrative representations only by narrativizing what Jean Baudrillard called the "implosion of meaning" or, worse, by envisioning a new division of opposites. Unfortunately, this is precisely the way it has been understood by many Japanese and foreign interpreters who have managed to recuperate, in the process, the very terms of cultural exceptionalism (*Nihonjinron*) which Japanese have always appealed to as a form of defensive reaction to distinguish Japan from the West, and as the surest protection from the desire of the Other. Yet this response, a consequence of Japan's latecomer experience, was an effort to make Japan appear as something more than a pale double of the Western ratio, a lack that needed to be filled, made complete somehow. What this reflex produced was a conception of Japan as a signified, whose uniqueness was fixed in an irreducible essence that was unchanging and unaffected by history, rather than as a signifier capable of attaching itself to a plurality of possible meanings. It is this sense of a Japan as signified, unique and different from all other cultures, that is promoted by the most strident and, we should say, shrill spokesmen for Japan's postmodernity. Yet the invocation of Japan as signified discloses the same reactive and fearful impulse that propelled the earlier attempt to show that Japan was as full and complete as the Western self. The contemporary reproduction of this conception of Japan, now clothed as uniquely postmodern and therefore superior to the West, has resulted in the banal and scandalously racist fulminations of Kurimoto Shinichiro, who has presented Japan's economic success as the sign of ethnic uniqueness (and, thereby, reaffirmed Nakasone's own views concerning the baleful effects of American racial heterogeneity), and the absurdist conviction of Yoshimoto Takaaki that consumption constitutes a new form of resistance against the powers of the status quo—capitalism—as if to imply the possibility of rearticulating reification as a revolutionary force for our time, but managing only to unintentionally replay Marx's famous observation that history the second time around leads only to farce, without even the hint of irony. Even the more measured discourse of Asada, as presented here in his exposition of "infantile capitalism," risks recuperating the binary opposition of the West and Japan, modern and non-modern, that plagued the earlier discourse on modernity and which he is pledged to put under erasure. What seems clear from these several papers is that when any consideration of Japan's postmodernity is yoked to the larger discussion concentrating on Japan and the West, and when the postmodern "scene" in Japan is seen as merely another way to express Japan's cultural uniqueness in order to explain its superiority to the West, the discourse on the postmodern can never hope to be anything more than an inexpertly concealed attempt to cover up the aporias that dogged the earlier modernist discourse, even as it seeks to fulfill the role of a simulacrum.

Which brings us to the question of the modern in the construction of Japan's postmodern "scene." What these papers show, above all else, is a general conviction that any effort to define the scene of Japan's postmodernity requires undertaking the dangerous task of re-tracing the meaning of the modern as the Japanese have confronted it since the fateful decision to transform society in the image of Western "enlightened" wealth and power. Nearly all of the papers consider the spectacle of the modern and how the Japanese have tried to extract the guarantee of stable meaning from a ceaselessly changing landscape and wrenching social transformations in daily life. Combined, they offer what Masao Miyoshi calls the "chronopolitical" dimension of the current controversy on postmodernism in Japan. The chronopolitical refers to the relationship between the premodern, modern, and postmodern or non-modern, according to Sakai's reading of Takeuchi's discourse. Yet a concern with chronopolitical relationships recalls the earlier Japanese discourse on modernism, and how it sought to resolve the problems of identity and difference induced by the introduction of new forms of knowledge, modes of production, and social relationships. The various ways this discourse attempted to relate these terms not only prefigured later discussions on postmodernity but bequeathed to them an unfinished agenda which still demands completion. As a result of this genealogy, the questions that still preoccupy Japanese today, in the search to define the space of the postmodern as a radical difference, echo the earlier discussions pre-possessed by the relationship of Japan's new modernity to the past, to the West of the present, and to a shapeless future. It is precisely be-cause Japanese did not always accept the Western conceit of a privileged unilinear relationship attesting to succession and progressive development that the discourse on the modern was able to provide a range of sanctions for both resistance to the requirements of the "universal" ratio masking a Western imperial ethos and surrender to it. Hence, Miyoshi shows how received literary forms, derived from an oral tradition, were able to resist being totally incorporated into imported and imitated Western forms, while Karatani and de Bary demonstrate how, through "inversion," Japanese literary criticism became the site of contestation. And J. Victor Koschmann discloses, in the often perilous itinerary followed by the thinker Maruyama Masao in the postwar years, the way Maruyama and his generation of "modernists" sought to constitute a modern subjectivity in Japan free from the domination of Western metaphysics as a condition for imagining the "intervention of the pragmatic will." Comparing Maruyama's conception of a subject that is no longer "hypostatized" or "essentialized" to Richard Rorty's "praxis-oriented form of social engineering," Koschmann sees in Maruyama's discourse a still productive alternative to Western theories of subject-centeredness and a lasting reminder of the earlier modernist project. In this connection Ōe Kenzaburō remains the eloquent modernist spokesman who has consistently resisted aspects of postmodernist theories as they have traveled to Japan.

By the same measure, Asada Akira reads the prewar Kyoto philosopher Nishida Kitaro, whose conception of the "topos of nothingness" (*mu no basho*) became the ground for "denying the self" altogether and establishing the "place of emptiness." Accordingly, Nishida "regarded the imperial court" as the occupant of this "place of extreme nothingness," empty and insubstantial yet capable of operating as a whole that ceaselessly incorporates the parts in the interest of harmony. Asada is convinced that this image derived from the prewar Kyoto school is currently serving in the capacity of an enabling principle to promote the reactionary conservatism of contemporary Japanese political society. This argument, as Tetsuo Najita shows, was at the heart of the writer Mishima Yukio's later (1960s) denunciation of contemporary society and his desperate call to revive imperial sovereignty before Japan lost all cultural mastery. Finally, H. D. Harootunian argues that we have in the figure of Takeuchi Yoshimi and a number of Japanese thinkers an ambiguous silhouette of intellectuals who accepted Japan's modern status and rejected the spurious claims of returning to a premodern tradition. Nevertheless, Takeuchi sought to envisage a realm that was neither modern (West) nor premodern (Orient), capable of simultaneously resisting being incorporated by the past and absorbed by the present in order to imagine a future free from the constraints of both. Their effort resembles the "chance" which, according to Stephen Melville, "would then be to know" themselves "as living within quotation marks and not thereby ceasing to live." Japan's chance and risk, Melville concludes, is "to live between itself—refusing to find itself in the embrace of the postmodern even as it poses the possibility of a movement beyond modernism."

≡≡≡

Most papers collected in this book were originally written for a workshop organized by a group of scholars—mainly Japanologists—in the spring of 1987. With the help of the Social Science Research Council, The University of Chicago, Cornell University, and the University of California, San Diego, the participants met in Boston and later separately in Chicago and Ithaca to discuss the papers. The Japanese version of the collection was published in a special issue of *Gendai shiso* in December 1987, and the *South Atlantic Quarterly* published the English version in the Summer 1988 issue. The papers by Isozaki Arata and Ōe Kenzaburō were added for this book with the belief that the practitioners—one in architecture and the other in fiction —would expand the scope of discussion so far limited to academic scholars. We are grateful to Jonnathan Arac and Michael Ryan for participating in the workshop as discussants. We express our debt to Stephen Melville who not only commented on the papers but also wrote a paper himself, which serves here as a postscript. Knowing how difficult it is to be an outsider, we indeed appreciate his assuming the role of the Other during this conference. Finally, we thank Melissa Lentricchia and Emily White of *SAQ*, Cathie Brettschneider of Princeton University Press, and Reynolds Smith of Duke University Press for their assistance that has been well beyond their usual territory of performance.

Note on Japanese Names

Japanese names throughout the book, except those of Japanese-Americans, are written in Japanese order—surname first—the style Japanologists have adopted in their studies in English. In Karatani Kōjin, for example, Karatani is his family name, and Kōjin his given (or "first") name. Even when the writer adopts a sobriquet, this order is followed. To complicate things, however, writers are known in Japan sometimes by their surname and sometimes by their "given" name. Natsume Sōseki (Natsume Kinnosuke), for instance, is usually known as Sōseki, not as Natsume, whereas a more recent writer like Mishima Yukio (Hiraoka Kimitake or Kōi) is known as Mishima. It seems that as a writer comes to be accepted into the "great tradition" (usually a while after his death), he comes to be known more by his given name than his surname. This book follows the current usage in this regard.

Postmodernism and Japan

Tetsuo Najita

On Culture and Technology
in Postmodern Japan

The rise of modern subjectivity and man-centered individualism is seen here not merely as an avoidable mistake, but as a phase in the course of human emancipation and maturation—though a phase whose intrinsic shortcomings have now become obvious.
—Fred R. Dallmayr, *Twilight of Subjectivity*

I am not lovingly gazing toward an Oriental essence—to me the Orient is a matter of indifference.
—Roland Barthes, *Empire of Signs*

Where will Japan take the postmodern retrospective perception that individualism was a "mistake," that the yearning for emancipation and freedom promised by humanist notions of subjectivity will not be satisfied? Dallmayr does not ask this question of Japan specifically, for he addresses himself to modernity in general and to a modernity as articulated within the framework of a theory of subjectivity and of knowledge identified with a humanist history since the Renaissance.[1] Yet the relevance of Dallmayr's question for modern and postmodern Japan is clear. What is beyond, or what comes after, possessive individualism and radical subjectivity? Is it community at home, the Japanese ways of doing things, that provides the site and process of postmodern certitude? Can phenomenology identifiable with Husserl and Heidegger, and perhaps Sartre, frame an alternative intellectual orientation? If the intervening force after the "obvious" failings of subjectivity is social consciousness as articulated by Lukács (not as inevitable, but as reflexive human intervention), then where might the source of reflexivity be located? Dallmayr points his readers to the problematic of nature as alienated subject, and, further, to the complex discussions about the dialectical epistemology of subject and object that emerged out of the Frankfurt School. His assessment of our intellectual history beyond the "obvious," however, remains uncertain, not unlike the sense of the postmodern in Japan, where, similarly, we sense a profound uncertainty about what might lie beyond the "intrinsic shortcomings" of individualism and subjectivity.

In the second epigraph, Roland Barthes expresses skepticism regarding subjectivity in terms of cultural knowing.[2] Since for Barthes subjectivity, either individual or cultural, aside from being a fabricated semiotic system, is actually only a myth, the Oriental Other quite logically is not knowable to him and therefore is a matter of "indifference." More importantly, Barthes's comment is about the Other as unknowable just as "we" (any "we") are unknowable to ourselves: hence the reflexive significance of admitting the limitation of cultural knowing, "until everything Occidental in us totters and the rights of the 'father tongue' vacillate." In his brilliantly laconic and at times annoying semiotic reading of contemporary Japan, Barthes reveals a radical and ironic skepticism that the Japanese have not been able to indulge, engaged as they have been in the relentless course of high-growth economics. What will cultural reflexivity mean to a Japan that can now afford its share of skepticism, and then some? Will it seek to "export" what it "knows" for certain about itself to observers who do not "understand" Japan? Will it mediate and manage its cultural knowledge through institutional channels not yet clear? Or perhaps, under the projected conditions of low-growth economics, the Japanese will admit, along with Barthes, that the "Occident" is a matter of indifference to them, not because self-known cultural essence is beautiful and true and knowable, but, consistent with Barthes's semiosis, because what might constitute Japanese culture as the basis of self-knowledge is also unknowable, changeful, never fixed, always an open text containing a "surplus of meaning," and hence never beyond doubt, and that, therefore, even the rights of the "father tongue" will always vacillate. In truth, as most of us are aware, the history of modern Japan reveals quite a different pattern in cultural epistemology, so as to make this Barthian possibility seem unlikely.[3]

For Japan, the West as the resource of technological knowledge has hardly ever been an object of indifference, except in certain egregious instances when, driven by uncompromising patriotic and nativist impulses, society has retreated from its—technology's—hold. And culture as the resource for firm, unshakable self-knowledge has rarely been characterized as ultimately unknowable, certainly not since perhaps Dogen and the early phases of Zen Buddhism in the thirteenth century; on the contrary, culture has been thought to be perfectly knowable, understandable from within, not requiring translation—not even the mediations of "language" and other "signs." A matter of the human spirit—*kokoro*—cultural certitude broadly conceived in terms of various historical and aesthetic verifications has served to frame technology within what is known for sure. Cultural self-knowledge, in other words, must be firmly grasped as a prior condition if technology is to acquire proper grounding. Culture precedes and frames technology, informs its ideology, grants it power, and, alternatively, generates contests over its own meaning.

The postmodern condition in "post-postwar" Japan will probably involve a working out of the deep interplay between technology and culture, the historical and the universal, otherness and self. The presumption that culture, history, and self are knowable has already generated intense and sometimes polemical discussion, since claiming to know is not the same thing as convincing others of what that knowledge is. In this arena of debate, culture is defended as radical individual commitment (as in Mishima Yukio's "defense" of culture), or explicated in the social-scientific terms of a refined, irreducible, and distinct "structure" or basic "pattern" (as in Nakane Chie's "vertical" society and Doi Takeo's "dependency" theory of childrearing), or presented as ideal "form" (as in Kobayashi Hideo's work on Motoori Norinaga). Or, as we hear more regularly of late, culture is "managed" by an impersonal administration so that it might be contextualized for "proper" understanding.[4] Rather than see an end or resolution to these interpretations, postmodern Japan will witness an intensification of debate over the claims of cultural self-knowledge.

For the postmodern condition is an extension of the modern past; the differences between the two are a matter of degree and quality. The postmodern is termed as it is precisely because of the unlike-lihood of a clear revolutionary break between the "modern" and what might lie beyond. As a phase "after" modernity, the postmodern retains the skepticism generated within the modern: namely, that "modernizing" development does not fix into place ethical or human purpose in history. For example, ever since the memorable debates among American and Japanese academics in Hakone in 1960 on the modernization of Japan, we have been alerted by the commentaries of Japanese intellectuals, notably Maruyama Masao and Toyama Shigeki, among others, to the high probability that beneath high-growth development there was a human experience that really did not coincide with the theory of modernization and the rationalization being advanced primarily by Western social and historical scientists.[5] Between Maruyama's insistence on the central importance of creating political value—i.e., political "fiction," as he referred to it and for which he is remembered—and the proposition among several American scholars that modernization is measurable history, there issued a dissonance that will undoubtedly spill over into the postmodern when the measurable threatens to become marginal and the possibility of "fiction" appears to have precious little outlet in the context of high-growth structures: a point made with painful directness in the satirical film *Household Game*, in which the demands of contemporary knowledge infiltrate the family household in the guise of a "tutor"—a shaman of sorts—who throws the rules of household civility into total disarray. The postmodern marks a moment when the simple questions are retrospectively asked of rapid modernization: "What is the meaning of all of this? What's it all about?" These questions were first raised by Japanese scholars at the Hakone Conference of 1960 at just the moment when Japan was about to launch its new history of high-growth economics in order to "double the national income." When this history of high growth had all but come to a close, the political scientist Ishida Takeshi echoed in 1984 the views of his mentor Maruyama at Hakone: ". . . any examination of development concepts must address the question of the purpose of development, i.e., development for what?" At issue for him was not only how a society might go about achieving goals that are already established, but, more importantly, how does it, politically, set goals for itself to begin with.[6]

However banal these questions may seem, they contain within them the realization that the history of development will not change drastically into something new, and that, therefore, the postmodern is likely to be a continuation of development, only less of it. "Is this all there is to it?" we might then ask. "More growth at less speed?" The rhetorical implication that this cannot be the case is hedged by the conservative perception of the postmodern as being "postrevolution." The very term "postmodern" is informed by a deep skepticism and uncertainty as to how dramatic transformations are to take place within our history, an observation that has been made from any number of viewpoints, but in sum reveal the awareness that the classic guideposts of historical change are not reliable indicators. Increased technological production has not fueled the social dialectic. Indeed the dialectic has not fired, to say nothing of its having misfired. The systematic reproduction of consumer goods has homogenized society, making everyone, as is often expressed with much pride in Japan, a member of the "middle class." Increased technological productivity, as this view would have it, does not generate a social dialectic but, on the contrary, neutralizes and disarms it.

Accordingly, the state is not about to wither away; instead, it has gained in sophistication, has become the preeminent apparatus that defines and promotes national interests, and has sustained the conditions of its own locus by managing culture. As the writings of Louis Althusser and Jürgen Habermas suggest, large-scale political organizations, such as parties, appear to be appendages of the state and of its interests rather than independently representative of the public good.[7] And, equally troubling, the persuasive capacities of independent political criticism are now held in suspenseful doubt. Indeed, what constitutes the "private," the basis of the autonomous subject that Maruyama prized and theorized about, has become enormously problematic, resonating in this regard with the "post-individualist" theme expressed by Dallmayr. The avenues available in moving from subjectivity to civil society at large no longer appear so innocent as they might have before, in, say, the decade following the end of the Pacific War. Education in particular has become a focus of debate and attention; in addition to scientific instruction, the kinds of social norms being taught and perpetuated have come under critical scrutiny. And, more broadly framed, the question of the primacy of culture in relation to technology has resurfaced in the bold and assertive terms of indigenous exceptionalism, or, the genre of writings often referred to as "Japanism"—*Nihonjinron*.

≡≡≡

The issue of culture in relation to "reason" (as knowledge) recalls for us the discourse on otherness with which Japanese civilization has been intensely engaged over the recent decades. One slant of this discourse reveals a Japanese self-conception that says: We are more than what we say of ourselves as a "truthful" and "compassionate" people, and that margin of plenitude comes from the moral and historical epistemology of the Other. Among Tokugawa intellectuals this meant reserving a vital scholarly place for the Confucian "classics" vis-à-vis the considerable intellectual and emotional enticements of nativism or *kokugaku*. It is true that devotees of rational Confucian epistemology could not but agree that while they could know Chinese thought, they could not become Chinese—that knowing and being were not identical, and, therefore, as an extreme example, that the ideographic system of writing should be abandoned in favor of the indigenous syllabary or a radically revised ideographic system in keeping with indigenous grammar. The act of translating Chinese sentences—*kanbun*—into Japanese ones—*kakikudashibun*—presumed the possibility of bringing something of the Other into the home culture.

The previous formula could be altered to read: What we are capable of knowing from whatever source outside ourselves may indeed be true and valid, but the real margin of plenitude is in our indigenous culture. The quest for Western science and technology in the mid-nineteenth century was grounded in this sense of cultural certitude. The earliest textbooks on Western science from the beginning of the Meiji era (e.g., Fukuzawa Yukichi on physics) were translated into Japanese through the assignment of ideographic equivalences. Japanese self-consciousness expressed itself with a primary reference to continuous "culture" and not to technological "work"—the latter, in the final analysis, being like Confucian knowledge attributable to the Other. Translation as considered here refers not only to making knowledge accessible; it speaks to the construction of a relationship of authority framed in terms of the culture within, the exceptional or essential elements often relied on by Japanese to explain their ultimate "difference" from every other culture around the globe. The question of independence and dependence has always loomed large within Japan's modern experience. This has been especially true as regards the relative autonomy of culture in relation to technology and of culture as the margin of plenitude in the self-conscious Japanese subjectivity. For Japanese, self-knowledge, derived from a prelapsarian encounter with the gods and the land they created, always forced a difference between the plenitude of being and otherness, whether the Other was China or the West.

If we might adapt Victor Turner somewhat, the marginal in the formulation I have suggested here in the case of Japan is not the liminal Other, but the term for cultural order and selfhood itself. One does not "pass" through and return from it to the world of rationality and order; the margin is not "anti-structure" but order itself. It is the constant tone, like some sort of deep "bass note" (to rely on Maruyama Masao's phraseology of *koso*); or the essential ideal form that continues over time, that does not require translation, that plays a legitimate role in cultural, historical, and aesthetic philosophy.[8]

The problematical relationship between culture and knowledge of the Other was articulated with particular intensity in early twentieth-century Japan. As in the case of Tokugawa Confucianism, the Other was clearly also "within" the historical process, although obviously much more powerfully so in the structures and processes of industrial production and the technological knowledge such production required. It was in this particular moment of reflexivity immediately following the first industrial revolution that some of the key terms were formulated that would establish the ideological place of "culture" in relation to "technology." Beginning in 1910, we detect a wide range of critiques against the previous transformational synthesis of the Meiji era that subordinated culture in relation to the new knowledge of Western technology. Along a broad front, we find critics saying that what changed in history was the unexpected and forceful infusion of technology into a particular social history of the late Tokugawa era that contained a momentum, some would say a dialectical one, of its own. History was thus grievously distorted and culture was placed under permanent siege. From this early perspective, technological progress, the measurable improvement of efficient production, was determined to be a different order of things from aesthetic and cultural forms, for these latter did not (and ought not be allowed to) change and were to be evaluated by norms other than functional measurements of progress.

Sometimes radical and rarely innocent, these criticisms were often informed by a cosmopolitanism of the early twentieth century that has often been repeated in recent decades. It derives from a perception of the globe as being a cultural map with "fixed" places for easily identifiable and describable national cultures. There is also a sense that while all of the many distinctive cultures added something of significance to the world cultural order of things, so that the ideal of a global civilization was entirely appropriate, still not all of the places were of equivalent status, some being relatively more appreciated and respected than others. Responding in good measure to queries from outside observers as to Japan's "distinctive" place as a culture beyond its merely derivative and mimetic components, a discussion unfolded as to the nature of Japan's cultural contribution and hence its proper "place" in the context of the globe. As the only Asian nation to have adopted industrial technology, Japan would have to clarify its cultural identity as a nation outside the ordering cultural framework shaped by Western nations. Since not all Western nations are alike, even though comparably industrialized, so too Japan, while industrialized like Western nations, could also project to the world its Asian identifications and the self-conscious readiness to "return" to them —*nyu-a*, as this return was referred to.

What resulted from this assertive cosmopolitanism articulated from an Asian and Japanese point of reference was an extraordinary outburst of creative production. From Okakura Tenshin's declaration "Asia is one" in his *Ideals of the East* (1903) and Nishida Kitarō's *Studies of the Good* (1911) to the scholarly writings of Tsuda Sōkichi's *The Thought of Japanese Commoners as Seen through Literature* (1916–21), Abe Jirō's *Studies in the Arts and Crafts of the Tokugawa Era* (1920), Naitō Konan's *Studies of the Cultural History of Japan* (1924), Watsuji Tetsurō's *Studies of the Japanese Spirit* (1926) and *On Climate and Culture* (1935), and Kuki Shūzō's *The Structure of Tokugawa Aesthetic Style* (1929), there is to be witnessed a creative expressiveness based on a cosmopolitan conception of culture that calls for reappraisal in the present postmodern context.

Within expressive cosmopolitanism, moreover, was a voice of lament: we hear a deeply felt concern regarding the aggressive pulls of technology. Culture was not in ideological control of technology, but most probably the opposite—culture was in a state of steady retreat. The cost of rapid technological growth, the celebrated writer Natsume Sōseki wrote as early as 1911, was enormous and painful.[9] While technology was clearly a labor-saving intervention in Japanese life, it had not brought individual or social well-being and happiness, but pervasive "nervous exhaustion." Discounting as superficial the new image of a powerful Japan as a result of the victory in the Russo-Japanese War of 1905, Sōseki pointed to the central issue of postindustrial Japan as a "crisis" of culture. Technology as a system of knowledge and production belonged to the Western Other, and had been directly imported into the native historical stream, rendering much of that history artificial. Within the modern Japanese bosom resided, in Sōseki's view, a crippled personality, akin to the heroine in one of de Maupassant's novellas who leaps from the window to show her fidelity and is utterly dependent on the care of others for the rest of her life.

A variant of Sōseki's view can be discerned in Tanizaki Jun'ichirō's ironic essay of 1933, "In Praise of Shadows."[10] Again it is technology that is identified as the intrusive Other, and doubt is expressed as to whether "culture" is indeed in control of it. Technology and its concomitant theories of positivism and progress represented expansive epistemologies that had drastically distorted the ethical and aesthetic sensitivities of the Japanese. Writing fiction, creating a Japanese world in a sea of technology and war-making industries, may thus be seen as fueled by the agony over the corrosive impact of Western knowledge on Japanese cultural forms. Rather than pretending that culture is in some kind of accord with technology, we should be self-consciously identifying with culture as an internalized space of resistance. Tanizaki urged a strategic cultural retreat into the interior spheres of "dimness," "shadows," and the "stillness" of dark places, where technology could be held in abeyance and where the mystery of creativity might still be found.

For the overlapping generations that these two writers belonged to, technology was the powerful Other within Japanese social history. And the knowledge that went into its functional processes, such as administrative law and applied science, came to represent a form of "self-colonization," while authentic spaces that remained within were summoned to serve as the basis of cultural self-knowledge and, hence, of resistance. Culture, while not dominant over technology, could remain separate from it as authentic internal space, or ideal "form" that might be identified with whatever technology could not invade. The separateness of culture informed the revival of folkcraft (what came to be known more generally as "traditional technology") and represented a turning back against the Meiji industrial revolution and the modernizing laws, institutions, and epistemologies that were put into place in order to achieve that revolution. Indeed, the more Japanese intellectuals reflected on the industrial revolution that they had come through, the more they became persuaded that they were becoming colonized not only technologically (in outwardly measurable matters of energy and production), but intellectually and culturally as well. Cosmopolitanism, in the final analysis, would not help, because the cultures in the global scheme of things would remain "Western" in orientation. That there should be a "retreat" into internal "form" and "shadow," therefore, makes sense—though it does not make change.

=====

Within the framework of postwar modernization theory, the bifurcation between culture and technology was mapped over in terms of progressive development. After the Pacific War, much of the history that did not fall within this pattern was interpreted either as "traditional" ideas that somehow went wrong, or as romantic tendencies in literature that were marginal, idiosyncratic, and uninfluential. Yet it was within this overarching framework of modernization that the place of culture was reasserted with a positivist point of reference, laying claim to culture as being the controlling force over technology. The Meiji industrial revolution, which had been identified as the Other within, now came to be articulated as postwar technology expressive of a distinctive culture within. Technology came to be ideologized in terms of "culture" to a degree that had not been the case before the Pacific War, when, as suggested above, culture tended to be appreciated as an ever-shrinking haven within which to find creative solace. In the postwar era, and especially with high-growth economics, whether the issue was industrial organization or the decision-making process or hiring and firing practices or meritocracy in education or quality control on the production line, technological excellence and achievement were clothed in traditional cloth—sometimes to the point of absurdity, so that even Westerners have been led to believe that *bushido* is the basis of Japanese technological and entrepreneurial practices. How else are we to explain the absurd popularity of Miyamoto Musashi's *Gorinsho* (a sixteenth-century handbook on the warrior's code) on Wall Street? In one way or another, technological excellence has been represented as an extension of cultural exceptionalism, not as resulting from the tension of the Other within culture.

How did culture come to assume such a preeminent and seemingly unproblematic role in relation to technology in postwar as compared with prewar Japan? The explanations are complex, and do not lead easily to summary formulations. Analyses by Japanese social scientists on basic cultural "structures" have played an important role;

the pattern may be traceable to Ruth Benedict's classic, *The Chry-santhemum and the Sword*, in which the methodology of reducing cultural configurations to a basic stylized structure upon which to build a comprehensive interpretation of culture has enticed consider-able imitation.[11] In brief, Benedict argued that, given the basic struc-ture of Japanese culture, the Japanese were, indeed, totally foreign to the Western view of social existence, and, therefore, policy-makers should keep uppermost in mind this foreign otherness in the enemy in shaping political guidelines for the war and its aftermath. Bene-dict's explanation framed the cultural psychology of wartime Japan-ese fighters. It did not explain, however, how or why Japan had become proficient in the technological and entrepreneurial senses. Postwar Japanese social scientists—the impressive and provocative analyses of Nakane Chie in *Tate shakai* and Doi Takeo in *Amae no kozo*—provide clarifications on these latter themes left largely unex-plored by Benedict. Like Benedict, their explanations rely on basic sociopsychological structures and patterns that could be objectively identified but not be directly knowable by outsiders. They proceed from the presumption that the Japanese are "unknowable" except to Japanese, and that the role of social science is to mediate and de-fine their self-knowledge in terms accessible to the world of others. It was the very distinctiveness of Japanese vertical or dependent rela-tionships, in groups, and in harmony, that was the basis of sure self-knowledge among the Japanese and that made them effective in the organized processes of high-growth economics. The "scientifically" reduced structural forms and relational axes explained the distinc-tiveness of a Japanese culture which outsiders could not directly know or participate in, and could at best approach through the medi-ations of social-scientific interpreters. Just how effective this Japan-ese "inversion" of Benedict has been can be appreciated by the consis-tent use of this perception of Japanese exceptionalism (unknowable but not inscrutable) in terms of group harmony and vertical loyalty to explain Japanese technological and organizational proficiency.

While the foregoing is only a partial insight at best, it appears to me that the place and meaning of "culture" underwent significant change from prewar to post-high-growth Japan. Western social sci-ences have played an important mediating role here, and the subtle ins and outs of this process are a subject that I must admit is controversial. It would seem certain, however, that the question of cultural hegemony over technology will persist as a central issue of debate in the postmodern condition of low-growth economics, as will, and perhaps more importantly, the issue of whether culture is plural and hence "unknowable," or whether there is a homogenous culture that can be reduced to refined structure and pattern. The issue of whether culture can be "exported," in the manner prescribed by Ezra Vogel in his *Japan as Number One: Lessons for America* (1979), will no doubt also loom large in importance, as will the "responsibility" and the role of the state in all of this.[12]

It may be worth observing again that culture and technology in the prewar discourse of self and Other tended to retain separate and autonomous positions, with culture providing alternative spaces to technology. Watsuji Tetsuro's idealized domestic architecture, after all, served as a cultural enclave separate from the cement edifaces that had come to dominate the urbanscape. Yanagida Kunio's "anthropology," to cite another example, was oriented to the ethnographic documentation of the culture of the forgotten Other, the abiding rural people facing the relentless expansion of technology and bureaucracy. In general, "culture" was not an "object" that could be scientifically identified. It was rather phenomenologically perceived and appreciated. It contained ideal "forms" that withstood the passage of time, including the corrosive forces of modernity and development. Culture, in this sense, was "anti-modern"; it was articulated selfconsciously in this manner so as to distinguish internal truthfulness from the otherness within. The prewar concern being fundamentally ethical, the proposition that culture served as the controlling ideological norm of technology was rarely advanced; whereas in the postwar period, especially under high-growth economics, technology has been ideologized with strong and pronounced references to distinctive cultural characteristics.

One of the tensions that is likely to surface in the postgrowth or postmodern context is the resistance to this ideological use of culture from any number of points of views. But it seems in looking back over the 1970s that Mishima Yukio's strident criticism of high-growth economism—and the mindless consumerism and homogenization of society spawned by it—marked a clear place for culture in post-growth or postmodern Japan. His is a voice against modernity, and, therefore, resonates with references to the prewar "defense" of culture. It is well to recall that in his widely read essay, "On the Defense of Culture" (1969), Mishima defended cultural "anarchy" against the bland mechanical orderliness produced by modern technology. Focusing on the symbol of the *Tenno*, for which the translation "emperor" is a misnomer, Mishima insisted that its status as akin to a constitutional monarchy was a totally artificial, Western, construct. Otherness within Japan begins with the constitutionalized definition of the *Tenno*. Not standing for law, bureaucratic regularity, or ritualized, circumstantial pomp (all attributed wrongly to the *Tenno* by pre- and postwar constitutional systems), the *Tenno*, according to Mishima, had always stood instead for a radical cultural principle of creativity and the realization of potential in each individual. Denying that a limit should be placed on the range of this principle, Mishima argued that the *Tenno* represented a culture that allowed "anarchy" within "aesthetic terrorism." At issue was the status of culture and individuality within it, not the political role of the monarchy in legitimating bureaucracy and technology.[13]

There is a prophetic element in Mishima's eccentricity. In emphasizing the need to separate "culture" from "politics," beginning with the *Tenno* symbol, and to situate culture as prior to and decisive in establishing individual authenticity in relation to technology and bureaucracy, which were mechanical and artificial, and, more importantly, homogenizing and dehumanizing, Mishima drew on the prewar discourse on culture but projected his view as a challenge to the new consumer culture spawned by high-growth economics. That Mishima should identify with Oshio Heihachiro and the intellectual tradition of radical idealism is best seen within this frame of reference. While such an identification may seem anachronistic and totally out of place within modern society, it would not appear to be so if these anachronistic references are seen as a critique against modernity and the constitutionalization and management of culture that have come with it. Rather than serving as a "closure" to that idealistic past, Mishima's suicide may also be seen as a principal moment in the postmodern debate on the place of culture in relation to technological modernization, precisely because he did seek to free authentic cultural mastery from the constraints of capital and technology.

The resurgence of the prewar discourse on culture as an intellectual enclave against or at least separate from modernity, and not the underpinnings of technology, may also be witnessed in Kobayashi Hideo's parting contribution to contemporary Japan, namely his *Motoori Noringa* (a work on the great nativist scholar of the eighteenth century) (1976), though Kobayashi's *Motoori* should not be confused with Mishima's *Oshio Heihachiro* (the philosopher-activist who led a rebellion against the Tokugawa government in 1837). Yet there is a similarity in Kobayashi's plea to that of Mishima's that culture self-consciously be kept separate from measurable, materialistic modernization. Kobayashi gives us a "defense" of culture against modernization that is quite at odds with the "use" of culture to explain and exonerate it. The issue for Kobayashi is epistemological to begin with and ethical in cultural consequence. The modern bifurcation between inner and outer, between interior feeling and exterior knowledge, Kobayashi finds misleading and given to artificial manipulation and gimmickry. While this manipulation produces measurable results, the consequences over the long haul are deceptive, dehumanizing, and sap the cultural self of its creative energy and vision. We see in Kobayashi's summation of his life's prodigious scholarly work a summons that Japan reidentify with the spirit and the way of truthfulness—*naoki no kokoro, makoto no michi, magokoro*—that were prized by intellectuals in pre-industrial Japan, such as Motoori and his colleagues in national studies. Because there are limitations as to how much Japan can develop as a high-growth economic society, Kobayashi seems to say, Japan must refer outside the field of modern technology to within itself, to the epistemology that relates feeling with knowledge, mind with object, self with nature.

≡≡≡

The very success of high-growth economics in Japan's 1960s and 1970s has left unanswered questions as to meaning, as to whether culture controls technology, or whether culture is, actually, totally separate as "form"—and hence as experience, in which case technology is in fact a pervasive, freestanding artifice and not dependent on culture. Having passed through breathtaking high growth, and having withstood the several severe "shocks" in that process, Japan now faces the prospect of controlled low growth. The social consensus sustained by high growth will no doubt wane, and questions as to the meaning of recent history are likely to accompany the process. What are the social and cultural consequences of that history? Where has it placed Japan in the cosmopolitan world order of things? Is Japan better understood, appreciated, than before high growth? If not, then why not? Has the quality of life within Japan improved in a basic sense? Has the natural landscape been damaged beyond repair? Is high-growth economics what the postwar period was about and for? These questions refer to competing claims as to the true meaning of "postwar" history. If "postwar" history is over, as most critics in Japan contend, the debate over its meaning has just begun. And this debate is informed by the awareness that high-growth economics is over; that flexibilities at home and abroad that absorbed that historical process are less available and in a process of decline; and that the problem of governance, accordingly, must attend to the question of managing culture, mediating and containing the meaning and distribution of culture as the consensus powered by high-growth economics loses its cohesiveness.

Whether culture is situated in relation to technology, as defined by social-scientific structure and pattern, or as detached from technology, as in aesthetic form and historicist moments, both proceed from the proposition that culture is sure self-knowledge and may therefore serve as a basis of certitude despite technological change and modernization. Neither, in other words, admits to Barthes's theoretical stance that the individual and cultural self, is, ultimately, truly unknowable and therefore belongs to the realm of "silence." While Barthes was startled to find "silence" worked into Japanese life at many different points, he failed to note that this silence is part of the universe of sure self-knowledge and, hence, of "culture," and not an admission of its unknowability. The English edition of *L'empire des signes* is cataloged singularly as "Japan—Civilization": the irony is obvious since this subject was a matter of "indifference" to Barthes.

And as for Japan passing into the postmodern "twilight of subjectivity," the "retreat of signs" still seems to lead to the certitude of cultural knowledge as an ordering reference.

Will postmodern conditions generate a challenge to that retreat to certitude on the ground that such a basis of certitude is chimerical? How might Japan articulate the constancy of uncertainty that is theorized to be central to the postmodern experience? As Jean-François Lyotard has argued, there are no controlling "codes" in postmodernity: what is true and false, orthodox and heterodox, loses its boundary lines.[14] Or, more pertinent perhaps, the true is less scientific and methodologically accurate, as it is ideologically controlled. And if history is not fixed in terms of a true narrative, how then will the possibility of new "surpluses" uncovered in historical texts and events be dealt with in post-high-growth Japan?

As the rhetorical questions posed here would suggest, the postmodern condition may be seen at once as an opportunity or a curse. It is an opportunity in the sense that it throws into doubt the very claim to truthful "form" embedded in historical experience that historians, social scientists, and literary critics may uncover and present as refined and stable "structure" or "pattern." The texts and events of human history may be reopened as if they were unfamiliar; they may be rediscovered in terms of new meanings. But the postmodern is also a curse, because it is inherently "conservative" in the sense that there is no certainty as to how history undergoes change, which in turn allows for the distinct possibility of mechanical reproduction, or the continuous reconstitution of things as they are, only more or less. The future will not yield Maruyama's "fiction," if this were the case. And since there is no privileged position in relation to history, there will be a variety of "custodians" of culture, among which the state will undoubtedly be a strong and self-conscious player. The epistemological tendency to affirm cultural self-knowledge as true, either as structure or form, and, as I've emphasized in this essay, containing the capacity to ideologize technology, is a theme that has already surfaced for review and reflection. What becomes of historians and their argumentations about the dead in all of this remains very much to be seen.

Notes

1 Fred Dallmayr, *Twilight of Subjectivity: Contributions to a Post-Individualist Theory of Politics* (Amherst, 1981).
2 Roland Barthes, *Empire of Signs*, trans. Richard Howard (New York, 1982), 3.
3 Ibid., 6. See also Paul Ricoeur, *Interpretation Theory: Discourse and the Surplus of Meaning* (Fort Worth, 1976).
4 Mishima Yukio, *Bunka boei ron* (*Discussion on the Defense of Culture*) (Tokyo, 1969). Nakane Chie's influential work is *Tate shakai no ningen kankei: Tan'itsu shakai no riron* (Tokyo, 1967), or *Japanese Society* (Berkeley, 1970). See also Doi Takeo, *Amae no kozo* (Tokyo, 1971), or *The Anatomy of Dependence*, trans. John Bester (New York, 1973); and Kobayashi Hideo, *Motoori Norinaga* (Tokyo, 1965–76).
5 The Conference on Modern Japan, "Modernization of Japan: Proceedings of Preliminary Seminars at Hakone, Japan, 1960" (unpublished).
6 Ishida Takeshi, "Rethinking Political Development: The Japanese Case," *Annals of the Institute of Social Science* 25 (1983–84): 1–8.
7 See Peter B. Evans et al., eds., *Bringing the State Back In* (New York, 1985); Louis Althusser, "Ideology and Ideological State Apparatuses," in *Lenin and Philosophy and Other Essays* (New York, 1971), 1–135; Jürgen Habermas, *Legitimation Crisis* (Boston, 1975) and *Toward a Rational Society* (Boston, 1970).
8 Victor Turner, *The Ritual Process: Structure and Anti-Structure* (Ithaca, 1966).
9 Natsume Sōseki, "Gendai Nihon no kaika" ("The Enlightenment of Modern Japan"), in *Gendai Nihon shiso taikei 32: Han kindai no shiso*, ed. Fukuda Tsuneari (Tokyo, 1965), 53–72.
10 Tanizaki Junichiro, "In'ei raisan" ("In Praise of Shadows"), in Fukuda, *Gendai Nihon*, 114–46.
11 Ruth Benedict, *The Chrysanthemum and the Sword* (Boston, 1946).
12 Ezra Vogel, *Japan as Number One: Lessons for America* (Cambridge, 1979). My review of Vogel's book appeared in the *New York Review of Books* (21 February 1980) and in translation in *Misuzu* 242 (August 1980).
13 See especially Mishima's response to Hashikawa Bunzo in *Bunka boei ron*, 61–64.
14 Jean-François Lyotard, *The Postmodern Condition: A Report on Knowledge*, trans. Geoff Bennington and Brian Massumi (Minneapolis, 1984).

Marilyn Ivy

Critical Texts, Mass Artifacts: The Consumption of Knowledge in Postmodern Japan

Japan has come to exist within the American political unconscious as an almost comforting figure of danger and promise—the danger of foreign capital and the promise it offers if domesticated. Comforting because, even though threatening, Japan is *there*, stable, the free world equivalent of Russia, the trade-war adversary against which Americans can strategically constitute themselves. Americans know, almost without inquiring, about Japanese business practices, the crazily lopsided trade deficit, the openings of auto plants in the Midwest, robots and Walkmans, the dedication of the work force. The news presents a repetitive and reconfirming scenario of Japan as a sign of impossible, dehumanized productivity, of dystopic capitalism. So repetitive, in fact, that there is no need to think about Japan; it remains backgrounded, mute, yet available for appropriation in an emergency. Only rarely does reporting on Japan break the benumbing focus on trade, competition, and productivity. When it does, it usually portends trouble. Prime Minister Nakasone Yasuhiro's party speech to his Liberal Democratic party comrades on 22 September 1986 provided one of those rare, and unfortunate, opportunities for Japan to break the surface of consciousness. In that now infamous speech, Nakasone remarked that "in America there are many blacks, Puerto Ricans and Mexicans, and on the average America's level [of intelligence] is still extremely low."[1]

These remarks caused a storm of protest in the United States, and from minority groups in Japan as well. Coupled with the later American government report on the comparative edge of Japanese schools, Nakasone's speech raised fundamental fears about knowledge and intellectual competition. Nakasone complained that the press reported his remarks out of context, and in that assertion he was correct. Most reporting did not reveal the startling remainder of his lengthy speech. I'd like to linger for a moment on that unreported remainder.

Nakasone's speech, in its entirety, is a delirious sweep through historical time and cultural space. His ostensible theme is the place of an international Japan in the world today and the Liberal Democratic party's role in attaining that place. But along the way he makes an excursus not only through Japanese history, but also through global space, invoking a theory of parallel development proposed by the anthropologist Umesao Tadao, director of the National Museum of Ethnology. Not only is feudal Japan compared to France and Germany (Japan emerges with a vastly superior literacy rate), but Nakasone traces as far back as Africa and *Australopithecus* to assert a polygenic theory of human origins. There is talk about Asia, about the world's oldest pottery (Japanese), about the impact of marauding Central Asian nomads on the Chinese and Holy Roman Empires, about SDI, nuclear power, about monsoon Buddhism and desert monotheism, the high-level information society, and talk about Mexicans, Puerto Ricans, and American blacks. He ends his speech with an appeal to search out the racial origins of the Japanese: only by knowing their self-identity can Japanese know their "difference" from the rest of the world.

In their manifesto on capitalism and schizophrenia, *Anti-Oedipus*, Gilles Deleuze and Félix Guattari state that "All delirium possesses a world-historical, political, and racial content, mixing and sweeping along races, cultures, continents, and kingdoms. . . . All paranoiac deliriums stir up similar historical, geographic, and racial masses."[2] Nakasone's speech is a classically paranoiac attempt to confirm Japanese world parity in an increasingly fragmented international and domestic milieu, to restore the honor of the Japanese race by comparing it to other races. Positing parallel lines of development—lines that don't converge—he arrives at a pure place of racial identity from which to constitute hierarchies of difference.

Within this delirium, however, is a canny recognition of the crucial importance of knowledge and information, with education and literacy as the clearest confirmation of Japan's contemporary superiority. Nakasone's narrative of knowledge conjoins prehistoric past and high-tech future in a series of assertions about the status of knowledge in Japan today. Thus he announces: Politics must suit contemporary society. How can it do that? First of all, society's rhythm and tempo are extraordinarily fast. Politics must match that pace. That's because Japan is now, Nakasone continues, a "high-level information society," a "dense, agitated society" (*nōmitsu gekidō shakai*), in which half the population and productivity of the United States is gathered in an area the size of California. No other nation has the abundance of information that Japan does, and in no other nation "does information come so naturally into one's head. . . . [T]here is no other country which puts such diverse information so accurately into the ears of its people. It has become a very intelligent society—much more so than America."[3]

What is striking about this passage is the linkage of speed, information, and intelligence. The "density" and "agitation" of the people directly reflect the accuracy, automaticity, and abundance of information. There is an assertion of the naturalness of the process, almost an evocation of information as environment, as Nature itself. Information comes naturally into one's head, yet the nation is responsible for providing this information. Information is transparent, devoid of ideological taint. The transparency and consensus of Japanese knowledge allow it to exceed, productively, the heterogeneous and racially divided cultural masses of the rest of the globe. Nakasone thus creates a narrative of legitimation in which Japanese superiority depends on density of information and capacity to read. His serial linkages of transparent information, culture, and racial superiority, and his notions of the high-level information society are ones that increasingly condense aspects of a Japanese situation many would call postmodern.

═════

Almost all formulations of the postmodern agree in detecting a crisis of representation. This crisis is grounded in the extremity of the contemporary moment, one defined by the dominance of multinational corporations, the nuclear sublime, and the extraordinary speed and replication of information created by computerization. In this contemporary postmodern moment, the virulence of capital has turned everything into pure commodified signs. National borders give way as information circulates at blinding speeds. Mass media, television, and advertising create "hyperreal" space, a space of "simulation," in Jean Baudrillard's terms. The real, the referent, no longer exists: all is simulation. Signification is torn apart. Knowledge is a matter of TV games, as the philosopher Jean-François Lyotard states.[4]

Lyotard makes this changing status of knowledge in postindustrial societies the focus of his work *The Postmodern Condition*. He outlines the new status that knowledge has in an ultra high-level information society, a condition defined by dispersal and a multiplicity of language games, but in which the "performativity" game of techno-science still dominates. Computerization marks all aspects of knowledge and transforms it into an "informational commodity," as Lyotard calls it—knowledge as something to be exchanged, consumed, but not used for its own sake. In Lyotard's analysis, knowledge has become the major stake in the global struggle for power.

We can thus sense more clearly the edge to Nakasone's rhetoric, in which he grasps the necessity for politics to keep pace with the dense and homogeneous communications flows in Japan. And indeed, this supposed Japanese consensus, this communicational transparency (no illiterate blacks or Puerto Ricans there!) is precisely the necessary condition for knowledge to be optimized as informational commodity. That is why, it is said, the Japanese are winning the race (speed and competition, again) in computerization and knowledge production: because of their transparent communicational consensus, the Habermasian ideal; and cultural emphasis on performativity, the language game of technoscience. Intimations abound, however, that things are out of hand: the ever-accelerating speed of information; saturated levels of consumption; an abundance of knowledge that threatens to become excess; the overproduction of goods for export; the corrosive solvent of multinational capitalism. Nakasone's very insistence on appealing to an increasingly discredited narrative of legitimation, in which the productive consensus is justified in racial terms, indicates the lag between his politics and this postmodern situation as Lyotard describes it. Thus the state increasingly attempts to circumscribe this capitalization of knowledge and to appeal to metanarratives of (discredited) legitimation.

The dissemination of knowledge, as well as knowledge itself, is thus both a given and a problem in Japan today. The problem of knowledge as an informational commodity comes up repeatedly in Japanese texts devoted to analyzing the postmodern condition. Many of these works have themselves become objects of mass consumption. The self-referential loop doesn't stop there, but goes beyond that to the spate of works which now explain *why* these texts on knowledge have become mass commodities.

In this particular report on knowledge I want to focus not on scientific knowledge as Lyotard does, but rather on the conjunction of the mass media and popular concerns with knowledge. Lyotard makes a distinction between "learning" (and its subfield "science") and "knowledge." "Learning" designates denotative statements that have to do with declaring what is true and what is false. But "knowledge" has to do with the totality of language games—not just denotative statements, but also statements on justice, beauty, "know how," and so on. In this sense Lyotard's "knowledge" comes close to some definitions of culture or even discourse. I want to focus neither exclusively on Lyotard's knowledge as learning nor on knowledge as discourse, but rather on a more limited conception of knowledge: on knowledge as *chi*, the Japanese word that indicates knowledge as acquired through intellectual cultivation, but which recently has come to designate something akin, I think, to "theory" in American literary-critical circles. It has become a catchword and synonym for what is being hailed as "new knowledge." If knowledge in the postmodern condition has become an informational commodity, then Japan presents the spectacle of a thoroughly commodified world of knowledge.

Perhaps the most telling moment in this equation of knowledge and product was the sudden and unprecedented popularity of a book about poststructuralism by a young scholar named Asada Akira. Entitled *Kōzō to chikara* (*Structure and Power*), it appeared in 1983 without benefit of advance publicity, yet in a matter of weeks it had sold close to eighty thousand copies, its author had become a sensation in the weekly magazines and newspapers, and the media announced the advent of "new academism." Office workers, university students, artists, musicians—everyone bought the book. Although academics in Japan have a much more fluid relationship with the popular press and mass culture than those in the United States, sales figures still surpassed anyone's grandest expectations. In short, they were phenomenal, and Asada and his book came quickly to be known as the *AA genshō* ("Asada Akira phenomenon"). The media soon included other scholars in this select "new academic" group; what they all had in common was a specialty in some branch of semiotic, structuralist, or poststructuralist thought. Simultaneously, this kind of new knowledge was proclaimed postmodernist in an equation of poststructuralism or deconstruction with the notion of postmodernism.

What kind of text, then, is *Structure and Power*? It is a lucid, yet not easy, exposition of major streams of poststructuralist thought, focusing particularly on Lacan, Bataille, Deleuze, and Guattari. Many of the analyses start from a consistent notion of structure, in which symbolic orders oppose order and chaos, culture and nature (for example, in the thinking of Lévi-Strauss); they then proceed to show how the thinker under consideration goes beyond or destroys a fixed notion of structure. Deleuze and Guattari's presences are strongly felt, particularly in those essays that explain how capitalism decodes and deterritorializes traditional symbolically coded orders. Asada's criticism is more poststructuralist than deconstructive, as he works more with notions of structure and relations of exchange than with language itself in its rhetorical twists and turns; Deleuze and Guattari (and, in the background, Lacan, Nietzsche, and Spinoza) have influenced him more directly than has Derrida.

Rather than the metacriticism within *Structure and Power*, however, I am more concerned with its reception, with the text as a sign for a certain condition in Japan today that some would call postmodern. Part of Asada's text has a polemical intention; it was directed toward a certain audience and aimed for certain effects. Many people bought Asada's text and read only the preface and the chart at the end of the book. This process of fragmented reading—of which I will say more in a moment—perhaps encapsulates the text's most salient gestures. For prefaces profess, as Derrida has shown, to reveal the contents of a book in another register, in a condensed mode; yet the contradiction of the preface, which claims to precede and introduce the body of the text, is that it is written after the text. *Structure and Power* also has a preface, or rather what is titled, appropriately enough, "In Place of a Preface." This quasi preface reveals the direction of the author's intention.

The preface was published previously, in 1981, in the Japanese journal *Chūō kōron* (*Central Review*) in a special issue devoted to discussing the status of the university today. In a somewhat expanded and changed form, then, it has become the substitute preface of this collection of discrete essays—all of which had also been previously published. The preface is really an inquiry into the possibility of the university, and into the nature of knowledge. This prefacing of a set of essays about structure and power with an essay on knowledge would seem to modulate toward a Foucauldian thematics, but there seems to be no explicit intention to move in that direction. Asada describes the preface as a preparatory movement initiating a "gradual sideways slippage toward knowledge." In writing this work, Asada states, he realized that he was surrounded by students, students of all kinds: students bored with their studies, students studying for exams, exams of all kinds—for technical schools, universities, graduate schools. He wonders, then, how his readers have become such docile and studious students. He focuses particularly on university students, who study only what is necessary in order to pursue their private lives: students forced to study for years in order to pass their university entrance exams, and who are now saturated with regimented knowledge. In the midst of these musings, Asada then clearly addresses his intended audience in the second person: This book is written to you who are standing in front of the gates of the university. What image do you have of the university and of knowledge? From these questions flows a set of choices: one can choose knowledge as object or means, or choose knowledge for knowledge's sake. Knowledge for knowledge's sake, however, often arrogates to itself the status of religion, clearly revealed by the sciences today. On the other hand, knowledge as a means degenerates into a bourgeois tool for advancement, as a mere route for success as bureaucrat or doctor, in order to live an upper-middle-class life. It is an impoverished choice.

This is the moment when Asada's argument turns, for, as he addresses his university-bound readers, neither alternative suits the style or the sensibility of the young. In fact, knowledge is a matter of style. The very attempt to reduce knowledge to a choice between alternatives betrays its inadequacy:

> Whatever is said, the matter is a problem of style, and it's to be expected that your sensibility [*kansei*] would reject both styles. When we say "style" or "sensibility," it has a very frivolous ring. But there are many occasions in which a selection of style according to one's sensibility is much more trustworthy than a subjective decision made according to reason. In that sense, I believe in the sensibility of the times.[5]

The text from that point on is a defense of knowledge as "play" (*tawamure*; *yūgi*), a game suitable for the generation that has been labeled apathetic and superficial. He denounces the metanarratives that have seemed compelling in the past—to search for truth in the struggle to create a prosperous future, to work and identify oneself with the corporate ethic, to create a revolution by leading the unenlightened masses. He (like Lyotard) proclaims the end of these metanarratives.

What replaces these metanarratives is play, a kind of local engagement, and a ceaseless turn to the "outside" (*gaibu*). He urges his readers to play with knowledge. Knowledge is that which appears in the interstices of a dualistic choice, a line of escape to the outside, a chance encounter. It is nomadic thought. From this description we can grasp the outlines of his conception of *chi*: Nietzschean "gay science," modulated through Deleuze and Guattari.

The rhetoric is emancipatory. But Asada is not just randomly directing his appeal to the neurotic Oedipalized subject of contemporary Japan, but to a very specific audience: young university test takers, those caught in the tightly programmed Japanese educational system, in which the exigencies of the exam system—the "examination hell"—almost completely determine the chances of knowledge. The Japanese examination system is a perfect allegory for Japanese late capitalism; the apparatus of the conveyor belt is the machine metaphor for the system which conveys children from good kindergarten to good company—a movement which has absolutely no essential basis, and which reveals, in the guise of a fantasy of security, the actual insecurity of the ceaseless progress of modern societies.[6] We can more clearly understand, then, the liberating intent of the preface which exposes at least one significant aspect of Nakasone's high level information society—Japanese education—as, instead, precisely the opposite: constricted and impoverished.

The well-known chart at the end of *Structure and Power* summarizes the theories and analyses so carefully laid out in the body of the text. Asada divides history into three columns: premodern, modern, and postmodern (suddenly the terms of the distinctions have turned into these), and under these three rubrics he subsumes various symbolic orderings and characteristics. In this charting, the postmodern becomes the "ideal limit" (*risōteki kyokugen*) of history and knowledge, again Deleuzean: the postmodern as the rhizomatic, the disseminated, the dispersed, and the multiple—that which is affirmative of difference as difference. The postmodern is the general economy of Bataille, marked by chance, play, escape, natural growth, schizophrenic differentiation, and anarchy—as opposed to the fixity, gambling, competition, planning, paranoiac integration, and hierarchy of the modern.

The preface is polemical, personal, exhortatory; the final table is comprehensive, structural. We can clearly perceive the appeal of both for its targeted audience. But what is the appeal of the body of the text, placed between didactic preface and charted conclusion?

Surely not the subject matter—after all there had been other books on poststructuralism, and most of them sold well under one hundred thousand copies! The simplicity of its exposition, its ability to present exotic European theories so that the masses can understand? Some critics have in fact pinned *Structure and Power*'s popularity on its simplicity. Its appeal, they say, lies in its catalog-like, schematic format; they have even compared it to the exemplary Japanese novel of consumer society, *Nantonaku, kurisutaru* (*Somehow, Crystal*), in its presentation of the brand names of vanguard French theorists. Yet Japanese I have talked with who bought the book do not consider *Kōzō to chikara* an easy introduction to poststructuralist thought. In fact, I think the reverse is true: much of its mass appeal lies in its perceived difficulty. But not just difficulty itself: Rather, its difficulty is linked to the youth and verve of its author, as well as with the liberating rhetoric of his prefatory or supplemental statements—a difficulty tied up with the myth of the author. The many interviews and articles which appeared after the publication of both *Structure and Power* and Asada's second book, *Tōsōron* (*On Escape*), thus give the sense of a myth in the making.[7]

A lengthy interview with Asada for the popular weekly *Asahi jaa-naru* (*Asahi Journal*) comprising the first article in the journal's series on "Wakamonotachi no kamigami" ("Gods of the Young"), reveals some of the attributes woven around the figure of the author: he was a piano prodigy who was expected to die young; there's not a single book in his apartment (there *is* a piano, however); he never reads a book from cover to cover, but only does "stand-up reading" (*tachi-yomi*).[8] What these legendary moments add up to is the myth of the *tensai*, the "genius," every student's wish fulfillment. The genius is a figure of knowledge without effort, of productivity without labor. There is no need for the genius to read and he owns no books; the books he produces become the replacements for the books he neither reads nor owns. There is thus a magical circuit which collapses production and consumption in an effortless generation of language. The genius is the perfect metaphor for the postmodern intellectual and the complete antithesis of the laboring student masses in contemporary Japan. It is not so much that the book is a remarkably easy exposition of poststructuralism, but rather that it is a textual sign, an artifact of magically produced "difficulty." If all commodities are fetishes, then *Structure and Power* is a particularly fantastic one, and what it fetishistically replaces is intellectual labor. The text's power and its resonance with the preface become clearer than ever.

Asada has in fact stated that he doesn't like to read books from cover to cover; he instead prefers to read partially, selectively. He believes that a book should be an encounter. One should wander through the bookstore aimlessly; it's a matter of suddenly recognizing which book is sending out a signal to you, and picking it up. "If you perceive that [signal] and you get the book, then it's the same as already having read it. You don't have to read the whole thing from cover to cover—I think it's all right just to put it by your pillow."[9] Comforting words indeed to beleaguered test takers and harried (new?) academics.

Many texts by the new academicians (or, as some prefer to be called, the postacademicians) repeat this emphasis on what could be called the technics of reading. Asada has compared the new technique of reading to eating hors d'oeuvres or snacks. Reading, eating, and consuming here become conflated—it's all a matter of incorporating something, but incorporating it lightly, without undue investment. There is thus a complex emphasis on techniques of reading and textual relationships in the new academic discourse. As we have seen, reading can be replaced by an "encounter" with a book, which sends out "signals"; one "picks up" the book. In place of reading one need only take the book to bed. The book becomes an object of desire. But this object of desire is precisely that of the commodity as an aesthetic object. As W. F. Haug states in his corrosive exposé of commodity aesthetics:

> When Marx says "commodities are in love with money" and that they ogle it with their price "casting wooing glances," the metaphor is operating on a socio-historical basis, for one category of powerful stimuli in the production of commodities for valorization is that of erotic attraction. *Thus a whole range of commodities can be seen casting flirtatious glances at the buyers*, in an exact imitation of or even surpassing the buyers' own glances, which they use in courting their human objects of affection.[10]

Haug's critique brings us back to the issue of consumption and to the anomaly of texts as flirtatious commodities. The new Japanese discourse on knowledge wants to go beyond the use value, the functional role of knowledge, in order to liberate desire (in relation to knowledge) as play and constitute a new notion of knowledge both beyond use value and knowledge for knowledge's sake; Haug would bring us back to the embodiment of knowledge in the commodity form of the book. To Haug, this "going beyond" use value is precisely "exchange value," which is valorized in the commodity form as the object (and mirror) of desire. This aestheticization is negative, deceptive.

At the same time, however, in the new academic emphasis on reading there is a valorization of texts as instrumental manuals. There seem to be almost two opposed discourses: one, on the text as an object of (consumer) desire, the other on the text as tool. The discourse on how to read (or perhaps how not to read) reflects the techno-scientific stress on "how to" or "know how" in general—not on the content of knowledge but on techniques for maximizing performance; it also reflects the closely allied imperative of maximizing speed. The new academics incorporate and closely mirror mass-mediated culture; they state that they package and present information similarly to TV commercials, in which information is tightly compressed and presented in fifteen-second bundles. The point is to get one's message across in as short a time as possible: speed determines knowledge. Or, alternatively, they compare their texts to computer manuals; the idea is to use the texts as charted modules for negotiating the mazeways of contemporary theory and society. Again, this manualization of the text seems at odds with the text as an object of desire. Yet we can see the parallels between the seductions of the text as a commodity, and the text as that which allows one to fulfill fantasies of painlessly acquiring knowledge.

A popular magazine article entitled "Postmodern Intelligence Speaks" describes how a person reputed to have supernormal powers demonstrated his ability to bend spoons in front of some assembled new academics. The idea that correct technique (which in this case was a detached relaxation, not an intense concentration) can lead to unexpected, even supernormal, results is similar to the approach to reading as "know how." Know how becomes the most essential factor in knowledge—something akin to the "Zen of spoon bending"—in consonance with the performative emphasis of technoscience. And this culmination of "how to" indeed becomes a fulfillment of desires for omnipotence and power within Japan today.[11]

This article also included the ensuing discussion among two academics (Nakazawa Shin'ichi and Asada Akira) and one nonacademic: Itoi Shigesato, author, television star, and the star "copywriter" (*kopii raitaa*) most associated with the avant-garde of Japanese department store chains.[12] It is no accident that the second "god of the young" to be chosen by the *Asahi Journal*, right after Asada, was this same Itoi. Many of the new academic stars explicitly invoke the conjunction of *chi* with commercial copywriting; they claim to present *chi* in the same terms as copywriters present their copy. They assert and affirm a direct influence both from television commercials and the linguistic compression of advertisements in general. There is a parallel between the new academic who has turned *chi* into a commodity and who mediates between the university and the masses, and the copywriter who mediates between the capitalist and the consumer.

≡≡≡≡

This fascination with copywriters and advertising in general shows up in the immense popularity of books that purport to describe and predict market trends, yet another example of the masses' specular self-reflection on their own condition. Recently a number of books have appeared, independently of each other, announcing the death of these self-same "masses" and describing the emergence of the "fragmented," the "micro," or the "meta" masses. These works contain surprisingly acute and comprehensive analyses of postmodern Japan. One of the best of these is *Now Is the Meta-Mass Age* (*Ima, chōtaishū no jidai*), published by the Parco Corporation, one of Japan's trendiest marketing, retail, and publishing ventures.[13] Not surprisingly, the text devotes much of its attention to the problems of knowledge and communication.

Meta-Mass describes the contemporary age as one that plays with "ruptured" (*bunretsu*), "counterfeit" (*giji*), and "displaced" (*zure*) communication. These themes are repeated in many other contexts that deal with the Japanese postmodern condition in terms that come from poststructuralist texts. The interlinked notions of play, slip-page, and performance are omnipresent in both academic and media discourse on current culture:

> In the meta-mass age, the relational scheme which would oppose the makers of information and the receivers of information, the intellectuals and the masses, no longer has any utility—and the initiative has passed from upstream to downstream. In this age aspects of communication have also been transformed. A new, light approach to knowledge mediates communication; without attempting to maintain deep person-to-person connections, com-munication rather finds a feeling of security in the condition of dispersal itself. Rather than the former "normal communication" of old, this is perhaps what we might call "discommunication." In short, the real situation of communication presents aspects of rupture, fictionality, and slippage. Yet the meta-masses are those that see this condition positively, as one of "play" [*asobu*]. In the meta-mass age, mass communication [*masu komi*] has lost its former functions, and has become instead "mass garbage" [*masu gomi*].[14]

In familiar Japanese fashion, this description of the deconstructive conditions of communication today ends in a pun: *masu komi* is the shortened, standard expression for "mass communication," and *gomi* is the term for "garbage" or "trash." By the shift of a phoneme, com-munication becomes its opposite: that which is left over, useless, and discommunicative.

The first aspect of the new communication (or discommunication) now addressed is that of knowledge: communication as a form of knowledge-as-play, brought about by the "commercialization of so-ciety" (*CM-ka shakai*). The editors tell us that this tendency to read diffusely—to pick something up and read only part of it, quickly—is related to the impact of TV and its commercials on Japanese society. Japanese television commercials are sixty seconds at the longest, and are usually not more than fifteen seconds long. Commercials (CMs) present the spectacle of seriality: one thing following another in rapid succession, without any meaningful linkage between them. CMs are tied together only by sheer seriality, and perhaps by their presentation of commodities (something which is, however, often subverted or elided in Japanese commercials). Commercials undercut the oppositional distinctions that define daily life—what is good and bad, ugly and beautiful, sacred and profane. In Japanese magazines as well, the distinction between text and commercial is often blurred; in fact, with their highly developed graphics, visuals, and advertising concepts, Japanese commercials often override program or text in interest. Trendy trade magazines (such as *Kōkoku hihyō* [*Advertisement Criticism*]), with their mix of cultural commentary, actual analyses of current advertisements, and dialogues between star copywriters and academicians or critics, now appeal to the meta-masses.

Meta-Mass maintains that Japanese culture today no longer exhibits the vertical cleavages of the past—the distinctions between high culture and mass culture, dominant culture and subculture, no longer apply. A hierarchical model of culture no longer fits reality; instead, culture today is a mosaic of cultural styles. Culture is dispersed, fragmented, and decentered. Intellectual distinctions are leveled; living proof exists in the person of Itoi Shigesato. Itoi is one of the most famous media stars in Japan today, with his own television show, numerous publications, and seemingly nonstop appearances in the popular press. What is the basis of this fame and media notoriety? Simply that he has written the copy for a famous series of ads produced by Seibu, Japan's largest and most innovative department store chain. These ads capture the "post-mass/meta-mass" sensibility in all its fragmented, tactile, and feeling-based diversity. And this special capacity of Itoi's reveals itself even more clearly in his ability to talk with intellectuals in all fields; he is able to exploit the shifting boundaries between serious knowledge and its playful consumption. Indeed, what we conventionally consider media—radio, television, and newspapers—are losing that role; instead, people like Itoi have become the media.

The upshot of this new milieu of communication and knowledge is this: one now consumes knowledge with feeling, with a sense of play and selectivity, exactly in the same way that one buys clothes. Style and appearance are all—and if knowledge doesn't make you feel good, then it's not knowledge. This approach to knowledge is exemplified by the formation of the academic yet avant-garde journal *GS: Tanoshii chishiki* (*GS: Gay Science*), with its reference to Nietzschean joyful knowledge. Joyful knowledge advocates what it represents, yet another loop in the already self-referential cultural condition of the meta-masses.

Once again in keeping with its origins in the advertising and marketing business, *Meta-Mass* singles out commercials as perhaps the most influential, if subliminal, means of conveying the sense of joyful knowledge. Japanese commercials often employ extraordinarily recondite and esoteric materials, words, and themes. For example, a composition by Erik Satie might form the background music for a watch commercial, the words "Russian formalism" might appear in a whiskey commercial, or the expression "postmodern" in a car ad. Commercials excel in presenting this sort of knowledge. They give viewers or readers the sense that they know something in an enjoyable way. This form of absorbing knowledge (along with the commercial message) does not prey on one's anxieties; it does not make a fool of the viewer. Knowledge is not separate from the presentation of the commodity itself; sign and commodity fuse in an almost perfect representation of the larger symbolic economy.

Any American who has gone to Japan and watched TV has been struck by the commercials—their blinding pace, their fragmentation, their high-tech construction, their wild and seemingly meaningless juxtaposition of language and images. To add to the perplexity of the newcomer, Japanese commercials often do not even refer to the product being sold; it is often difficult to ascertain either the sponsor or the product. For devotees, the commercials themselves often become highly valued aesthetic artifacts, and their creators respected and famous artists.

Japanese commercials carry out much of what postmodern art also attempts: a dispersal of meaning, a serial display of signifiers, a deconstruction of language and image. CM aficionados assert that in the best ones—those of Itoi Shigesato or Kawasaki Tōru, for example—a self-reflexive, subversive intent is at work, one that reveals the postmodern fragmented body. That, at least, is what the prominent culture critics Yoshimoto Takaaki and Kurimoto Shinichirō have claimed.[15] They maintain that the most advanced of these commercials subvert their own objectives. Yoshimoto in particular insists that the language of avant-garde copy expresses the situation of the sign in advanced capitalist society, negating the goal of selling. He overtly praises Baudrillard's notion of the simulacrum as particularly appropriate for analyzing contemporary Japanese capitalism. Copies appear, then, in a double sense: the words of the copywriter and copies of copies—copies without originals, without reference. In advertising, the referent is the product—when that referent is subverted or elided, one is left with the simulation of an advertisement, a serial succession of images where the ad no longer advertises anything.

We can understand aspects of this phenomenon by looking at the history of Japanese advertisement (which of course parallels American advertising in many respects). Classic advertising strategy demands that one product be superior to another product. But in the current era of hyperproductivity and replication, differences between products no longer suffice—differences in quality alone are not enough to ensure sales:

> So at that point a new pattern emerges, which assumes that . . . the difference between products is expected to be understood. This pattern is called symbolic product differentiation. Because there is functionally not much difference between products, advertisers have to try to present differences symbolically.
>
> When this reaches its furthest development, at the end the product ends up disappearing who knows where, and only the symbolic images which surround the business, the product, or the brand, remain. When it gets to this point, it's not the difference that a product possesses that is advertised; rather, the ad *qua* ad gains independence, and differences are established between *ads*.[16]

This process of accelerated differentiation (*saika*) mirrors the process in capitalism itself, capitalism in its advanced, postmodern form, where the principle of sheer equivalence liquifies all solid realities. The other side of that differentiation is the drive to accumulate, the repressive, productive, paranoiac side; yet in the contemporary postmodern situation the connections between the two become increasingly unreal. It is increasingly difficult to correlate production with expenditure.

That Japanese producers would throw their money into commercials which negate themselves and involve the viewer in a game of complicity reveals the strategic extremes to which capital must go in order to embody the desires of the consumer. The figure of the copywriter as cultural hero—as the embodiment of the creative, playful, and somehow subversive artist—also reveals that the world of advertising appears as a possible line of escape from the rigidified corporate and bureaucratic spheres in Japan. Much as the new intellectual seems to subvert bureaucratized, rationalized knowledge with *tanoshii chishiki* (gay science), the copywriter represents (in a double sense) a subversion of bureaucratic capitalism from the inside, in the radical form of mass advertisements. The sales figures for both the new academicians' books and those of Itoi's clients reveal, however, the same stubborn, self-referential impasse and the massive powers of recuperation of contemporary Japanese capitalism.

Usually advertising and commercial art are associated with a certain kind of realism; the avant-garde are those thinkers and artists who challenge this realism.[17] But in Japan, direct and crafted subversions of realism take place within advertisements themselves, according to Yoshimoto and many others, if by realism we are here referring to the reality of the product being advertised. While the copy of American commercials still tries to appeal to the rationality of the viewer by realistically comparing product A to product B (although recently, high-tech, Japanese style ads are appearing in the United States), Japanese advertising (in particular, television commercials) appeals more directly to desire within the symbolic economy.

———

It is tempting to locate a specifically cultural difference in the Japanese postmodern condition, and the possibility of that difference must surely be taken into account. Could it not be that Japanese practices of representation are always already radically different from Western (American?) ones, and that these differences are reflected, albeit in an exaggerated form, in commercials? Analysts of Itoi's copy, for example, have compared his use of language to haiku, to something deeply, traditionally Japanese (although others have pointed out the radical departure from the ads of the 1960s that Itoi's copy indicated).

What meaning does the notion of the simulacrum, the copy, have in a culture where the notion of the origin, it is said, has not existed: where there is no transcendental signified? Where, it is also asserted, literature and art trace the form and flow of sensuous, detached, empty signifiers—rather than fix the meaning of external signifieds; where, in short, there is no logos? Perhaps "Japan" describes the uncanny convergence of a cultural predilection for language dispersal with a postmodern capitalism whose powers of deterritorialization and differentiation seem to effect the same kind of dispersal. Has the Empire of Signs met Marx's political economy only to spawn a postmodern Empire of the Political Economy of the Sign?

These are the questions asked by postmodernist critics in Japan today. If postmodernism takes its point of departure from a contemporary crisis in representation, then what does postmodernism mean in a cultural situation where representation itself is different? Or, in critical practice, if postmodernism is equated with deconstruction, and if deconstruction deconstructs Western logocentrism, then how does deconstruction work in a culture which is nonlogocentric? The critic Karatani Kōjin, using an example from Keynes as his basis, has drawn a parallel between David Riesman's "other-directed" (*tanin shikō*) person (who must ceaselessly take the intentions and calculations of the other into account), and Baudrillard's postmodern person, for whom the "original" (i.e., God) is now nothing but a simulacrum. Subjectivity is continually deferred. He then states that

> in Japan, however, "other-directedness" in this sense [of Baudrillard's simulacrum] is not anything novel. Even if this other-directedness is a deconstruction, appearing in the form of consumer society, of Western metaphysics, it holds no deep significance for us. It's always been like this. Western thinkers' persistent critiques of "creativity" and "spontaneity" only signify the strength of those notions.[18]

Elsewhere in *Criticism and the Postmodern*, Karatani questions the concept of consumer society with its stress on individual desires, rather than on the competition between corporate bodies and the driving force of technical innovation (for example, in the production of advertisements).[19] But in conclusion, he states that Japanese postmodern thinkers and writers are trying to hit a target that doesn't even exist; regardless of their intentions, their deconstruction ends up being absorbed by Japan's "anti-constructed construction" (*hankōchikutekina kōchiku*). This failure of deconstruction is not the fault of consumer society. It is the fault of *Japanese* consumer society. And thus the problem of the postmodern in Japan is brought back to specifically Japanese cultural differences.

Karatani has been pursuing this line of analysis in recent works, particularly those centering on the Edo period (1600–1868). He construes the fundamental problematic for Japanese culture as that of a foreclosure of "intercourse" (*kōtsū*) with an "exterior" and the closed discursive space that results. This closed discursive space does not have the subjectivity and structure of Western discursive space, and in encounters with alien forms of thought, certain indigenous intellectual projects (for example, those of Motoori Norinaga and Nishida Kitarō) have effected deconstructions prefiguring current Western-derived deconstructions.

This possibility of a Japanese native deconstruction—of a deconstruction before the fact—became one of the primary issues in a discussion among Asada Akira, Karatani Kōjin, and Jacques Derrida on the occasion of Derrida's visit to Japan in 1984. The *Asahi Journal* published part of the transcript of this discussion as "The Ultra-Consumer Society and the Role of the Intellectual."[20] Their conversation begins with a discussion of the deconstruction boom in America and Japan, particularly the consumption of Asada's works in the marketplace, and continues with a consideration of indigenous deconstruction. Karatani maintains that in Japan there is essentially no structure, and "when there's no structure, how is deconstruction possible?"[21] Although Karatani thus appears to deny the possibility of deconstruction in Japan—because there is no preexisting logocentric structure—at other points in the conversation he indicates that something like a deconstruction had already taken place in Japan; that it is, in fact, "much easier for us [Japanese] to effect a deconstruction in Japan than in America."[22]

Derrida responds to Karatani by questioning the possibility of a Japanese deconstructive tradition:

At the same time that something is constructive it must be deconstructive. This is not just something that applies to Japan, but France is the same. Deconstruction is not some universal system that is the same everywhere—this is in itself the meaning of deconstruction—that it's multiple, various. There are multiple kinds of deconstruction according to specific social and historical situations. We must say that it's not possible for it to be anything but this multiplicity. . . . I'd like to say two things about what Mr. Karatani has said about Japan. You say that because in Japan there's no construction, then it is easy for deconstruction to occur. But, first of all, I wonder if there really is no construction in Japan. Secondly, I wonder if deconstruction is such an easy thing. There are these kinds of questions.

On the first point, I think that Japan today is not such a simple matter. For example, contemporary Japan is not just made up of uniquely Japanese traditions, but it should be expected that Western models have deep roots and that these are integrated into Japanese culture. Even just talking about philosophy, in the universities Western philosophy has traditionally been taught, no? I wonder if deconstruction doesn't possess some capacity to play a role in relation to those kinds of things.

The second point—I wonder if deconstruction is truly so easy in Japan. I have my doubts about whether we can say that deconstruction is a direct element in Japanese-type thought. Certainly, Japanese often say that Buddhist thought or the Zen of Dōgen was already a kind of deconstruction, but I wonder if that is so. If that were really so, then why, for example, has Asada's book received such tremendous attention? If that phenomenon of Asada were nothing more than a repetition of deconstructive elements already found within Japanese thought, then it shouldn't have called down such an enormous response in contemporary Japan.[23]

The question of indigenous deconstruction in its connections with the mass consumption of Asada's texts leads quickly into a discussion of capitalism in Japan today. Karatani asserts that contemporary Japanese capitalism has gone beyond even Baudrillard's consumer society, into some other "extremely abnormal situation" in which "even the discursive space itself has been taken up into the interior of capitalism" in a "super-accelerated differentiation process."[24] Karatani strongly emphasizes the globally unprecedented speed of dissemination in Japan's information society, upholding a fundamentally negative view of the Japanese discursive situation. Asada and Derrida, while not wholly disagreeing with Karatani's assessments, are more willing to discover positive potentials in this situation, possibilities of "different traversals, strange interchanges," for "clinamen-like encounters," in Asada's words, or "chances," in Derrida's.[25] Derrida sounds a final note of hope at the conclusion, in response to Karatani's observation that the transcript of their conversation will be consumed by the reading public within one week:

> But this is a good example! In France there is absolutely no possibility that this kind of discussion would appear in a magazine published in such numbers. Let's not simply think of this situation in just a negative way. That's because this is one "chance."[26]

═══

Whether or not Japan's indigenous thought is deconstructive or postmodern before the fact, it is clear that a system of power now operates within Japan in an extraordinarily comprehensive, structured, and orderly way. And even if Japan is a closed discursive space, Japanese capitalism recognizes no closure in its global expansiveness and in its exploitation of the third world.

I am not sure if the Japanese consumption of knowledge today, and the entire space of information and media, is as positive as Yoshimoto and others would indicate. Do Japanese ads subvert power, or do they merely rationalize it, make it entertaining? Is their postmodern exaggeration of consumer fantasies a deconstruction of the reality of their object? Lyotard states that this kind of postmodernism, rather than subverting reality with its powers of pastiche, is perhaps the most realistic mode of all, the realism "of money. . . . Such realism accommodates all tendencies, just as capital accommodates all 'needs,' providing that the tendencies and needs have purchasing power."[27] Can consumption occur in an innocent, playful space? What are the connections between Japan's accelerated symbolic consumerism and its investments in the third world? Perhaps the realism of money has instituted a new regime of knowledge which overrides the differences among representational practices in Japan, France, and the United States.

One common interpretation of postmodern consumerism takes the Frankfurt School's position of critiquing the culture industry and mass consumption; another position tends to view positively the developments in knowledge, consumption, and media (for example, McLuhan), and stresses their utopian potential. Perhaps a third, more adequate, resolution would instead resemble Deleuze and Guattari's, which recognizes both the domination of capital as well as its unprecedented liberation of desire. In that resolution, then, the point is to work with, to play with this liberated desire, to push capitalism even further in the direction of decoding or deterritorialization. That is precisely what much postmodern art, criticism, and literature attempts to do—to take the media modes and commodity forms of late capitalism to new critical extremes in deconstructing hegemonic modernism: what Hal Foster has called a "postmodernism of resistance" rather than a "postmodernism of reaction."[28] As Paul Bové states in discussing Stanley Aronowitz's *The Crisis in Historical Materialism*:

> Radical theory can join other forces in preventing this apocalypse [the destruction of society] by recognizing the independence of nature and by theorizing desire as part of the counterlogic of postmodern society. The possibility and efficacy of such theorizing is strengthened by feminism and ecology and by the counterhegemonic speculations of writers such as Gilles Deleuze and Félix Guattari. . . . The shift of capital from production to consumption along with the development of advertising and other aspects of the "production of signs" has released desire from some of the more familiar and repressive forms of bourgeois reproduction. In other words, capital catches itself in a contradiction: the use of advertising to exploit desire to sustain consumer society has released desire itself as a "natural" force no longer contained by the repressions that directed all energy into production.[29]

In Japan, this liberation of desire assumes a striking resolution in relation to the strictly codified educational system and the rigidities of its examination process, and to the demanding system of production. In no other postindustrial nation is there more of a polarity between the ordering structures of capital and the accelerated flows of energy and innovation in consumerism. There is a necessity to understand both moments, the repressive one and the liberating one: to critique both Nakasone's narrative of transparent, abundant knowledge as the sign of racial superiority, yet to at least hold open the thought that "new knowledge" might bring forth positive possibilities, even in the specular form of critical texts consumed as mass artifacts.

Notes

1 Nakasone Yasuhiro, "Zensairoku: Nakasone shushō' no chiteki suijun' kōen" ("The Complete Text: Prime Minister Nakasone's 'Intellectual Standards' Speech"), *Chūō kōron* (*Central Review*) 101 (November 1986): 152. Nakasone's speech is transcribed in this issue, 146–62. All translations are mine unless otherwise noted.
2 Gilles Deleuze and Félix Guattari, *Anti-Oedipus: Capitalism and Schizophrenia*, trans. Robert Hurley, Mark Seem, and Helen R. Lane (Minneapolis, 1983), 88–89.
3 Nakasone, "Zensairoku," 152.
4 See Jean-François Lyotard, *The Postmodern Condition: A Report on Knowledge*, trans. Geoff Bennington and Brian Massumi (Minneapolis, 1984).
5 Asada Akira, *Kōzō to chikara: Kigōron o koete* (*Structure and Power: Beyond Semiotics*) (Tokyo, 1983), 5.
6 Ibid., 14. Asada bases many of his statements on the Lévi-Straussean distinction between "cold" and "hot" societies, or premodern and modern. In "cold" societies, "excess" is dealt with in cyclical festivals (of which the exemplary examples are sacrifice and potlatch); in "hot" modern societies, differentiation is ceaselessly produced in the form of capital: there are no real "festivals" (*shukusai*) in modern societies. Instead, what is "excessive" is realized in a different form, through capitalism's unending everyday forward progress, which itself *tries* to produce "abundance" or "surplus." In modern societies, "everyday life itself has become a continuous, profane 'potlatch' " (12).
7 This text contains the famous exhortation "*Nigero!*" ("Run away!") addressed to Japanese youth. It appears alongside the perhaps more lasting legacy of his restatement of (once again) Deleuze and Guattari's paranoid/schizophrenic distinction: the *parano* vs. the *sukizo*, a binary opposition instantly appropriated by Japanese popular parlance as the latest diagnostic typing for personality differences, right

alongside blood types and astrological signs. See Asada Akira, *Tōsōron: Sukizo kizzu no bōken* (*On Escape: Adventures of the Schizo Kids*) (Tokyo, 1984).

8 Interview of Asada Akira by Tsukushi Tetsuya, in *Wakamonotachi no kamigami: Tsukushi Tetsuya tairon shū, Part 1* (*Gods of the Young: Dialogues with Tsukushi Tetsuya, Part 1*), ed. Tsukushi Tetsuya (Tokyo, 1984), 6–21.

9 Ibid., 20.

10 W. F. Haug, *Critique of Commodity Aesthetics: Appearance, Sexuality, and Advertising in Capitalist Society* (Minneapolis, 1986), 19. The quote from Marx is from *Capital*, vol. 1 (Harmondsworth, 1976), 202; emphasis mine.

11 Transcribed discussion of Asada Akira, Nakazawa Shin'ichi, and Itoi Shigesato, "Posutomodan no chisei ga kataru: kakuritsu zero no koto o kanō ni suru, kore ga 'hau tsū no kyokuchi nan ja nai?" ("Postmodern Intelligence Speaks: Making the Impossible into the Possible—Isn't That the Culmination of 'How to'?"), *Samu appu* (*Thumb Up*) (20 April 1984): 52–54.

12 "Copywriter" is not a word that has common currency in the United States today, and the figure of the copywriter has no importance in mass culture. Famous advertising executives may publish hardcover books on their successful and creative ad campaigns, but outside of the trade, these books, if read at all, merely take their place in the executive success genre recently epitomized by Lee Iacocca.

13 Gekkan Akurosu Henshū Shitsu, ed., *Ima, chōtaishū no jidai* (*Now Is the Meta-Mass Age*) (Tokyo, 1985).

14 Ibid., 175.

15 Yoshimoto Takaaki and Kurimoto Shinichirō, *Aitai genron* (*On Mutual Illusion*) (Tokyo, 1983).

16 Asada, "Saika no paranoia" ("The Paranoia of Differentiation"), in *Tōsōron*, 12; emphasis mine.

17 To Lyotard, "realism's task is to preserve various consciousnesses from doubt," to stabilize the referent, "to reproduce the syntax and vocabulary which enable the addressee to decipher images and sequences quickly, and so to arrive easily at the consciousness of his own identity. . . ." He states further that realism's "only definition is that it intends to avoid the question of reality implicated in that of art . . ." (*Postmodern Condition*, 74–75).

18 Karatani Kōjin, *Hihyō to posutomodan* (*Criticism and the Postmodern*) (Tokyo, 1985), 33.

19 Ibid., 31.

20 Transcribed discussion of Asada Akira, Jacques Derrida, Karatani Kōjin, "Chōshōhi shakai to chishikijin no yakuwari" ("The Ultra-Consumer Society and the Role of the Intellectual"), *Asahi jaanaru* (*Asahi Journal*) (25 May 1984): 6–14.

21 Ibid., 8.

22 Ibid.

23 Ibid., 8–9.

24 Ibid., 10–11.

25 Ibid., 13.

26 Ibid., 14.

27 Lyotard, *Postmodern Condition,* 76. Lyotard distinguishes between this kind of "postmodernism" or "transavantgardism"—which he states is a "realism" which attacks artistic experimentation—and postmodernism as "that which, in the modern, puts forward the unpresentable in presentation itself"; the artist's and thinker's task is "to invent allusions to the conceivable which cannot be presented" (81).

28 See Hal Foster, "Postmodernism: A Preface," in *The Anti-Aesthetic: Essays on Postmodern Culture,* ed. Hal Foster (Port Townsend, 1983), ix–xvi.

29 Paul A. Bové, "The Ineluctability of Difference: Scientific Pluralism and the Critical Intelligence," in *Postmodernism and Politics,* ed. Jonathan Arac (Minneapolis, 1986), 17.

Isozaki Arata

Of City, Nation, and Style

At the very outset, I had to answer a question I put to myself. In brief, what style should I impart to the Tsukuba Center Building? By the word *style* I do not necessarily imply any of the styles that have prevailed in the past. No matter how abstract they are, when forms manifest themselves in a building, they become clearly recognizable characteristics, or a style. And, when this style has been set, all subsequent design problems resolve themselves almost automatically. But, in this instance, I felt compelled to make a complete reexamination of even this automatic routine.

No conditions pertaining to style were imposed on me. I received no instructions—formerly common in projects for public architecture of this kind—that the building should be Japanese in flavor, oriental in style, modern, functional, or efficient-rational. As long as one adheres to its nonvisual, indirect system of economic considerations, the contemporary bureaucracy is lenient in matters of style.

Perhaps I am overstating myself, but I sense the shadow of the nation in the task of designing a central set of facilities for Tsukuba Science City. Of course, in the past, I have been commissioned by prefectures and cities to design several other public buildings, all of which were needed by their locales and the operational systems of which were all generally understood. Since most of them have been cultural facilities, approaches to definite problems have been clear, as has been the outcome of the generalization of the styles resulting from work on the given project.

The Tsukuba Center is a complex of commercial and cultural facilities including hotel, civic center, concert hall, information center, shops, and plaza. In other words, its content is such that the building might have been the undertaking of a commercial developer. If it had, recouping the initial investment would have been a prime concern. Actually, the client responsible for the project is the national Housing and Urban Development Public Corporation, but recouping the initial investment nonetheless remained a major concern. And the budget and the system whereby the facilities are to be operated and the outlay is to be recovered were drawn up in ways far too complicated for us to understand.

Complexes of various functions, like this one, are often undertaken by the same public corporation to serve as the centers of and provide commercial services for its large apartment-building settlements. In such instances, however, concern with style is less urgent since buildings of this kind are determined on the basis of purely functional and commercial considerations. But, in my view, a center for Tsukuba Science City must be designed under distinctly special conditions related to the inception of the city itself.

Tsukuba Science City is the sole new town project to be nationally planned and completed in Japan since the end of World War II. Its planning is related to that of cities in general, and people in important positions in research, government, and planning participated in it. Countless committees were formed to study practically all issues that can arise in connection with urban design. At each stage of plan implementation, outstanding representatives from each field were called upon to join in a pooling of effort. As has been true with all other large-scale projects in other regions of postwar Japan, the outcome of the work has been a modern—far too modern, in a manner suited to the efforts of an honors student—attempt to help modernist thought and methods take root in Japanese soil. It is as if the Japanese national state had decided on its own initiative to stimulate modernization. The new town manifestation of this intent is Tsukuba Science City, a place to which such national organizations as universities and research institutions may take refuge from the overcrowded conditions of Tokyo.

The result is a city—if it can be called that—devoid of all urban characteristics. Indeed—and this is no joke—officially the place is still registered as Sakura Village; in other words, on the governmental records, Tsukuba Science City does not exist.

The idea underlying the plan of Tsukuba Science City is no doubt the concept of the garden city that originated with Sir Ebenezer Howard's criticism of the overcrowded, concentrated Western city. In spite of the contradictions inherent in its premise of incorporating cities into rural circumstances, for some reason, twentieth-century urban-spatial images—radical and conservative alike—have been dominated by this idea. It is only natural then that, believing it to be the accepted, modern style, the planners of Tsukuba Science City should have opted for low-density spaces dominated by roads and greenery. But, in the latter part of this century, against a background of increased motorization of human movement, the garden city has been subjected to criticism.

The central part of Tsukuba Science City reflects a new plan drawn up after the mid 1970s and incorporating the pedestrian deck, which is an extension of the policy of separating pedestrian and vehicular traffic. Nonetheless, the roads are bordered by broad sidewalks, with adjacent planted areas; wherever officially stipulated, the facade line must be recessed from these planted areas. A network of raised, intersecting pedestrian decks cuts through each of the central-zone blocks. The central plaza is located in a site of 18.6 hectares (about 170 × 120 meters) surrounded by roads on the east and south and pedestrian decks raised 5 meters off the ground on the north and west.

Planned to be a city protruding into a rural setting, this new town project has erased all recollection of its surroundings. If it has any memories of them at all, they are limited to views of Mount Tsukuba on the northeast and a few wormlike incursions of privately owned property that were not eliminated when apportionment adjustments were made. Aside from these, Tsukuba Science City is figuratively a vacant lot. Tangible and intangible obstructions to the creation of urban forms have been systematically eliminated. The dwellers of this city are newly arrived outsiders lacking all connection with the local scene. Using new inputs of information, they live in abstract houselike spaces. Is this the kind of living space the modern age has produced? Whether it is or not, there is no denying that a city (village) has emerged in this location, though I never visited it until, in connection with this design, on the basis of the proposal system, I was requested to come to explain my ideas. And, upon first encountering this desolate modern city designed and built by the textbook, I knew it was not the kind of place where I would want to live.

Our first report amounted to a reaction against modernist city planning and an attempt to discover how many of the following elements—which are missing at Tsukuba—can be recovered and incorporated on the relatively modest site and scale of this project.

Magic: The location of Tsukuba Science City in relation to Tokyo is in the unlucky northwest, the direction known as the Demon Gate.

Labyrinth: At Tsukuba, all views from the main roads to the innermost reaches of the byroads are perfectly clear, just like what Foucault calls the Bentham observation structure.

Theatricality: The buildings are the backdrop, the plaza the stage, and the people assembled there the leading players—at Tsukuba this kind of urban space is not to be found. In its place are endless rows of isolated expressionless buildings.

Complexity: Since everything at Tsukuba has been clearly compartmentalized according to function, the overall composition is totally lacking in the kind of unexpected pleasures to be had from the fortuitous combinations characteristic of true cities.

Ambiguity: As long as theoretical lucidity prevails in standardized urban and architectural spaces, the charm of contradiction-laden polysemy cannot emerge.

Symbol: Even though a reconsideration of what to symbolize and what to relate is essential, at Tsukuba I found no buildings designed according to deliberately symbolic methods.

Neighborhood: This is, of course, difficult to realize without an accumulation of a fairly large number of diverse facilities; nonetheless, it is unreasonable to expect friendly neighborhood bustle and vitality in zones cut into segments by wide thoroughfares.

It seemed to me that the reason for employing the proposal system to select an architect for the center facilities was dissatisfaction with current conditions at Tsukuba. And I felt somewhat odd to be put in charge of the design because people in authority were disposed to criticize a national-scale new town project—unprecedented in postwar Japan—that had called on the combined efforts of the entire urban-planning camp.

I have already mentioned my awareness of the shadow of the national state behind this project. Though political representatives kept quiet, other parties were apparently concerned that the center facilities symbolize the entire Tsukuba project in one way or another. As I have said, no forceful demands in connection with style were made. Still, some people felt the center should incorporate a tower standing on the city axis; others expressed a desire for symmetry as a sign of monumentality. Objections sounded stronger when, after it had settled down to its present form, the plan was criticized for want of monumentality. But from the very beginning I had insisted that we avoid relying solely on centrality and symmetry and always had an answer ready to such objections.

I think my being worried about selection of a style can be understood in the light of my discovery that the thing to be symbolized in this instance is Japan as a state. Willy-nilly, I was compelled to select a style that would stand for the whole Japanese nation, even though that style could be indirect and operative on two or three levels.

The national state and commercial merchandise discourse on architecture—including elements from past styles, in the process of development of modern Japanese architecture since the second decade of this century—can be plotted by means of a simple formula, the main axis of which is the style the national state found suitable for use. Indeed, as if in evidence of the government's importance in these matters, Western architecture was initially transplanted to Japan by means of the Tokyo Imperial University, a state institution. A similar concern with the kind of design, architectural methods, production systems, and styles Japan as a nation should use has persisted throughout the century. The Architectural Institute of Japan, which was formed after 1910, issued a prospectus entitled "What Should Be the Future Architectural Style for Our Nation?" In 1945, examining the competition entries of Maekawa Kunio and Tange Kenzō for a project for the "Great East Asian Coprosperity Sphere," Hamaguchi Ryūichi wrote "The Problem of the Japanese Architectural Style." After World War II, Nishiyama Uzo often spoke of what he called "the people's architecture." And interest in the same kind of topic pervaded the thought of the traditionalists and popularists of the 1950s and the Metabolists of the 1960s. In opposition to this patriotic trend was the commercial school of design, illustrating the Osaka capitalist philosophy, of such men as Watanabe Setsu, Yasui Takeo, Tange Kenzō, and Murano Tōgo, all of whom treat buildings as commercial merchandise. After the 1920s, modern architecture in the narrow sense, interest in the theories of production structures, and demand for new technical innovations pushed the national architectural style in the direction of a commercial style. Then, in the 1960s, the Metabolists effected a union between theories of architecture as commercial merchandise and architecture as representative of the national state. At about the same time, however, the nature of the Japanese state was undergoing a fundamental change; in other words, the nation was being managed on the basis of commercial theories and had fewer opportunities to express its own will clearly. In short, the state was withering away.

These circumstances are vividly illustrated by the business and government district adjacent to the imperial palace, in the heart of Tokyo. The majority of the buildings there now were completed in the 1960s, but two—and only two—older ones have stood the test of time and history: the National Diet Building and the Dai'ichi Life Insurance Building. Completed in the 1930s and designed on borrowings from the art deco (classic) style, these two are superior to all the many far larger and more glamorous new buildings in the neighborhood, and their superiority derives in part from the subtle changes taking place in the Japanese nation during the 1960s. In comparison with the old buildings, for example, the Supreme Court Building and the headquarters of the Tokyo Metropolitan Police seem much less powerful, even fragile. I suspect that the reason for the comparative weakness of these two newer buildings can be traced to the way in which the national state was being engulfed, nearly to the vanishing point, by capitalism at the time when they were being designed. Though he still exists as a living person, the emperor of Japan has divested himself of all claims to divinity and had vanished as the unifying element in the national structure. In a similar way, while still extant, the national state has vanished, robbing designers of a mainstay that their predecessors enjoyed. The architects of the Supreme Court Building and the Metropolitan Police headquarters seem to have been laboring under the delusion that it is possible now, as it was in the 1930s, to give visual expression to the social hierarchy of emperor, state, capital, and the people.

In the 1970s, amalgamation of emperor, state, and capital generated a prevailing structure in which architecture became commercial merchandise. And, when this happened, private individualism arose in opposition to the trend to lump all architecture in the commercial catalog. The opposition manifested itself in two ways. The first way was pursued by designers of residential architecture, who do their work in close contact with individual clients only. In opposing generalization—in the form of mass production or duplication —such architects seek their own, enclosed solutions to problems. By calling it art, they isolate the house from the social context and, at the same time, escape the temptation of mass production. A group of currently internationally famous architects can be fitted into this pattern. But they all run the risk of being isolated and, in this sense, seem pathetic. When their hothouse operations become fashionable, their designs are consumed faster. When people are interested only in novelty, consumption reaches such a peak that supply is depleted. And it becomes very difficult for the architect to preserve private individuality under such circumstances.

The other way to oppose the apparently fated trend for architecture to be swallowed up in either the sociopolitical (state) or the commercial (capital) context is to call on the assistance of a cultural context to avoid dealing with actual operative circumstances and to elevate architectural discourse to what can be called a meta-level. (The one category that might seem to transcend commercialism is religious architecture, which is, however, no longer ground for general architectural statement.) The process I mean may be figuratively described as putting the state and capital in parentheses and once again writing the word *Architecture* in majuscule.

This means making the first-person individual the core of architectural design. I was almost exclusively concerned with method in the 1970s because I emphasized the first-person individual. Although I concentrated on manner, I always designed houses—even if they were called works of art—to be appreciated, not from the outside, but from the inside. And, when they left my hands for the hands of their owners, those houses returned to the sociopolitical context. In other words, though I was responding to both the state and commerce, I did not talk about it.

Ultimately, thinking of this kind moves closer to cultural and philosophical contexts and is fundamentally unrelated to practicality. It occurs on the meta-level, where historically all Architectural, with a capital A, statements have taken place.

The emphasis on the first-person that I found a valid trajectory was in effect no more than a switch of context intended to allay a fall into the practical level, where many prohibitions are in effect. In other words, it is amateurism as opposed to the professionalism required of commercial architecture produced to conform to the prevailing social framework. The national state issues architects' licenses to ensure that such professionalism is maintained. But, unless some effort is made to broaden viewpoints beyond that framework, architects end up in the slavish position of doing no more than docilely creating the kinds of buildings society demands. Recent disputes appearing in *The Japan Architect* about "large-scale architecture" and "wholesome architecture" strike me as slightly domineering attempts to change course for the sake of self-justification on the part of designers who have become bound to the professionalism of buildings designed as commercial merchandise. Criticizing such an attitude on the basis of amateurism alone is probably leaning too far in one direction. Consequently, I have consistently adopted the stance of a thorough-going amateur on the level of architectural statement while striving to be professional as a commissioned designer. This ambiguity was the only free way to oppose the overwhelming commercialization of architecture that took place during the 1970s. The people who demonstrated interest in my proposals related to methodology did so only because they were able to see, behind my words, my actual professionally produced works. I am perfectly well aware that, without those works, people would have put less trust in my theories. And the knowledge makes me so heated that I have attempted to join a cultural context.

After a quarter of a century of thinking about these matters, I have at last attained an amount of self-confidence because I have seen that architecture can be adequately independent with its own inherent forms and styles and without breaking with the current of commercialization or adhering strictly to the amateurist viewpoint. In short, I have come to the conclusion that we must direct our attention to the powers of evocation inherent in forms and styles themselves. They are always to be found even in architecture conceived on the basis of economic criteria, by which they do not, however, necessarily abide. Instead, they tend to have evocative powers that disturb and twist the commercial circuit. In the broad sense, their operation is cultural. And, when these forms and styles are clearly manifested in architecture, they can generate various binding powers. This consideration brings us back to the presently unconsidered question of what kind of style a work of architecture should have. (The question is related even to simple classical styles.) Since the 1960s—that is, since the time I began my design career—when Japanese government and capital merged, no one has asked this question. In the face of the rapid commercialization of architecture that has taken place during that period, no doubt attempting to oppose the trend by emphasizing individuality was the utmost that could be done.

Sensing the national state behind the Tsukuba Science City Center project made me look back over the course of development in architectural statement in those years. Though considerations of this issue must not be simplified into attempting to determine the kind of style suited to use by the national state, I am afraid present circumstances are likely to short-circuit them in precisely that direction. With this likelihood in mind, I asked myself what style the center building should have.

———

It is easy to imagine how simple, clear neoclassicism operates. In the early part of the nineteenth century, national states employed this transparent style for facilities in such capitals as Berlin, Paris, and Washington, D.C., and in official buildings in regions more or less remote from governmental centers. Since it is based on a system of orders, the classical style can be freely enlarged or diminished at will. Neoclassicism adds calculated mass and volume to the classical system. To the last details, it adheres to overall proportions and is always lucid and transparent. It might be called the visualization of order, which extends to the interior as well as the exterior. Nothing could be better suited to the needs of governments—which need to enforce their will to the last details too—than this virtually perfect architectural style. And it is not only because of the ease with which it gives a monumental appearance that, for more than a century, governments have used it in their institutions. A still more important reason is that a style in which order is pervasive stimulates a clear awareness of the presence of the state structure throughout a domain.

Since 1950, however, as capital and government have tended to fuse in most nations of the world, modern architecture (having ceased to be avant-garde) has come to be considered suitable for the construction of institutions that formerly were housed in neoclassical buildings. In place of ruthlessly eliminated ornaments, modernist architecture employed icons from the world of industrial products. It was popular for its symmetry, which made possible buildings of a monumental character, and it preserved the continuity, transparency, and permeability of neoclassicism. Housed in a building in this style, a government organization was able to extend its image to the smallest details. Furthermore, the modernist style met the needs of government and capital alike to express identity clearly. Finally, it has been able to serve state and capital equally well because it is totally permissive of the theories of architectural commercialization.

But it was its very all-pervading transparency that first made me question the use of modern architecture. When they are stripped of governmental context, I am very fond of both neoclassic and good modernist architecture. The lucid system of neoclassicism, which predominated for a century and a half, is evocative. Tsukuba Science City is laid out on the basis of a modernist-style plan, creating clear, bright, urban spaces. It would be easy to link a modernist-style building to such a plan. But I believed it impossible to accommodate the Tsukuba Center with a transparent system. And this brings me back again to the shadow of the national state.

I have said the amalgamation of government and capital resulted in the disappearance of the state. I believe that this is the reason that Japan has been able to make extraordinary economic growth and to engage in stiff competition with other nations. But recent economic friction has made it necessary to reexamine the nature of Japan Incorporated. In short, international tension is evoking a reappearance of the state. During approximately a decade starting in 1970, while I was almost ceaselessly engaged in teaching, conducting exhibitions, and lecturing abroad, I became aware that Japan was beginning to be practically compelled by other countries to clarify its image as a nation.

My own vague image of Japan as a nation had a bearing on the choice of style I made for the Tsukuba Center building. By a process of elimination, I chose not to resort to the lucid, coherent institutional style, and mentioned my decision in the items of our original proposal. In my search for a shifting, revolving, flickering style, the process of elimination led me to reject other possibilities. I did not want to use anything associated with the idea of traditional Japan, which, if generally applied throughout the design, would have an effect similar to that of the neoclassic style.

I decided that the course to take was to allow the details to speak clearly but to generate new meaning by drowning each other out and to direct the evocative powers of a style, in which continuity is lacking and confusion is allowed to persist, toward the negative for the sake of motivation. This is the kind of image I assembled to represent the Japanese state, which, while existing, is highly reluctant to step out into the clear. The style is highly refracted and unclear but only in the parts that have no need of speaking out in a loud voice. The form of expression indicated by this style is clearly simile. If possible, the style should generate a different syntax as a consequence of double- and triple-layer operations.

After several trial-and-error selections, I decided upon a sunken plaza set on the urban axis and enclosed on two sides by two wings arranged to form an L. (See photo 3.) The axis proceeds northward, ultimately reaching a tower that serves as an observation platform. This arrangement may represent the sole nonmodernist compositional principle surviving at Tsukuba. The axis coincides with the entrance of, but passes through, the concert hall. The oval sunken plaza, which lies along the axis, has a cascade flowing down into it on the northwest side. (See photo 4.) The water drains out through the middle. Instead of a towerlike projection, I have used this sunken plaza as metaphoric expression of the hollowness of the center. The minute I learned that, by coincidence, the oval plaza is the same size as the piazza on the Capitoline Hill in Rome, I immediately set out inverting icons. At the Capitoline Hill, it is necessary to mount a flight of steps, on the axis, to reach the plaza, in the center of which, on a convex surface, stands an equestrian statue of the emperor Marcus Aurelius. At Tsukuba, a flight of steps leads down into the plaza, which has a concave surface for the drainage of water from the cascade. In addition, the parts of the pavement pattern that are black in Rome are white, and vice versa, at Tsukuba. I have used the pattern, which is an immediately recognizable cliché symbolizing the pavement of the forecourt of the Senate Building, for the iconographic confusion it introduces and to underscore the negative meaning of the central part of the plan.

Since the design was made public I have frequently been criticized, directly and indirectly, for having mistakenly made reference to the Capitoline piazza. Some said, by using deliberate reference to something that originates in the West, I violate cultural-context rights. Others have denounced the willful way in which I make additions and alterations to the original. Still others have warned me of profanity in the way I consumed the original. The only answer I have to these criticisms is that I was fully aware of what I was doing when I did it. But behind the objections I sense animosity toward the revival of orthodox styles and the desire to maintain firm relations with the

1. The Museum of Contemporary Art, Los Angeles. *Photo by Furudate Kat-suaki, courtesy of Arata Isozaki & Associates, Tokyo, Japan*

2. (below) Tsukuba Center Building, Tsukuba Science City. View of the hotel wing, looking east from the edge of the pool at the head of the cascade descending to the sunken plaza. The sculpture, entitled "Laurel and Papyrus," was designed by Nagasawa Hidetoshi. *Photo by Ishimoto Yasuhiro, courtesy of Arata Isozaki & Associates, Tokyo, Japan*

3. (opposite, top) Oval sunken plaza with cascade, looking west, Tsukuba Center Building. *Photo by Ishimoto Yasuhiro, courtesy of Arata Isozaki & Associates, Tokyo, Japan*

4. (opposite, bottom) Cascade flowing into sunken plaza, looking north, Tsukuba Center Building. *Photo by Ishimoto Yasuhiro, courtesy of Arata Isozaki & Associates, Tokyo, Japan*

2.

3.

4.

5.

5. (right) Bronze statue of laurel tree ("Laurel and Papyrus" by Nagasawa Hidetoshi) above cascade, looking west, Tsukuba Center Building.

6. (below) Facade of the concert hall, south of the sunken plaza, Tsukuba Center Building.

Photos by Ishimoto Yasuhiro, courtesy of Arata Isozaki & Associates, Tokyo, Japan

6.

cultural context to which the styles belong. As I have often said, the Katsura Palace, the Parthenon, the Capitoline piazza, and so on all live in a time and place equidistant from us. Anything occurring in the history of architecture—even the history of the world—is open to quotation. But the important point to notice is that, once quoted, things lose their original meaning and generate new meanings with an effect resembling the concentric circles rippling around a stone thrown in a body of water. If, as some people fancy, quotation must follow strict laws, it is only within the framework of revivalism. As far as consumption of the original goes, this is essentially the production structure on which human culture has relied from the outset; and there is no reason to prohibit it.

So I make reference, too, to the basic division of Western architectural facades in the tripartite horizontal segmenting of the walls into bands corresponding to the attic, the *piano nobile*, and the *rez-de-chausée*, all of which, together with window ornaments, though apparently eliminated in modernist architecture because of powerfully inclusive posts and roofs, actually survived, vestigially, as the open ground level *en pilotis*, the free floor and elevation plan, and the rooftop garden. The only difference between the two systems is that the older one relies on bearing walls and the modernist one on post-and-beam structures. There is no ethical reason preventing us from using either. Furthermore, since at Tsukuba they stand behind a double-level arrangement consisting of the front road and the inner pedestrian deck, the three divisions of the wall surfaces are an appropriate device.

Massive rustication of the concrete parts of the walls and a portico resembling sawtooth posts are the outcomes of my own personal obsessions. (See photo 6.) I would have treated them differently if authoritarian oppressiveness had been my goal. Instead, however, I conceived of them as facade elements on an urban scale. I have done no more than reaffirm the portico—which modernism abandoned—as a way of articulating elevations. And I chose the sawtooth form because it was used by three men—architects and artists—whom, though separated by two centuries, I greatly admire: Giulio Romano, Clauda Nicolas Ledoux, and Constantin Brancusi.

Cliché-like similes from historical styles are used extensively in the details, not as vague suggestions, but directly. I adopted this plan because of my feeling that, while emphasizing individuality, the building must be circuited toward the city, politics, and society. I have deliberately called on things that have been made kitsch as long as they retain evocative powers but have employed counterbalances to prevent any one image from dominating. (If I had not done this, the entire building would have become kitsch.) For this reason, elements seem to have been fragmented and then sutured together again. Or perhaps they look like so much historical refuse crammed helter-skelter into a framework. The reason for this is simple. Starting at one end, I crushed the clear system—of the kind usually preferred for institutional architecture—with the result that fragments overlap, setting up friction, betraying, and then being stitched again with a vague hope that a new statement will emerge from among the sutures. One by one, I buried the limitlessly subdivided parts, and all that remains now is the recollection of the interminable nightmare.

Addendum

If I were to say that Tsukuba Center Building is the expression of the absence of something, I would not be taken seriously. Yet actually, the central concept of the design is that very *absence*. Visually, there is a clearly defined center. In such a center, one would expect to find a symbol of authority or exalted position—of majesty, officialdom, the state, or the sovereign. But what happens if one chooses a method that omits that expected presence? This design is the result of my experimentation with just such an idle question.

All the details of this building are metaphorical. Several points in the whole plan, for example, allude to Velázquez's *Las Meninas*. When you visit the building, you will come upon the oval-shaped sunken plaza (photo 3). One portion is wrinkled and misshapen as if it had been gnawed at. Rather than descending directly to the lower level, you gaze around at the hotel on the east side (photo 2), and at the facade of the concert hall on the south side opposite (photo 6). You might find yourself wandering into these buildings, but nothing attracts you into descending to the oval plaza. You stroll around on the level above, enjoying the excellent view. Right below is the focal point. Oriented toward it are two water sources, one a smooth stone-faced waterfall (photo 4), and the other a cascade flowing over rough stones from a bronze statue of a laurel tree, a symbolic transmutation of Daphne at the water's edge (photo 5). These two streams meet and are drawn into one stream that disappears underground.

Although situated like the Capitoline piazza, with its crowning statue of Marcus Aurelius, every relationship is reversed here: this square is the lowest point in the whole—both rainwater and the line of vision are drawn toward and into the earth at the center.

If there is any ruling concept, it lies in this central point. Because it becomes the center of sight, it is the point one would expect to be given visualized substance. But the systems that protrude into this center instantaneously reverse the sight line, imposing a governing order over the whole. Here, the structure of the design has undergone an inversion process. And it is here that the metaphor of *Las Meninas* applies.

Velázquez's *Las Meninas* is a painting done from the perspective of the king and queen of Spain, whose portrait is being painted by the artist within the palace, El Escorial, where Velázquez was then in service. At the left is the painter himself and his canvas seen from the back. Beside him are the princess and several ladies-in-waiting seen from the perspective of the real subjects of the portrait, the king and queen.

Once we realize this, we notice at the center back of the painting a small mirror hanging on one wall of the room, and there the king and queen can be seen as they pose for the artist. If one does not notice this clever trick it is simply a painting of a group of ladies-in-waiting. If noticed, it becomes clear that the entire work is an attempt intended precisely to portray the royal couple in absentia. Though paintings are traditionally depicted from the perspective of the artist, this work is like a mirror image reflecting even the painter himself. But it is not a mirror image such as artists often use to paint self-portraits; the perspective is fictitiously set from the standpoint of the king and queen who are physically not in the scene of the painting at all.

If my trick of inverting the Capitoline piazza is criticized as no more than a conventional simile, I would vindicate myself by invoking the metaphor of *Las Meninas*. The architect has been hired not by a king, but by a state, and requested to do a portrait of the state. And yet the countenance of the state is not as clear as that of an existing ruler, and even if it were, I feel that I would not want it to emerge clearly. In order to deal with this ambivalence, I made the center simply a space—a void: I portrayed a metaphor in which all the usual spatial arrangements are reversed or inverted. Everything is situated around a void, descending and then vanishing into oblivion at the center. It is Michelangelo in reverse. At the same time, there is a miscellany of fragments scattered around the periphery of this center. And here again I would invoke the portraits of the ladies-in-waiting in *Las Meninas*. These women are all facing different directions, observing no unified pose or sense of dialogue with one another. Although they may be posed in the composition singly, they seem oblivious to any interrelationship of any apparent significance. This mysterious lack of integration is surely one of the reasons for the continuing fascination of Valázquez's work.

For most of the fragments I have cited historical forms, but once borrowed, they are torn out of the context of which they were originally a part and transferred into a newly created context. In the process of transfer, some elements have been greatly changed, some so thoroughly abstracted that they cannot be identified.

The Tsukuba Center Building possesses the complex structure of a long novel, and it is filled with so many direct and quiet concrete allusions to endow the details of fragments with an independent and powerful dynamic of their own. In other words, I had to make each detail self-sustaining so that it could stand without relation to others. But the explicit representation of these concretely manifested fragments is by no means consistent, nor do they converge on one point, but ceaselessly revolve in the periphery of that unoccupied center. If one were to give a metaphor for the void center, it might be that everything—line of vision, water, meaning, representation— is devoured by the earth itself as a result of its own form.*

Note

* This article was originally published in Japanese in *Shinkenchiku*, November 1983. The English version is in *The Japan Architect*, January 1984.

H. D. Harootunian

Visible Discourses/Invisible Ideologies

There are several discourses on the social
in twentieth-century Japan devoted to making sense of the effects of industrialization
and of new forms of instrumental knowledge,
including its vast propensity to differentiate spheres of learning into specialized disciplines reflecting more basic social divisions.
Yet among these discourses I hope to show
that none more clearly and enduringly sought
to resolve the aporia of social indeterminacy
(in which declining remnants of a precapi-
talist order coexisted in an antagonistic relationship with a capitalist society, worked
to prevent the fulfillment of an uncompleted
past) than the 1942 symposium on "overcoming the modern" (*kindai no chōkoku*).
This uneasy cohabitation of earlier modes of
cultural production alongside newer epistemological strategies in the same social space
(what Ernst Bloch, rereading Marx's conception of "unequal development," would call
nonsynchronicity) was further exacerbated
by a war against the West; it demanded a
resolution of the question of social deter-

minacy, concerning the principles bonding Japanese society, if the survivors of the past were not to be altogether eliminated by a capitalist present and its theory of social relationships. But what began as an effort to re-imagine the social as distinct from the prevailing social imaginary (how societies seek to represent the "real" by calling it reality and endowing its signification, even though the "real" remains outside of representation) in prewar Japan became, forty years later, a social discourse. In other words, a discourse which tried to account for history as a principle of social constitution was transformed into an arrangement in which the distinction between representation and the real was effaced in order to make society appear without history. Whereas the instituting discourse, calling for the overcoming of modernity, still conceded the importance of history for explaining the development of a traditional order into a modern society as a condition for moving to another level, the later "conquest of the modern," promoted by the government of Ōhira Masayoshi in 1980, sought to displace history, or simply to get outside of it, in an effort to proclaim a narrative in which premodern and modern elements comingle as if they now constituted a natural and timeless coupling.

Yet before this narrative pastiche was constructed to take the place of the older discourse on the social, the Japanese intellectual Takeuchi Yoshimi, in a desperate and lonely intervention to forestall the elimination of the social by the state, reread the critique of modernity in the early postwar period as a prerequisite for the resolution of the aporia between discourse and the social, in order to find a model of modernity that belonged neither to the West nor to a dead and discarded past. Takeuchi's text on *kindai no chōkoku* represented a superimposition on the symposium's text; it functioned as a palimpsest that allowed the critique of modernity to glimmer through while it blotted out the more strident justifications of war. Although he sympathized with the symposium and the task it set for itself, he was neither insensitive to its ineffectualness nor indifferent to its moral hypocrisy with respect to the war in Asia. But the palimpsest, bringing together different times and texts, risked duplicity, insofar as Takeuchi sought to combine views discordant and ceaselessly contradictory. *Palimpsest* gave way to the construction of a *pastiche*, which had no need for articulating a reasoned defense or synthesizing seeming opposites, since the operation was founded on the composition of random chards of life and history, which obeyed no other logic than the frame that contained it.

This last moment was inaugurated by the Ōhira brain trust in a remarkable text announcing the advent of a new age of culture. Whether or not it can be considered a postmodern moment depends entirely upon how the category is understood. If, by postmodern, we are willing to recognize that it aims to condemn the modernist separation of politics and culture, thereby attributing the cause of disorder to this momentous division, then it is possible to read as postmodern all of those efforts that seek to reinstitute the regime of a political totality at the expense of dissolving the social, without resorting to the more coercive methods usually associated with established forms of totalitarianism. According to Claude Lefort, postmodern polity manages to eliminate the opposition between the state and civil society by dissolving the social into the "pure generality" of the political.[1] Its discourse will radiate the signs of its unity and, hence, of the homogeneity of the objective domain. By manifesting the presence of the state throughout the social space, it conveys, through a series of representatives, the principle of power informing the diversity of activities, and incorporates them into a model of common allegiance. It carries out this operation by "diffusing itself throughout the circuits of socialization, by elaborating signs whose representative function is no longer identifiable," by taking actors, turning them into subjects and inserting them into systems so that the discourse almost speaks through them and almost abolishes the space, implicit in modernist ideology, between enunciation and that which is enunciated.[2]

While the postmodern would, in its denunciation of an adversarial culture, says Hal Foster, "confound cause and effect" in order to reaffirm prevailing political and economic arrangements, its conception of order would conform to all of those efforts to *re*-present a totalized polity in the simulacrum of the social, even as the social is effectively eliminated. This will become evident from a reading of the *Bunka no jidai* (*Age of Culture*) text. This text proclaims, in comparison to earlier attempts to imagine an "overcoming" of modernity, that the time has come for "conquering the modern" (it is important to note the tone of militancy of this forced march) in order to implement the new age of culture. This new age of culture will constitute the final contraction and reversal of the categories of the "real" into a dense, seductive, and entirely cynical communal or consensual order which appeals to cultural uniqueness for its certainty even as it is held together by commodities and signs signifying signs. Jean Baudrillard has proposed, quoting Ecclesiastes in one of his more hallucinatory texts, that the simulacrum is " 'never that which conceals the truth, but is, instead, the truth which conceals that there is none.' " "It is the generation by models of the real without origins or reality: a hyperreal," "the map that precedes the territory." By this measure, the so-called real can easily be produced from "miniaturized units, from matrices, memory banks and command models," to form a pastiche which can be reproduced indefinitely and which need not appear rational, since it is not measured against any idea or "negative instance."[3] Under these circumstances, culture remains an operational instrument largely or principally at the disposal of state control, and is projected to conceal bureaucratic "rationality." As a result, the earlier modernist critique of 1942, and even Takeuchi's later courageous intervention, became a postmodern "therapeutic," not to mention a "cosmetic," employed to justify a return to the solidarity of the traditional family and the truths of morality and a Japanized culture. In this scheme, modernism is reduced to a style and consigned to a moment in history, a moment which has now been "conquered" and condemned as a "cultural mistake." Elements enlisted from premodern and modern experiences are easily combined and conflated to erect a false unity, whereas culture and history are smoothed over to appear natural, difference is subsumed by identity, and the Other is finally banished from the social order.

In contemporary Japan there has been a relentlessly obsessive "return" to "origins": an orchestrated attempt by the state to compensate for the dissolution of the social by resurrecting "lost" traditions against modernism itself, and by imposing a master code declaring "homogeneity" in a "heterogeneous present." It is precisely an effort to install a master code, an effort systematically announced in the official statement of the Ōhira government but surely prefigured in the discourse of countless intellectuals, including Yoshimoto Takaaki,

Nakane Chie, Murakami Yasusuke, Hamaguchi Eshun, Kimura Bin, and others too numerous to mention. This master code would eradicate the scandal of difference, for all times to come, in the name of an "affirmative culture" rooted firmly in reified values. Such a culture has characterized the program of Japanese governments since Ōhira's prime-ministership proclaimed an end of the modern—that is, since the postwar era and the "advent of an age of culture."

In the case of the *bunka no jidai* program, all hope of a referent is discarded. Moreover, this loss of reference is accompanied by a rejection of the point of certainty outside of society, in favor of an affirmation of discourse solely as discourse, now extricated from the social, to mask the "bureaucratic fantasies" of: abolishing the historical in History; restoring the logic of a "society without history" and identifying "the instituting moment with the instituted"; denying the unpredictable and the unknowable; and firmly establishing an order that will not "tolerate the image of an internal social division." This order claims to be homogeneous, whether racially or socially, inasmuch as everybody belongs to the "middle stratum" despite all the differences which exist in fact.

≡≡≡

In July of 1942, a group of distinguished intellectuals, academics, and critics were summoned to Kyoto by the Literary Society (*Bungakkai*) to discuss the theme of "overcoming the modern." All of the participants believed that the debate, convened six months after the outbreak of the Pacific War, would mark the end of "modern civilization" in Japan and would reveal the outline of a "glorious new age." Composition of the debate was divided along a line that distinguished two major intellectual groups: the Literary Society and the Romantics. Among the better-known participants were figures like Kobayashi Hideo, Nishitani Keiji, Kamei Katsuichirō, Hayashi Fusao, Miyoshi Tatsuji, Kawakami Tetsutarō, and Nakamura Mitsuo. Under the shadow of war, the debate's principal purpose was to discuss the larger "world-historical meaning" of the event itself, and how this understanding might relate to the vision of a future that no one could immediately perceive, but which all anxiously sought to envisage. One of the organizers of the conference, Kawakami Tetsutarō, stated this overall concern most clearly in his concluding remarks. He proposed that, apart from the question of the success or failure of the discussions, it was an indisputable fact of immense importance that such an intellectual encounter had taken place within the first year of the outbreak of the war. He felt that the discussions reflected a struggle between "the blood of the Japanese, which truly motivates our intellectual life," and "Western knowledge, which has been superimposed upon Japan in modern times." He was convinced that the ensuing conflict would be a desperate and bloody one.[4]

If the intellectuals who discussed the question of modernity in Kyoto believed that the task before them was to envisage a social order beyond the contingencies which plagued contemporary Japanese society, they also saw the war as the agent capable of finally conquering the modern. This is not to say that there was complete unanimity or consensus among the participants, but all could agree that the war, however they felt about it, now made it possible to construct a new social imaginary that would "overcome" the innumerable contradictions of Japanese society. For the most part, "modern" meant the West, its science, and the devastating effects it had inflicted on the face of traditional social life. A number of writers, like Kamei and Hayashi, recommended that the inappropriateness of science and even technology had, in fact, alienated the Japanese from their founding myths and their gods, to such an extent that the real meaning of "overcoming" required the reintegration of the Japanese with the spirit of the *kami* (gods) and the elimination of the effects of reason, with its ceaseless propensity to divide and separate. Here was revealed the ideology of the debate, insofar as the discourse was made to suppress all of those signs which, many believed, threatened to imperil and even destroy the sense of certainty concerning the nature of the social: that is to say, signs of genuine historicity, of contemporary daily life, of precisely all of those things fractioned and fractured through the "dispersing effects of socialization, autonomization, differentiation" and signs—which, in other words, now promised to make society in the 1930s "alien to itself." In this respect, the "secondary discourse"—the "folding over of the primary, manifest discourse"—could easily become an ideology in search of a representation which, by invoking a juxtaposition of tradition, modern, and a transcended modern, could establish a society "without history" at the heart of a historical society. This goal was never fulfilled for a number of reasons, but was, as we shall see, at the heart of the later projection of a holonic society in the new age of culture.

While the debate's most perceptive participant, the critic Kobayashi Hideo, early expressed an ambivalence toward any effort to overcome the modern, as he felt that Japan was already modern, this sense of timeless essences unmediated by history constituted a principal part of his own intervention. Kobayashi proposed that conceptions of progressive history inevitably misled modern men and created false expectations by deluding them with a "poetry of the future." But forms of beauty remind societies of a timeless quotient, perhaps, though he never said it, a "poetry of the past," which has successfully overcome history, especially those conditions attending the production of the particular object. Beauty, he insisted, never "evolved" in a progressive, purposeful manner, and can never be understood from the historically motivated perspective of the modern.[5] Thus, Kobayashi called for a knowledge of essences; these essences could be easily identified with enduring artifacts from "tradition," inasmuch as they had survived the limitations of their own history and outlived the moment that had given them expression. Yet his understanding rarely strayed from a more familiar Platonic conception of beauty as a form of eternal truth. Overcoming the modern did not mean an "advancement" to a new period, but a reunion outside of history with the eternal forms of truth and beauty, possibly an encounter with the unrepresentable, the sublime. Such a view supported a program calling for the traditional cultural ideals, allowing them their own space and time, not because they were necessarily and uniquely Japanese, but because they had survived time, as tradition, in such a manner that they might serve as sources of renewal, creative inspiration, and identity in a world insisting on the sameness of the modern. For Kobayashi was most troubled by the fear that Japan would become a replica of Western society. He dramatized this concern by enlisting Marx's own irony, which itself constituted an ironic gesture; Kobayashi described the modernization of the West as a "tragedy" and the second manifestation of it in Japan as a "comedy." The quintessential comedians of Japan had not yet captured the stage, he remarked, but they would soon.[6] Only art, he observed, would save Japan from the contingency that he associated with history, despite the effort to represent the historical as the succession of reason and progress, and to make it appear orderly.

The debaters concentrated on one further issue. In interrogating the meaning of civilization, identified with the Meiji achievement, participants like Kamei Katsuichirō and Hayashi Fusao drew attention to its epistemological consequences—the specialization and compartmentalization of knowledge. Kamei observed that this effect generated a profound loss in the sense of "wholeness" in life among the Japanese, and constituted a serious disruption of traditional spirituality. Specialization had proceeded at a relentless pace in the twentieth century, driven by a relentless utilitarianism that accompanied the idea of progress willfully promoted by the Meiji Enlightenment. In this fateful process, Kamei remarked, the real "philosophers of life" were destroyed—by which he meant those courageous figures like the Christian leader Uchimura Kanzō, who had resisted the assimilation of modes of specialization and instrumentality for a unified vision of knowledge, in which all things were informed by an intrinsic and divine spirit. Kamei spoke for most of the participants of the debate when he called for the restoration of a philosophy of "wholeness" and the "unity of knowledge" as it related all things, creatures, and beings, a unity he believed had been the mark of Japanese civilization from the time of its origins. In his harsh condemnation, Meiji civilization and enlightenment had introduced "deformed specialists" into contemporary Japanese culture and had produced incalculable consequences for the quality of life, which only the war would be able to arrest and unmake. This rejection of rational knowledge resulted in the conviction, articulated by the former Marxist and writer Hayashi Fusao, that the "civilization and enlightenment of the Meiji period meant the adoption of European culture, and resulted in the submission of Japan to the West."[7] Although the Meiji achievement represented the last opposition of the East against the West (for only Japan managed to withstand the Western wave that had already swept over India and China), the price paid for this resistance was the incorporation of the rational instruments of the enemy. The time had come for a final confrontation between the East and the West if the plague were to be exterminated, if, in fact, this epistemological domination were to end.

The debate singled out something called "Americanism" as the principal force empowering the global expansion of utilitarian instrumentality and extinguishing the spirit everywhere it was applied. The participants specifically referred to the immense importation of what they described as "hedonistic" and "crass" materialism among Japan's urban youth after World War I, exemplified by faddish groups calling themselves "modern boys" and "modern girls." This critique showed how the visible marketing of mass culture reflected the absence of a deeply rooted sense of cultural purpose in the United States, rather than an obsessive concern with the circulation of commodities and the reproduction of consumption. The danger of this "Americanism" lay in its capacity to spread a new "universalistic" culture of simple materialism, and to destroy the foundations of older, ancient societies, whose values had withstood the test of time and had survived until this latest onslaught. Due to the duplicity of Meiji civilization, Japan confronted the spectacle of a consumer society driven by a desire for commodities which could never be satisfied, even in the last instance; moreover, it faced the concomitant loss of quality and the beauty of scarcity and restraint. In the final analysis, the problem appeared to be how Japan might retain its own technological accomplishments yet preserve those irreducible elements from culture which, it was believed, made Japanese Japanese. When faced with the choice between traditional and modern modes of production, none of the participants ever conceived of turning back the clock, so to speak, and returning to a simpler and undifferentiated agrarian order. But they were clearly concerned with trying to constrain the "machine" into the role of the servant, rather than the master, and to restrain what all perceived as the ceaseless commodification of their lives.

When Takeuchi Yoshimi wrote his long meditation on this wartime symposium concerned with the critique of modernity, like so many of his contemporaries in the postwar period he did not mean simply to recall the half-forgotten discourse of an earlier time in order to remind Japanese of an intellectual episode lost to history. Nor was he primarily interested in salvaging the reputation of many of the symposium's participants, especially those associated with the Japan romantic faction, recently discredited because of their supposed complicity with fascists and ultranationalists. Takeuchi acknowledged that it was customary after the war to refer to the debate and its title—"Overcoming the Modern"—as "infamous" (*akumyōdakai*), and he wondered if the great "havoc" it allegedly had caused was not simply a case of overdetermined criticism, since the intellectual content of the proceedings was nonexistent.[8] As a result, he thought it best to offer a new reading of its text, as a condition for resituating his own critique of modernity in the postwar discussions of the questions of modernism, subjectivity, the promise of political democracy, and the problems of war responsibility. While he sought to provide a genealogy for his own developing critique of the forms of modernism, it would be wrong to accuse him of anti-modernism or some variation of an invertebrate traditionalism. He was nonetheless convinced that, once the earlier text had been stripped of its unjustified ideological associations and the charges of complicity in Japan's war goals, it would reveal a prescient awareness of the problems Japan encountered when it fatefully decided to transform society into the Western image. By the same measure, he was equally certain that the war and the postwar reconstruction of a new order dramatically necessitated his decision to retrace the steps of this earlier discourse, in order to imagine the terms in which writers and intellectuals understood the modern and why they felt an urgency to overcome it. Writing in the 1950s, Takeuchi recognized that the war did not bring an end to the modern in Japan, as many in the *kindai no chōkoku* debate had fully anticipated; it merely laid the groundwork for an even more powerful modern order that was already on its way to completion.

Takeuchi connected with the symposium at the moment when its participants recognized that the shock of the opening of hostilities was manifest in an "intellectual shudder"; for they knew they were now committed to a struggle between "Western knowledge" and the "blood of the Japanese." He heeded most closely the symposium's ardent pledge to dissolve the "autonomization" of cultural spheres. This autonomization had come to dominate the landscape and to separate genuine cultural production by intellectuals from political practice.

With this move, Takeuchi believed that it was possible to differentiate the symposium's consequent ideological associations from its sub-stantive and critical discourse, which had effectively problematized the question of Japan's modernity. Supplementing what he believed to be missing in the text of the symposium, Takeuchi carefully sepa-rated ideology from thought, or, as he stated it, extracted thought from ideology. He confessed that this operation might well be impos-sible to accomplish; yet if he did not attempt the effort to understand thought as reality and if he did not take the risk to acknowledge its independence from event, he could not possibly tease out the thought "buried" in those discussions. More importantly, Takeuchi's decision to uncouple thought from event called attention to a recurrent propo-sition of the critique of modernity, which was to escape (outside of) history altogether. By burying the symposium as an event in a past history, Takeuchi advised, and pacing the difficult ground of its thought, it might still be possible to give life and presence to its legacy in the present.

Takeuchi hoped to install as a living presence in postwar Japan the critical possibilities inherent in the self-perception of the "blood of the Japanese, which has acted as the true motive power of our intel-lectual activity and its rivalry with Western knowledge, which has unhappily been superimposed on it. . . ."[9] If recognition of this seem-ing bonding prompted a record of a bloody struggle, the motivation for releasing Japanese intelligence from its Western dependence was no less compelling in the first year of the war than it was nearly two decades later. The disjunction between native wisdom and Western rational knowledge opened up, for Takeuchi at least, a space within which to reassess a modernization process that slavishly aped the West while subverting Japanese intelligence. Such a reassessment also offered to sunder the virtual identification of the two as a condition for a reunion with suppressed alternatives, for rediscovering the path the Japanese had not taken. This was a well-known, major driving force in Takeuchi's own writings, and it prompted his valorization of the modern Chinese writer Lu Xun, who represented best the choice all Asians encountered in selecting routes to modernity. Lu Xun's example projected an image of defending a modernization process which relied neither on Western models nor on reified traditional forms, but on the energy of the masses. Furthermore, his example constituted for Takeuchi an eloquent reminder of the promise inherent in the play of cultural differences rather than of sameness.

It was for this reason that Takeuchi, whose sympathies were often with the left, devoted so much energy to resuscitating the tarnished careers of prewar right-wing activists, such as Kita Ikki and Ōkawa Shūmei. Takeuchi saw in these prewar intellectuals analogies to Lu Xun, especially in their thinking about Japan's modernity. The kinship of these various writers and thinkers, as well as of other Asians such as Tagore and Gandhi, lay in a common refusal to accept either a Western model of modernity or its reified double in traditional and archaic forms—this was, he believed, the meaning of *kindai no chōkoku* the symposium hoped to convey. Here, Takeuchi agreed with Kawakami Tetsutarō, the symposium's principal organizer, who announced that the times necessitated giving substance to the idea of a new spiritual order. Since the late nineteenth century, the specialization of knowledge had prevailed and the cultural sphere was fragmented into autonomous disciplines. However one attempted to avoid such autonomization of the fields of knowledge, one inevitably ran counter to the "rule of special terminology," theories concerned with epistemology and methods, and the historical stages of manufacturing. Within this framework, Takeuchi recognized that the effect had been to erect barriers between different areas of culture, causing mutual isolation and preventing genuine self-understanding; "communication requires striking a wall in order to talk to inmates inhabiting the next room of the same ward."[10] The reference to the ward, and its special association with disease, was not lost on Takeuchi, and functioned as a constant metaphor throughout the 1930s to call attention to the baneful effects of Westernization.

Hence the symposium was represented as a "lone beacon of light piercing the wall of each person's isolation, and illuminating what had already been before them, but they had not been able to see." Takeuchi acknowledged with the participants of the symposium that they were all modern intellectuals and writers, driven by necessity to assess the actual cost of Japan's assimilation to the West, even as they knew the impossibility of separating themselves from what had apparently become common sense. The problem was to find a way to conceptualize a modernity that was made in Japan, not in the West. Rather than launch an anti-modern attack, the symposium ought to have imagined a modern order in Japan that would be accountable to native intelligence and indigenous experience. To overcome the modern, then, meant liberation from the West and from the constraints of a model of modernization that insisted upon a sameness which had successfully suppressed the Other and the play of cultural difference. According to Takeuchi, it was this critique which compelled so many of the participants to examine their own modern endowment in Japan, and which represented a "beam of light" illuminating the path to follow in the postwar era.

If the modern had a consistent meaning, it referred to historicism (according to Suzuki Shigetaka); therefore, overcoming it demanded a program of getting out of the straitjacket of developmental historical emplotment and rejecting the legacy of *bunmei kaika*, the Meiji commitment to an enlightened civilization of rational utility and instrumentality. Yet, on closer examination, these two targets represented different sides of the same coin: if one started from an assessment of the theory of historical development, whether Marxist or non-Marxist, it would lead directly to a critique of the Meiji commitment to an evolutionary and progressive conception of historical development. Or, if one began with a rejection of Meiji instrumentalism, it would invariably lead back to its authorizing historical mission. In other words, both historicism and rational utility, as embodied in the state, inevitably led to modernism and its double—Japanism (*Nihonshugi*). Within the framework of this critique against historicism and utility, Takeuchi situated his own text as a condition for connecting the charge to overcome the modern with his present. If *kindai no chōkoku* was to make sense for his own moment, it was necessary to problematize how the symposium grasped the structure of modern Japanese thought at the time that it convened. While Takeuchi rejected the temptation of differentiating the two moments, he acknowledged that something was lacking in the original text which he proposed to supplement. This missing element was the incapacity of the symposium to distinguish between an intellectual struggle with the West, leading to war, and Japanese colonial expansion in Asia.

By problematizing the structure of modern Japanese thought, the symposium disclosed a profound aporia, a doubt and a "necessary hesitation" before the claims of Westernization and modernization. This doubt produced theories leading to conflict as a form of resolution. It was the task of the present to discover where such theories went wrong. Takeuchi proposed reversing the normal course of history in order to uncover the particular blindness that had prevented both the past and the present from finding an adequate resolution of Japan's relations with China and Asia, without making this resolution a condition of an intellectual revolt against the West. In this respect, the debate on modernity represented a kind of "condensation of the aporia of Japan's modern history." [11] At the heart of this discourse of doubt, Takeuchi noted, were a number of binary oppositions demanding resolution, such as restoration and renovation (*fukko* vs. *ishin*), loyalism and expulsionism (*sonnō* vs. *jōi*), opening the country and keeping it closed (*kaikoku* vs. *sakoku*), national essence versus civilization and enlightenment (*kokusui* vs. *bunmei kaika*). [12] According to Takeuchi, the symposium failed in its inability to make the aporia itself—the doubt—the object of consciousness. The reason for this failure was its refusal to separate an intellectual struggle from the idea of total war. Hence the doubt dissipated "like scattered clouds," and the symposium's promise to overcome the modern degenerated into an explanatory "label" for a public ideology of war. "The dissolution of the aporia," Takeuchi wrote, "prepared the intellectual ground for the post-war devastation and the colonization of Japan." [13] Takeuchi argued that, while the symposium could hardly serve as a source for creative thought, it is, nevertheless, necessary to set right the aporia as a central theme if Japanese are to restore creativity to thought. Advising contemporaries to return to the ground traveled by people like Ōkawa Shūmei in order to understand why the Sino-Japanese conflict really differed from a struggle with Western intelligence, Takeuchi was convinced that the energy invested in Asia was an extravagance that inhibited the formation of thought according to tradition. The problem for contemporary Japan was not in sustaining "myths," referring to Etō Jun's defense of them, but in avoiding an "easy knowledge" emptied of self-reliance and incapable of conquering or overcoming myths.

Among his contemporaries, it was the modernists Takeuchi wished to contest, especially those adherents of political democracy who dominated postwar discourse down to the early 1960s. His critique against modernism revealed an impulse to decenter the agency of a subject who made history, as well as to release a suppressed other —the energy of the masses—in the hope of realizing a new kind of history. In the process of reinstating the human subject as the agent of a new history, he believed that postwar modernists evaded any confrontation with the idea of the folk, owing to the wartime valorization of *minzoku* (a racially specific folk). Despite this unhappy episode, the folk or the masses, whom he increasingly identified with Asia, remained a historically viable constituency, in contrast to the reified conception of subject authorized by a theory of ideal types. In his words, the folk had always been the "real antithesis" to civilization and enlightenment and modernism, since the time the country had been opened to the world. The refusal of contemporary modernists to come to terms with the folk, regardless of their unfortunate ideological appropriation during the war, was not substantially different from the policies of the prewar state to mobilize the masses for capitalism and a ruinous war. Yet they alone, as the China of Mao Zedong already showed, offered the hope of a genuine revolution in contemporary Japan.

To overcome the modern in this postwar context, therefore, meant liberation from the very mediations used to articulate a program for contemporary Japan. Takeuchi's text sought to show in this environment that the war did not forestall or even foreclose the real critique offered by the *kindai no chōkoku* symposium, and that, in their identification of an aporia, the participants had hoped to avoid closure itself. In a remarkable presage of what was to come, he feared most that the alliance between modernism and Japanism would recenter the subject, armed precisely with those practices which hitherto had been identified with instrumentality and utility. In this transformation of a class model, the bourgeoisie—the object of earlier critiques—was redefined now as Japanese and human; it established its regime of truth under discursive practices that functioned to maintain its rational advantage and to provide a culturally exceptional justification for its economic privileges against the West. Even when

Takeuchi wrote his essay, postwar Japan was, in fact, in the process of realizing the very form of historical narrative that earlier writers had identified as the problem: the ideological form of modern Western society, the inevitable slippage into sameness. The struggle in postwar Japan, as it had been earlier, encompassed differing "systems of narrative" and the necessity of establishing one that was particularly resistant to assimilation.

For Takeuchi, overcoming modernity meant finding a way to reunite thought with the practice of the people, tapping the energy of the masses which had been suppressed throughout the long night of Japan's modernizing history. Here, he believed, might be found the promise of a genuine Japanese revolution. Convinced that the model for this reunion with the practice of the people was already exemplified by the Chinese revolution, he was emboldened to propose that Asia itself should become a method for transformation, which would successfully avoid either the course of Japan's slavish dependence upon the West or its reverse in the reification of traditional forms. Postwar Japan had failed to resolve the claims of modernization for those, like himself, who looked increasingly to Asia for a release from the West: his government and people still looked down upon China and other Asian nations. But, he warned, quoting the critic Odagiri Hideo (who had written earlier about *kindai no chōkoku*), since "we have not worked to settle the past with our own hands," calling attention to the American Occupation's control, "so the past is beginning to take reprisals against us."[14] To avoid this dark future, indeed, sameness itself, Takeuchi plunged into political action in 1960 in order to complete what he believed to be unfinished business: to bring about the Japanese revolution he feared might already have been lost.

In 1980, thirty-five years after the end of a disastrous war the Japanese fought to "overcome modernity," the government of Ōhira Masayoshi announced a plan for the eighties and beyond, to the twenty-first century, in the establishment of a new age of culture. The new age of culture marked a "conquest of the modern" which referred to the postwar epoch between 1945 and the late 1970s. The text established a comprehensive chronology of the genealogy of Japan's modernization since the Meiji restoration. Before the war, periods seemed to follow fifteen-year cycles: 1885–1900 constituting a time of politics and the installation of the political framework for modernization; 1900–1915, when capitalism was formed; 1915–1930, a time of culture —Taisho culture—which saw the efflorescence of the "democracy movement"; and 1930–1945, a "time of conflict" which led to war. After the war, the same pattern of periodization resumed. The fifteen years from 1945–1960, principally guided by Prime Minister Yoshida Shigeru, represented the "age of politics," which reestablished the political infrastructure for Japan's subsequent progress. The span of time between 1960 and the late 1970s, inaugurated by the Ikeda cabinet and continued by Satō, initiated the "age of economy" with the expansion of "high economic growth" (*kodo keizai seicho*). Once the Japanese people entered this stage and experienced the benefits of economic abundance, they were ready to pursue the "fruits of spirit and culture." What the text excludes is a discussion of why the cycle ends here, why the last stage of "conflict" would not inevitably be repeated.

According to the text *Bunka no jidai no keizai un'ei*, in each age there is an appropriate requirement (*yosei*) that must be satisfied; for Japan, standing at the beginning of the 1980s, the time has come to meet the demands of culture and spirit. This means "implanting" in the folk the superiority of specific cultural values. Yet, on closer inspection, it becomes apparent that the values this program seeks to instill are derived from a "managerial" experience which now promises to displace, if not eliminate outright, the possibility of social surplus, manifest in mass democracy and its necessary valorization of human rights. The managerial dimension is, in fact, masked by appealing to a revitalization of values associated with the older quest to salvage a traditional way of life.

At the first meeting of the group selected to envisage the new "age of culture" (April 1979), Prime Minister Ōhira proposed that

> thirty years after the war, Japan has pursued the goal of economic abundance and pushed on ceaselessly without looking aside. We have reaped remarkable results. As for these results, especially in the century since the Meiji, they represent the great essence of modernization and industrialization advanced by the model of several European countries.[15]

Moreover, the resulting "unprecedented freedom and abundance has stimulated reflection on the important side of human character, which had been lost sight of under the regime of industrialization and modern rationalism." When people turned to the pursuit of a "restoration [*kaifuku*] of warm human relationships in the family, workplace and local regions," they would see that "material civilization based on modern rationalism had reached its saturation point [*howaten*], and the time had arrived to transcend the modern [industrialization] to an age that stresses culture."[16] Writing from this perspective, Ōhira's brain trust stated that, in an age that demanded "modernization" and "economic growth," the objective and model were provided by the West, which "disregarded our traditional culture and fixed for us progress and standards and goals pursued by others." In the new age devoted to culture, the text intoned, the requirement would be the installation of a genuinely "comprehensive Japanese culture." But, in order to confront the end of modernization and overcome the modern, it was necessary to systematically assess anew the "special quality of Japan's culture."

What counted as the special quality of Japan's culture was reflected in the determined opposition to a structure which "contrasted sharp distinctions between two things," such as those between God and Satan, winner and loser, white and black in European and American cultures. Resembling the child's game of scissors, rock, and paper, Japanese culture has always been characterized by the avoidance of binary oppositions, thereby emphasizing the model of a three-legged contest or the structure of a circle "where none are superior and there are no absolute winners or losers."[17] As a result of this tradition, Japanese have rejected both a totalistic holism (*zentaishugi*) which disregards the individual, and an extreme individualism that promotes the "self differentiated from the other" (*tasha*), found throughout European and American societies. This contrast demonstrates Japan's "cultural particularity," which has been described as a relationalism (*aidagarashugi*) that privileges the relationship between human and human, between part and whole, as expressed in words like *ningen*, "between people," *nakama*, "within relationships," and *seken*, "within society." Japanese, therefore, emphasize the importance of essence (*ki*) embedded in human relationships, and subsequently stress the centrality of one's participation in a larger complex —*bun*, as found in terms like *kibun, jibun, hombun, mibun, shokubun,* etc. Discerning the quality of *bun* requires exhausting oneself in it and is thus linked to *en*, binding ties, as represented in the following relationships: *ketsu-en, chi-en, gakuen,* and *sha-en*.[18] All signify the characteristic of the "*nakama* society" or the "*ie* society," a social constellation held together by fundamental and culturally irreducible relationships that determine how one is to behave with reference to others within the confines of Japanese society.

When Japan is compared to either the holism or individualism of the Western world, the special features of this relational social order are even more apparent. This form of social imaginary, the text implies, has remained unchanged since the Stone Age, despite historical upheavals, and constitutes Japan's claim to exceptionalism. Since it was now believed that the Japanese had already reached a high level of technological and industrial achievement, the "citizenry should no longer make the modern its goal." Instead, they must define their objectives through the mediation of a more precise opposition between the "Western thing" and the "Japanese thing."[19] It should be stressed that where the earlier prewar discussion had forcefully tried to reify tradition in an effort to counter the onslaught of the modern, the new postmodern inflection changed the terms of discourse entirely, and thereby undermined the whole critical program which had informed it. While the invocation to overcome the modern summoned powerful associations of an earlier anti-modernism, its presumed connection with the later *bunka no jidai* vision was, at best, spurious, since the earlier discourse aimed principally at contesting the imperial claims of Western epistemology, while its "successor" has been unfailingly associated with it. At its most intense moments, the earlier discussions produced a critique which called into question a rational, instrumental knowledge and its differentiation into spheres of specialization as a condition for social and historical progress. If prewar thinkers agreed on nothing else, they nonetheless shared a profound distrust of politically rational forms, represented by and in the bureaucratic state and its corresponding conception of a civil society. To be sure, the associations evoked by the new age of culture immediately suggest their genealogical descent from this prewar discourse.

Yet it is the purpose of the postmodern ideology to secure this effect of an uninterrupted and seamless process. The ideology inscribed in the call for a new age of culture seeks its authority in a science of society, which derives its authority from the earlier reconstruction of social theory before the war. Any effort to unpack the genealogy of the postmodern would reveal the origins of the present more clearly in the postwar period and postwar experience, rather than in the 1930s, and the resemblance of its own narrative to little more than a pastiche, rather than an uninterrupted "history."

The "scientific" authority of the postmodern ideology derived from the social science developed in the postwar period, which matured in the texts of Nakane Chie, Doi Takeo, Kumon Shunpei, and Murakami Yasusuke, notably in *Bunmei to shite no ie shakai* and other texts that successfully eliminated historicity as a condition for eliding and conflating disparate elements into essence. According to Murakami et al., for example, a continuity of essences linked the prewar concerns for traditional social relationships to their postwar retention as a primary principle of social organization. But they also recognized that the prewar effort to retain the principles of a "household society" was compromised by a "trial-and-error process aimed at synthesizing differing principles of European and Japanese society in order to industrialize."[20] The accomplishments of this "synthesis" escaped dismantling by war and defeat; instead, they were reinforced by this experience. In fact, the "revolution" sparked by the American Occupation and the transformations it introduced affected only the "outer layers of thought" and failed to alter the "basic patterns of people's behavior." The household (*ie*) and the view of the family-state that prevailed before the war disclosed their "brittleness" precisely because they constituted an "adulteration" of the fundamental model of social relationships. Although the household—*ie*—was "dismantled," the *ie* society remained intact, and it even replaced the destructive features of the older social imaginary with a "functional, household-type corporate body." Even after the war and the vast changes implemented by the occupation, Japanese society was able to resist the blandishments of "individualism" because it was constituted by a variety of "*ie*-type groups," such as enterprises, firms, household businesses, and religious organizations. However, this model of the social was less an enlargement of the household than a homology of the "peasant collective organized to press demands" (*ikki*) or the "village" (*mura*).[21] A typology of social patterns founded on the model of traditional peasant organization would operate functionally to contain the "new middle classes" (*chukan, nakama*) once the economy and polity were reconstructed after the war. In this way, the values of an agrarian order have been made to serve the requirements of a postindustrial society.

While this "scientific" argument tried to instate a continuity in social relationships since the remote past (the period of "clan society"), according to its authors it was possible to concentrate on the status of the group *only* at the expense of effacing historical differences between prewar experiences and the principle of the new middle class, proposing that what survived was a "functional form" and not its adulterated content. This move required rereading the history of the prewar discussions so as to establish a shared identity between an anti-modernism which, before the war, was fueled by "enlightened and progressive intellectuals" and epistemological colonialism, and, after the war, was stimulated by "progressive intellectuals" bent on establishing a democratic society on the model advocated by the American Army of Occupation. This is not to say that Murakami et al. did not see differences between earlier concerns for community and the postwar reestablishment of a household-type society. They readily acknowledged that the model of society before the war had suffered from "brittleness" and "adulteration," and was ultimately surpassed by a new pattern free from history and competent to organize the new middle class. Moreover, this new social arrangement guaranteed exemption from the very changes, the so-called "age of conflict," which had led to the dissolution of the "family-state" (*kazoku kokka*), although not to the dissolution of its "form." Once a *mura*-type state is put into place, according to Murakami, a pattern will be established that will not change, even after the attainment of "high economic growth." In the context of this surge for economic abundance, a new middle class will be formed according to: (1) an equalization of the distribution of income, (2) homogenization of "life-forms," and (3) an advance of "main-streamism" (*chūryuka*) at the level of life-consciousness.[22] Writing in the late

1970s (the *Ie shakai* . . . book was published in 1979, at precisely the moment its authors were beginning to prepare the statement on the age of culture), Murakami et al. saw the attainment of moderately high levels of personal income and a corresponding increase in the standard of living—consumption—as conditions for imagining a new "middle class," one in which opportunities, and capacities for fulfilling them, would level all the distinctions marking older forms of class division. The effect of homogenizing social and economic differences within the population, to create a broad or mass middle stratum managed by principles governing the household-type system, resembled Nakane Chie's earlier social-scientific analysis which showed how groups in Japan "formed on the basis of commonality of attribute" invariably possess a strong sense of exclusiveness founded on this commonality. It is important to note that this sense of leveling, made possible by organizing people according to the village collectivity, functioned only at the intermediate levels beneath the government which, according to Murakami, is free from the "influence of the family-state." It would produce not only a high rate of growth preceding the age of culture, but it would also sustain this style of life against the corrosions of historical change. In short, the household-type society would secure the promise of similitude, now read as homogenization (a move made earlier by Nakane), against the spectacle of difference—history. Along the way, writers like Nakane and Murakami have also noted how other groups in Japanese society have conformed to this typology of interaction, and concluded that when, say, the family is compared to its counterpart in Western industrial societies, it revealed a far greater degree of social solidarity than that found in "individualistic Western societies."

This vision of the social order was presented as a natural necessity mirrored in Japan's history. Even though history was extensively emphasized to enhance the argument for the endurance of the *ie* society, nothing seems to have changed very much since the *uji* period of Japan's prehistory. Yet this discounting of historical change, denying history as the site of genuine difference, prefigured the assertion that, once the modern has been surpassed, the age of culture and the new middle class will finally realize their exemption from the uncertainties of change and the caprice of history. This reworking of what Hegel elsewhere had called a "history-less history," firmly at the heart of Japanese social science, promised to relieve the present from the determinations of the past and the unpredictability of the future. By the same measure, it authorized the state ideologues to separate themselves from the discourses of the prewar period, even as they claimed genealogical kinship with them. They must do so as a condition for producing their own "scientific" discourse and for revealing this genealogical "past" as merely ideological, or, as they described it, "adulterated," "trial-and-error," and "brittle." What this science managed to project as "natural" to the Japanese was a vision of a society in which, as Hamaguchi Eshun and Kumon Shunpei stated elsewhere, the "dynamics" of the "Japanese managerial system" are applied to the totality.[23]

By contrasting the Ōhira program to the wartime debate, we can conclude the following: (1) Whereas the earlier discourse seized upon the surviving traces of tradition as the condition for calling attention to an organic totality (*zentai*) that had always been in place since the beginning of the folk, the later, postmodern version transmuted these reified elements of fixed and enduring social relationships into functional prerequisites which authorized a "holonic path" (*zentaishi*) ever capable of harmonizing differences.[24] (2) Before the war, social theorists produced their critique in an atmosphere of urgency, fearful that the modernist transformation would soon eliminate the spiritual traces of an authentic life. But the planners of the new age of culture and the twenty-first century acknowledged that the thirty-five years from 1945–1980 were spent reconstructing a political infrastructure competent to augment high economic growth—as if to suggest that considerations of spirit (that is, culture) appear only after the folk have achieved "abundance." This means that, while the earlier discourse wanted to alter the order of priority, so as to situate culture at the head of the signifying chain for determining subsequent political and economic content, the postmodern state sees culture as merely a product of the chain of signification, determined by a technocratic bureaucracy devoted to rational and instrumental control. (3) Both the premodern discourse against modernity and the postmodern ideology sought to repair the split or lack of fit between the social and the political as a means of avoiding social surplus; however, the earlier discourse sought the solution in rethinking traditional structures, while the latter has made the business firm the model for the wider sociopolitical order. (4) Despite the extravagant claims for a new age of culture and spirit, the new program differs dramatically from the expectations of the earlier discourse precisely in its thorough commitment to materialism and commodification, which the prewar debaters would have rejected *tout court*. It should be recalled that one of the purposes of the earlier discussion was to prevent the contamination of the spirit of creativity—culture—by the materialism of the commodity fetish, which the United States and its shallow sense of culture signified. In the new age of culture, scarcity of goods will have been eliminated and abundance will serve as the bond for reinforcing forms of "Japanese-like" social relationships between human and human, in order to secure the promise of a unified and homogeneous community.[25] (5) The new cultural age juxtaposes the "Japanese thing" (*Nihontekina mono*), rather than "tradition," against the image of modern Western society. Although the prewar symposium was concerned with the aporia between tradition and modernity, and was fearful of the eradication of the former by the latter, the debaters were still willing to risk the realization that these modes of social existence constituted moments in an ongoing history that characterized all societies, not simply Japan and the West. Still, the new representation appeals to the ethos of an exceptional culture (identical with "nature") in order to explain the irreducible and unique source of Japan's status as a world "industrial power" and a global "economic giant." And no doubt it dispels older associations which had yoked modernity and progress to the West and tradition and stagnation to Japan. Yet, clearly, the new representation no longer conforms to the simple opposition between traditional and modern, seen as moments in an evolutionary narrative. Rather, it reveals the operation of a newer division between what the *Bunka no jidai* text describes as the "Japanized View" and the "Westernized View," now facing each other as absolutes standing outside of history, accountable only to an unchanging "nature" (read as culture) and "race."

After the "conquest of the modern," the Ōhira government's proclamation of a new age of culture disclosed the formation of a new discourse, whose ideological implications, concealed and invisible, differ vastly from the putative anti-modernism of the wartime debate and from Takeuchi's recommendation to make Asia itself a method for the modernist transformation. In the case of the debate and Takeuchi's subsequent gloss, the question did not relate so much to whether Japan ought to be modern or not, since it was already a modern society according to Kobayashi Hideo; rather, the issue was the appropriateness of the modern West as a model for Japan and, indeed, for the rest of Asia. If the debaters were blinded by the necessity to make sense of a war which they quickly misrecognized as a struggle to rid Japan of the baneful effects of psychological and epistemological colonialism, so that it might lead Asia to a new order under Japanese tutelage, Takeuchi was able to separate this identification of an Asian war of liberation from the modernist critique in order to reapprehend the status of both in the postwar period. Unlike the debaters, Takeuchi made no effort to suppress his antipathy for the prewar and postwar states, and he linked this criticism to his general renunciation of the Western model both had recklessly adopted. He believed that such an assault on the postwar political order was necessary, since it was beginning to show signs of reproducing the discredited past with even greater intensity. Takeuchi never lived to see the polity promoted by the Ōhira government, nor even to imagine the rush among responsible intellectuals to "scientize" reified conceptions of the totality, renamed by people like Nakamura Yūjirō as *sensus communis*. Yet he was still certain that unless Japan was able to find a ground outside of its recent historical experience of modernization, then the call to overcome the modern would signal the completion of a process which he and others before him had sought to arrest and redirect from the imperial claims of identity to the place of radical difference. Whereas the war defeated the aspirations of the *kindai no chōkoku* symposium, the "second chance" envisaged by Takeuchi met a similar fate in the period of "high economic growth."

In the vacated space, the new age of culture declares a kinship with an imagined past from which it derives authority, and a separation from a history of cultural mistakes. This is no familiar dialectic, which, in its movement, ceaselessly incorporates moments of its past as it supercedes them in the itinerary toward the end of history. It is, instead, a truncated version and cynical closure which proclaims the end of the historical with the "conquest of modernity," that is, the twilight of the Hegelian idol.

To this end, the program of the holonic society aims to eliminate the distance between the discourse on the social, marking both the prewar debate and Takeuchi's rereading, and a social discourse—the practice of socialization—by collapsing the former into the latter. Hence the new discourse conceals the distance between the representation and the "real," which consistently imperiled the modernist ideologies of the *kindai no chōkoku* symposium and Takeuchi's replay. At the same time, this discourse renounces all those efforts to "realize the representation in the form of the totalization of the real," which has always threatened totalitarian ideologies.[26] Its strategy constantly calls forth the "ruses of the imaginary" in order to dismiss them; even though it is a process that is both "unconscious" and "without history," it must still account for the effects of knowledge and history by binding them into new configurations in the service of tasks that are always the same. In Japan, and perhaps other societies showing the symptoms of postmodernity, the "group" is fixed as a "positive entity," and envisaged as both the expression and objective of social communication; it operates effectively to obscure the apparatus of domination from the masses, who are without power. The representation of the group—the broad "middle stratum" to which all Japanese belong—as put forth by the Ōhira brain trust and inscribed in countless articulations by serious social thinkers, excludes from its domain the question of the "origin" (or takes it back to a remote and mythic time too far removed from contemporary Japan), as well as the "legitimacy and rationality of the oppositions and hierarchies" that have been instituted in each sector and continue to exist. Seeking to elicit a belief in the "mastery" of the very experience of socialization which means being Japanese in the present, the new representation attempts to conceal itself as a representation and divert attention away from itself as discourse.

Employing advanced techniques of communication, the new discourse pretends to propagate information, to make the contemporary order into (what has been called) an "information society" (*jōhō shakai*); in this ceaseless communication of unwanted information, it does not take hold of the Other at a distance, but uses information and the technology of communication to include its representatives within itself. In this way, the individual is situated in the group, an imaginary group (called "relationalism"—*aidagarashugi*), inasmuch as individuals are "deprived of the power to grasp the actual movement of the institution by taking part in it." If this new faith in social communication and group centeredness still leaves open the possibility of social division, even when attempts are made to disguise it as a "flaw in the dialogue between classes," the representation of social relationships is made unconscious for the express purpose of assuring both the facilitation of communication and "the implication of the subject in the group." The effect is expressed in the ready way people call attention to the identity of their group in the obligatory utterance "we Japanese," which seems to prefigure and preface all discourse between Japanese and the outside world. But, however efficacious the expression "we Japanese," it is invariably posterior to the conditions of a network already in place, in which the agents are linked together in a national subjectivity devoid of regional, class, or even gender distinctions, "by being deprived of any mark of their opposition to one another."

We have also seen that the new representation derives from the model of the organization of the firm, which is applied to the rest of the social formation; but it no longer tolerates a division between managers and those who carry out their orders. One need not recall the countless books and articles that have recently bombarded us, which testify to something called the "Japanese style of managerialism," with their "inspiring" accounts of quality-control sessions, the cooperation of managerial-worker teams, heroic self-sacrifice, stirring examples of the boss rolling up his shirt sleeves to pitch in with his workers, etc., to accept this picture of an arrangement which has effectively eliminated the division between labor, management, and the mode of production, linking them together within a structure capable of functioning on its own, rationally and independently of human choice and desire: the model for robotics.

With this in view, we can see how, in the Ōhira vision, supplemented by numerous social-scientific and cultural texts, the organization constitutes the reference of the real, a representation that is disseminated throughout the whole of society. According to Claude Lefort, "[t]he incantation of social communication is complemented by an incantation of information."[27] Experts abound everywhere, he says, dispensing the truth of everything, since everything can be said. But this proliferation of information, deemed necessary for carrying on daily life in contemporary Japan, marks the indeterminacy of knowledge and places a high valuation on perpetual novelty, the newness of the new, the latest and most recent bit of knowledge: this is the sign that is mobilized everywhere these days, in order to stave off the threat of the historical. Which brings us back to Baudrillard and the role of consumption: if consumption is generated not by locating a need whose origins lie in an individual or group, but by representing a "system of objects" which stands in place of the social as an illusion, the resulting simulation is an effort to present the historical again by making change invisible and promoting the new. What is consumed is always new and everything is within the means of everybody, whatever one's capacity to pay for it. Every dream is marketable and directed toward everyone in society, not merely the few, thereby effacing the difference between one consuming subject and another, since they are made to appear to belong to a common world populated by objects which they must consume. Only the signs of human beings—the "system of objects"—are perceived. But to employ communication and organization in order to stimulate consumption means that ideology has completed its task, by making invisible the "great closure,"[28] since it no longer needs to make statements about the nature of man or society as *the* condition for a discourse on the social.

Notes

1   Claude Lefort, *The Political Forms of Modern Society*, ed. John B. Thompson (Cambridge, Mass., 1986), 215; see also Ernesto Laclau and Chantal Mouffe, *Hegemony and Socialist Strategy* (London, 1985), 93–148, for a brilliant critique of the "positivity of the social."

2   Lefort, *Political Forms*, 216.

3   Jean Baudrillard, *Simulations*, trans. Paul Foss, Paul Patton, and Philip Beitchman (New York, 1983), 1–2.

4 Matsumoto Kenichi, ed., *Kindai no chōkoku* (*Overcoming the Modern*) (Tokyo, 1979), 166.
5 Ibid., 219–20, 222, 226.
6 Ibid., 219.
7 Ibid., 107, 239.
8 Ibid., 275.
9 Ibid., 290.
10 Ibid.
11 Ibid., 338.
12 Ibid.
13 Ibid., 339.
14 Ibid., 284.
15 Ōhira sori no seisaku kenkyūkai hokōkusho (Reports of the Policy Research Bureaus of the Ōhira Cabinet), in *Bunka no jidai no keizai un'ei* (*Economic Administration of the Age of Culture*) (Tokyo, 1980), 21.
16 Ibid.
17 Ibid., 4.
18 Ibid., 4–5.
19 See Kawamura Nozomu, *Nihon bunkaron no shuhen* (*The Environs of Discussions on Japanese Culture*) (Tokyo, 1982), 147–48, for a perceptive discussion of this juxtaposition of the "Japanese thing" and the "Western thing." See also *Bunka no jidai*, 16.
20 Murakami Yasusuke, Kumon Shunpei, and Sato Seizaburō, *Bunmei to shite no ie shakai* (*Household Society as Civilization*) (Tokyo, 1979), 466.
21 Kawamura, *Nihon bunkaron*, 259–62; Murakami et al., *Bunmei to shite*, 473–78.
22 Kawamura, *Nihon bunkaron*, 259.
23 Hamaguchi Eshun and Kumon Shunpei, *Nihonteki shūdanshugi* (*Japanese-Style Groupism*) (Tokyo, 1982). This is, in fact, the central argument of this ideological tract, masquerading as "managerial science."
24 *Bunka no jidai*, 12–15, 104.
25 Actually, this achievement of a unified and homogeneous community, expectantly announced by proponents of cultural exceptionalism (*Nihonjinron*) and secured by following the so-called "holonic path," signifies the accomplished existence of a unified national subjectivity everywhere in Japanese society. While such a goal is still incomplete, there is good reason to believe that the publicly instituted tendency of the state to secure the promise of uniformity and homogeneity —by reminding both Japanese and foreigners of the uniqueness of such irreducible values as consensus and group-centeredness—is very much the point of all those "scientific" declarations, which attest to the primacy of the *ie* throughout Japan's history. Needless to say, the *ie* permits the constitution of an "imaginary Japanese" in discourse, and thereby eliminates any explicit connection with the usual divisions, such as class, gender, and regional affiliation, to gain forceful representation in the ideal of a "mass middle stratum." The idea of an "imaginary Japanese"

is suggested by Michael Bommes and Patrick Wright, "Charms of Residence?: The Public and the Past," in *Making Histories: Studies in History-Writing and Politics,* ed. Richard Johnson et al. (Minneapolis, 1982), 264–69. On "group as subject" and the requirements of the *ie*-centered society, see Murakami et al., *Bunmei to shite,* 257–58.

26 Lefort, *Political Forms,* 225–29.

27 Ibid., 233.

28 Ibid., 235.

Naoki Sakai

Modernity and Its Critique: The Problem of Universalism and Particularism

Even though I will predictably reach the conclusion that the postmodern, an other of the modern, cannot be identified in terms of our "modern" discourse, it should not be utterly pointless to put into question what constitutes the separation of the modern and the postmodern—that is, what underlies the possibility of our talking about the modern at all. Similarly, it is essential to deal with another other of the modern, the premodern, with reference to which modernity has also been defined in a great many instances. This series—premodern-modern-postmodern —may suggest an order of chronology. However, it must be remembered that this order has never been dissociated from the geopolitical configuration of the world. As is known very well by now, this basically nineteenth-century historical scheme provides a perspective through which to comprehend the location of nations, cultures, traditions, and races in a systematic manner. Although the last term has not emerged until fairly recently, the historico-geopolitical pairing of the premodern and the modern has been one of the major organizing apparatuses of academic discourse. The emergence of the third and enigmatic term, the postmodern, possibly testifies not so much to a transition from one period to another as to the shift or transformation of our discourse as a result of which the supposed indisputability of the historico-geopolitical pairing (premodern and modern) has become increasingly problematic. Of course, it is not the first time the validity of this pairing has been challenged. Yet, surprisingly enough, it has managed to survive many challenges, and it would be extremely optimistic to believe it has finally been proven to be ineffectual.

Either as a set of socioeconomic conditions or as an adherence of a society to selected values, the term "modernity" can never be understood without reference to this pairing of the premodern and the modern. Historically, modernity has primarily been opposed to its historical precedent; geopolitically it has been contrasted to the nonmodern, or, more specifically, to the non-West. Thus, the pairing has served as a discursive scheme according to which the historical predicate is translated into a geopolitical one and vice versa. A subject is posited through the attribution of these predicates, and thanks to the function of this discursive apparatus, two kinds of areas are diacritically discerned: the modern West and the premodern non-West. As a matter of course, this does not mean either that the West was never at premodern stages or that the non-West can never be modernized: it simply excludes the possibility of a simultaneous coexistence of the premodern West and the modern non-West.

Already a cursory examination of this sort about modernity amply suggests a certain polarity or warp among the possible ways to conceive of the world historically and geopolitically. As many have pointed out, there is no inherent reason why the West/non-West opposition should determine the geographic perspective of modernity except for the fact that it definitely serves to establish the putative unity of the West, a nebulous but commanding positivity whose existence we have tended to take for granted for such a long time. It goes without saying that the West is not simply and straightforwardly a geographic category. One need not refer to historical details to discover that the West has expanded and shifted arbitrarily for the last two centuries. It is a name for a subject which gathers itself in discourse but is also an object constituted discursively; it is, evidently, a name always associating itself with those regions, communities, and peoples that appear politically or economically superior to other regions, communities, and peoples. Basically, it is just like the name "Japan," which reputedly designates a geographic area, a tradition, a national identity, a culture, an ethnos, a market, and so on, yet unlike all the other names associated with geographic particularities, it also implies the refusal of its self-delimitation; it claims that it is capable of sustaining, if not actually transcending, an impulse to transcend all the particularizations. Which is to say that the West is never content with what it is recognized as by its others; it is always urged to approach others in order to ceaselessly transform its self-image; it continually seeks itself in the midst of interaction with the Other; it would never be satisfied with being recognized but would wish to recognize others; it would rather be a supplier of recognition than a receiver thereof. In short, the West must represent the moment of the universal under which particulars are subsumed. Indeed, the West is particular in itself, but it also constitutes the universal point of reference in relation to which others recognize themselves as particularities. And, in this regard, the West thinks itself to be ubiquitous.

This account of the putative unity called the West is nothing new, yet this is exactly the way in which Jürgen Habermas, for instance, still argues about Occidental rationalism. He "implicitly connect[s] a claim to *universality* with our *Occidental understanding of the world*."[1] In order to specify the significance of this claim, he relies upon the historico-geopolitical pairing of the premodern and the modern, thereby highlighting a comparison with the mythical understanding of the world. Within the cultural traditions accessible to us—that is, within the cultural traditions anthropologists have reconstructed for us—myths of archaic societies "present the sharpest contrast to the understanding of the world dominant in modern societies. Mythical worldviews are far from making possible rational orientations of action in our sense. With respect to the conditions for a rational conduct of life in this sense, they present an antithesis to the modern understanding of the world. Thus the heretofore unthematized presuppositions of modern thought should become visible in the mirror of mythical thinking."[2]

He takes for granted a parallel correspondence among the binary oppositions: premodern/modern, non-West/West, mythical/rational. Moreover, for him, the very unity of the West is a given; it is an almost tactile reality. What is most surprising is that while admitting the need for the non-West as a mirror by which the West becomes visible, Habermas obviously does not ask if the mirror may be extremely obscure. Whether or not the image facilitated by ethnographers and anthropologists is the true representation of what is actually there, is not at issue. What is worthwhile noting is that he deals with the non-Western cultures and traditions as though they were clearly shaped and as though they could be treated exhaustively as objects. Even when he tackles the problem concerning the incommensurability of other cultures, the whole issue of unintelligibility is reduced to the intelligibility of the problem of incommensurability. For Habermas, it signifies no more than that of cultural relativism, a pseudoproblem in itself.

Habermas argues with epistemological confidence in order to reinstall epistemological confidence in us and make us trust in universalism again.[3] That is, given the most persuasive and possibly most rigorous determination available today of the term "ethnocentricity," one might say he is simply ethnocentric. But if the intrusion of the term "postmodern" bears witness to the inquietude surrounding our identity, if this putative unity of the West, the us, from which and with whom Habermas wishes to speak is being dissolved, what does the fact that his epistemological confidence is not shaken imply? If the possibility of a certain enunciative position, the us, the Occidental *us*, with which his theory of communicative action is so closely interwoven, is in fact threatened, would one be justified to say his epistemological confidence indicates something else? Are *we* then allowed to say it points to an inquietude about *us* that has been repressed?

═══

From this perspective, it is understandable that the discursive object called Japan has presented a heterogeneous instance that could not be easily integrated into the global configuration organized according to the pairing of the modern and the premodern. It has been repeatedly deplored or extolled that Japan alone of the non-Western cultures was able to adopt rapidly what it needed of Western nations in order to transform itself into a modern industrial society. Hence, a sizable amount of intellectual labor has been invested in order to render this peculiar object innocuous in the discursive formation. In the United States, the consequences of this labor have usually been collected under the name of the "Modernization Theory." In addition to overtly strategic requirements of the State, there was a certain implicit but no less urgent demand to which the production of social-scientific and humanistic argument was submitted. Following Max Weber, who also saw clearly the mission of discursively ascertaining the putative unity of the West and who executed that mission most skillfully, some modernization theorists pursued the mission of ascertaining the unity of America as the central and perhaps commanding part of the West.

What modernization theory has accomplished by introducing the opposition of universalism and particularism into the study of other cultures is, first, to reproduce the same kind of discursive formation within which the unity of the West is constituted—but, this time, with the center explicitly in the United States. Second, it has generated a new kind of historical narrative which preserves the dictates of nineteenth-century historicism but rejects its overt reliance upon the notion of national history. Here, I must hasten to add, this does not mean that the new historical narrative was less nationalistic or in an antagonistic relation with nationalism. This version of universalism is, like some other universalisms, decidedly nationalistic. Yet, in this new narrative, nationalism had to be articulated differently. On the one hand, modernization theorists certainly inherited the European legacy of a historical time that coincides with the transition, gradual or rapid, from particularity to universality, from abstract universality to concrete universality, and ultimately coincides with the process of increasing rationalization, of reason realizing itself. On the other hand, they saw universalistic elements as being dispersed; instead of stressing the dynamics of conflict between the self and the Other, the attempt was made to show that any society is potentially capable of rationalizing itself. But it is also explicit that, in rationalizing itself, that society becomes similar to America. Or, to put it slightly differently, progress always means Americanization. In this respect, modernization theorists expressed the vision, most successfully implanted in the mass consciousness of postwar Japan, that modernization was implicitly equated to Americanization. While, prior to this, modernization had been more or less equated to Europeanization, modernization theory at large worked in the service of shifting the center from western Europe to America.

Obviously it is utterly beside the point to ask which vision of modernization is more authentic. What this reading hints at is that, while the modernization process may be envisioned as a move toward the concretization of values at some abstract level, it is always imagined as a concrete transfer from one point to another on a world map.

Thus, universalism and the concept of modernity were even more closely interwoven with American nationalism than before. But it is important to note that, because of this double structure, universalism often appears free of the well-recognized defects of nationalism. Of course, the claim to universality frequently serves to promote the demands of nationalism. Because of the double structure, an incessant oscillation is generated between universalism and particularism; possibly a certain provincialism and the aspiration toward universalism are two sides of the same coin; particularism and universalism do not form an antinomy but mutually reinforce each other. As a matter of fact, particularism has never been a truly disturbing enemy of universalism or vice versa. Precisely because both are closed off to the individual who can never be transformed into the subject or what infinitely transcends the universal, neither universalism nor particularism is able to come across the Other; otherness is always reduced to the Other, and thus repressed, excluded, and eliminated in them both. And after all, what we normally call universalism is a particularism thinking itself as universalism, and it is worthwhile doubting whether universalism could ever exist otherwise.

However, there are certain conditions that have to be met in order for this universalism to be possible. The center of the West being assumed to represent the most densely universalistic social formation, it ought to be ahead of less universalistic and more particularistic societies in the historical time of rationalization; it must be the most *advanced* particularity, since universality is equated to the ability to change and rationalize its social institutions. Embedded in this format is an equation according to which one can infer, from the relative degree of economic rationality, the society's investment in universalism. In other words, unless a society performs well in such a sphere as economy, it would not be able to claim it adheres to universalism. Hence, when the society is perceived to be ahead of other societies, this universalism effectively and powerfully legitimates that society's dominion over others. But if its economic and political superiority in rationalization to the others is not perceived to be certain, it rapidly loses its effectuality and persuasiveness. By the weight of its commitment to universalism, the society's self-esteem would eventually be put in jeopardy. Universalism would then appear to be the burden under which pressure the image of the society as a totality would be crushed.

≡≡≡

The term "postmodern" obliquely attests to this sort of internal contradiction which modern universalism has come to realize. A recent publication, *The Fracture of Meaning* by David Pollack, is one of the best instances in which to observe what would happen when a naive universalism is confronted with such recognition. It reacts to the perceived change of environment by reinforcing the already existing rules of discourse according to which universalism has been naturalized. What is significant here, however, is that, whereas those rules were previously implicit, assumed and accepted silently, they have now to be stated and loudly announced. It is in this point that the importance of Pollack's work lies, and, furthermore, his investigation of the Japanese aesthetic constitutes a deliberate attempt to conserve the kind of framework embedded in the accumulated knowledge on the non-West, particularly the Far East. What makes his work even more interesting is his gesture of respecting and taking seriously the kind of theoretical critique, sometimes called poststructuralism in academic journalism, that has been most effective in disclosing a specific, Eurocentric and humanistic power relation in the production of knowledge. Pollack's dauntless determination to eliminate and neutralize the critical impulse of "poststructuralism" is betrayed at almost every point where the authority of such names as Jacques Derrida and Roland Barthes is appealed to. Yet one must be sensitive to the ways in which his argument collapses, since these reveal much more about the persistence of that obsolete but arrogant discursive formation called "modernity" than about mere technical mistakes.

In demonstrating a uniquely Japanese dialectic called *wakan*, "Japanese/Chinese," by means of which the subjective identity of Japan has been installed, Pollack manipulates the master metaphor, an old trope repeatedly used in Western studies of the Far East for nearly a century, of "a frog from the bottom of its well, who would define its world almost exclusively in terms of its walls."[4] Up until the mid-nineteenth century, China was Japan's walls in opposition to which Japan's existence was defined. And, he adds, the United States has recently taken over that role. Just as Japan previously defined itself as China's other, so today it defines itself as America's other. In both cases, Japan's self is parasitic in one sense and relational in another. Putting aside the problem of whether or not every possible form of subjective identity is parasitic and relational, he proceeds to display many "scientific facts" which, without exception, testify to a distinctive gap between Japanese and Chinese languages. And he begins more detailed descriptions of a uniquely Japanese culture "with the simple and very modern-sounding premise that culture and language reflect and are informed by the same structures."[5] Yet, based upon this premise or upon one of the implications of this premise that both culture and language must be able to be isolated as unitary systems in order for these unities to "reflect and to be informed by the same structures," the gap between China and Japan at the level of representation is inscribed upon and merged with the difference between the two at the level of the real.

In linguistics, some systematic unity of regularities has to be posited as a necessary presupposition in order to analyze and organize so-called empirical information. What constitutes the possibility of linguistics as a systematic and formal corpus of knowledge is this positing of language unity which should never be confused with the actual substance of a language. But the systematic unity of a language does not exist in various linguistic activities as "the spine exists in the body of the mammal."[6] Hence, it is misleading to say that linguistics discovers and identifies the unity of a particular local or national language after the examination of data. On the contrary, the positing of such a particular language unity is the necessary condition for the possibility of linguistic research. The nature of language unities such as Japanese or Chinese is basically discursive.

This is to say that a language unity cannot be represented as a circumscribed space or closure. The metaphor of "a frog in the well" is not necessarily irrelevant; it is rather accurate and extremely persuasive in the context of contemporary Japan where the outside world seems to be a mere image projected on the walls erected by national mass media. However, if this metaphor is linked to a typical epistemological cliché of cultural solipcism, all these unities would be reified, and this is what happens with Pollack. In part this results from his inability to maintain the difference between a category of analysis and an object of analysis. But, more importantly, this seems to be a consequence of the general lack of theoretical critique about modern discourse.

For instance, the three unities of Japanese language, Japanese culture, and the Japanese nation are repeatedly used almost interchangeably. As if obediently following the models of Japanese imperial historiography (*kōkoku shikan*) or more recent discourse on Japanese uniqueness (*Nihonjinron*), Pollack projects the stereotypical image of contemporary Japan into its middle ages and antiquity. In order to stress how different the Japanese are from the Chinese, and to demonstrate the dialectic interaction of the two nations, he frequently resorts to the kind of circular argument in which Japanese culture is identified by referring to the identity of Japanese language; Japanese language is then identified by referring to the national identity of the people; and finally the Japanese people are identified by their cultural and linguistic heritage. He is not aware that this series of tautologies is a feature of a historically specific discursive formation. What Pollack does not see is that there is no logical ground on which the three categories correspond to each other in their referents. As I argued elsewhere,[7] it is only in recent history that the putative unity of Japanese culture was established. An object of discourse called culture belongs to recent times. For Pollack, these three unities are

transhistorical universals: *The Fracture of Meaning* most explicitly
endorses cultural essentialism. His argument amounts to the task
of determining Japan as a particularity, whose sense of identity is
always dependent upon the Other. Needless to say, this Other is a
universal one in contrast to which Japanese particularism is rendered
even more conspicuous. By extension, this determination of Japan
implies that Japan has been from the outset a "natural" community,
has never constituted itself as a "modern" nation.

Pollack argues that, despite the evident linguistic heterogeneity
between China and Japan, the Japanese adapted Chinese writing,
which generated an endless anxiety over their own identity.

> It would no more have occurred to the Chinese, for example,
> than it would to us to find a "problem" in the adequacy of their
> own script to represent their thoughts. And yet our investigation
> begins precisely with the problem of the adoption of Chinese
> script in Japan's "first" text, a problem that will become para-
> digmatic for all that follows.[8]

Japanese uniqueness, he asserts, is best manifested in the fact that
Japan had to borrow a foreign script. Plainly, the title of the book, *The
Fracture of Meaning*, comes from this understanding. But the reader
will be caught by surprise when he reads the following: "Clearly, the
notion of a 'fracture' of the semiotic field of culture is not unique
to Japan; nor is modern semiotics, after all, a subject particularly
associated with Japan."[9] Evidently David Pollack did not mean to say,
"It would no more have occurred to the Chinese, for example, than
it would to us to find a 'problem' in the adequacy of their own script
to represent their thoughts." Of course, he did not *mean* it, for, after
all, the meaning is fractured not solely for the Japanese, but for us
all. But does not the pretence of not admitting that the script is never
adequate to thought lead to the formation of an ethnocentric closure?
Does not the recognition of the meaning's fracture purport that,
because not only writing but also speech is exterior and inadequate to
thought, the script is always foreign and that it, therefore, pierces the
imagined closure of ethnic, cultural, and language unity? Does not
Derrida say that, when one speaks or writes, one is always external
to one's putative identities?

In order to criticize Japanese particularism and possibly what Pollack thought of as Japanese cultural essentialism, he had to construct an image of Japan which would never adopt and include others. This is to say, he first had to create an object which he could later bash. But, in this process, he mistakenly defined this peculiar object in terms of his own cultural essentialism. As a result, cultural essentialism has been accepted as the basic vocabulary belonging to the subject who studies rather than as an attribute to the object studied.

This kind of inversion repeatedly takes place in Pollack's book. When the overall methodological construction of this work is examined, one cannot help noticing another inversion. In the introduction, Pollack states: "I am concerned with the Japanese interpretations of what they saw as essentially 'Chinese,' rather than our own interpretations or those of the Chinese themselves."[10] In accordance with the metaphor of "a frog in the well," these three fields, or three wells —Japanese, Chinese, and ours—are juxtaposed. Each field seems to form a hermeneutic horizon, as Pollack asserts the hermeneutic nature of his study. However, he says in the conclusion: "I am concerned here with a dialectical process . . . so that this study becomes more than anything else a hermeneutics of Japanese culture, a study of the ways in which the Japanese interpretation of themselves and their culture evolved over time."[11] Here the Japanese field is chosen, and he says he is concerned only with the dialectic of Chinese and Japanese seen from the viewpoint of the Japanese, so "neither China nor even the idea of China was necessarily involved in its operation."[12] He deals with China only insofar as it is represented by the Japanese.

What he is unable to comprehend is the fact, without reference to which the metaphor of a frog in the well would not work, that the frog can never see his own well on its walls. For the frog, the totality of his well can never be visible. Therefore, it would never know that it is confined in a tiny space; it is not aware that what it believes to be the entire universe is merely a small well. In order to know that its universe is merely a well, the image of the well must be projected on the walls. Thus for the frog (Japanese) the totality of the well (Japan) is basically invisible and has to be recognized only as a representation projected on the walls. If China is dealt with only as a representation,

Japan should be dealt with in exactly the same fashion. Furthermore, if the Japanese do not have some representation of Japan and their confinement or subjection to it, they could not even recognize that they are Japanese; they would not be able to identify themselves with Japan. As China is simply imaginary for the Japanese, so Japan is also imaginary for them. If Pollack wishes to talk about the synthesis of China in the Japanese culture, he must first talk about the synthesis of Japan in the Japanese culture. There should be as much dialectic between the Japanese and Japan as between the Japanese and China. Of course, his cultural essentialism is totally blind to the problem of subjectivity.

One of the ironic implications of this metaphor is that no one can confidently claim to be free from the fate of the frog. The frog believes that there is no other and different world outside its small world. So its knowledge of its small world is supposed to be universally valid everywhere. But how can the world of those who laugh at the frog be guaranteed not to be another well? The haughty and self-confident smile on their faces will freeze as soon as this question is posed. After all, is the Japan which Pollack describes any different from the China which the Japanese imagined on the walls of their well?

In a sense, *The Fracture of Meaning* is haunted by a sense of insecurity which seemingly stems from an implicit knowledge that somebody may ask this question anytime. What has been undertaken to repress this sense of insecurity is the setting up of an enunciative position from which the author speaks in universal terms—a ubiquitous and transcendent stance from which he views things. It is arranged to appear natural that Pollack's words are automatically registered as metalanguage. His language posits the *us* with whom he wishes to speak, and his *we*, the speaking subject of this metalanguage, coincides with the West and with America in particular. Thus, once more, the West assumes its ubiquity and universality in the midst of its particularity. Needless to say, Pollack's argument presupposes that the opposition of theory (universal) and the object of theory (particular) corresponds to that of the West and Japan.

A privileged object of discourse called Japan is thus constituted in order to show *us* the supposedly concrete instance of particularism, in contrast to which *our* universalism is ascertained. Japan is defined as a specific and unitary particularity in universal terms: Japan's uniqueness and identity are provided insofar as Japan stands out as a particular object in the universal field of the West. Only when it is integrated into Western universalism does it gain its own identity as a particularity. In other words, Japan becomes endowed with and aware of its "self" only when it is recognized by the West. It is no accident that the discourse on Japanese uniqueness (*Nihonjinron*) mentions innumerable cases of Japan's difference from the West, thereby defining Japan's identity in terms of deviations from the West. Its insistence on Japan's peculiarity and difference from the West embodies a nagging urge to see the self from the viewpoint of the Other. But this is nothing but the positing of Japan's identity in Western terms which in return establishes the centrality of the West as the universal point of reference. This is why, despite the gestures of criticizing Japanese exclusivism and ethnocentricity, Pollack in fact eagerly embraces and endorses the Japanese particularism and racism so evident in *Nihonjinron*. As a matter of fact, his entire argument would collapse without this openhanded acceptance of particularism.

Contrary to what has been advertised by both sides, universalism and particularism reinforce and supplement each other; they are never in real conflict; they need each other and have to seek to form a symmetrical, mutually supporting relationship by every means in order to avoid a dialogic encounter which would necessarily jeopardize their reputedly secure and harmonized monologic worlds. Universalism and particularism endorse each other's defect in order to conceal their own; they are intimately tied to each other in their accomplice. In this respect, a particularism such as nationalism can never be a serious critique of universalism, for it is an accomplice thereof.

Still, the relationship between the West and the non-West seems to follow the old and familiar formula of master/slave. And during the 1930s when "the times after the modern" (*gendai*), somewhat similar to our postmodernity, were extensively examined, one of the issues that some Japanese intellectuals problematized was the West and the non-West relationship itself. In offering a diagnosis of the times, many, including young philosophers of the Kyoto School such

as Kōyama Iwao and Kōsaka Masaaki, singled out as the most significant index the rapport between the Western (European) and the
non-Western (non-European) worlds. A fundamental change, they
observed, had taken place in the world since the late nineteenth and
the early twentieth centuries. Until the late nineteenth century, history seemed to have moved linearly toward the further unification
of the world. The entire globe was gradually organized according to
the singular framework which ultimately would allow for only one
center. First of all, history appeared to be an unending process of unification and centralization with Europe at the center. Hence, it was
understandable and partially inevitable to conceive of history simply
as the process of Westernization (Europeanization). In this historical
scheme, the entire world was viewed from the top, and was thought
of as being Western in the sense that the rest of the world was taken
to be that which was doomed to be Westernized. Essentially, as is
best represented by Hegelian historicism, "the history of the world
was European history." [13]

However, toward the late nineteenth century, Kōyama claims, the
non-Western world began to move toward its independence and to
form a world of its own. As a consequence of this transformation,
what had hitherto been taken for the entire world was revealed to be
a merely modern (*kindai*) world, a world among many worlds. This
possibility for historical cognition and praxis, informed by the fundamental historical transformation of the world, was then called "World
History." In this *world history*, it was assumed that historical changes
simply could not be comprehended without reference to the already
established spatial categories: climate, geography, race, nation, culture, etc. Only within the framework set up by those categories was
it possible to understand historical developments and make sense out
of various changes which were to be incorporated into a larger unit
of narrative. What this simple but undeniable recognition pointed to
was that history was not only temporal or chronological but also spatial and relational. The condition for the possibility of conceiving of
history as a linear and evolutionary series of incidents lay in its not
as yet thematized relation to other histories, other *coexisting* tempo-
ralities. Whereas monistic history (*ichigenteki rekishi*) did not know
its implicit reliance on other histories and thought itself autonomous

and total, "world" history conceived of itself as the spatial relations of histories. In world history, therefore, one could not think of history exclusively in those terms which referred back only to that same history; monistic history could not deal with the world as it was apprehended in world history since the world is primarily a sphere of heterogeneity and others. To what extent Kōyama's world history was capable of facing heterogeneity and others, and whether or not world history would ever be able to be exposed to them in their heterogeneity and otherness will be examined later. But I should note that this notion of otherness and heterogeneity was always defined in terms of differences among or between nations, cultures, and histories as if there had been no differences and heterogeneity within one nation, culture, and history. For Kōyama, heterogeneity and otherness were at most moments of *international* differences.

An oblivion of spatial predicates, which reveals itself as the truth of monistic history at the moment of the emergence of world history, comes from certain historical conditions. Unless the historical and cultural world is seriously challenged and influenced by another, it would never reach an awareness that its own world can never be directly equated to the world at large, and would continue to fantasize about itself as being the representative and representation of the totality. Eurocentric history is one of the most typical cases of this: for it, the world does not exist. But Kōyama also adds Japanese national history to the list. Japanese national history is another example of monistic history in which, in spite of the fact that Japan has been challenged and influenced by other histories and cultures, it has yet to arrive at the knowledge that history resides in those interactions with others, due to its island situation (*shimaguni-teki jōken*).

What Kōyama brought into awareness is the fact that the very identity of a history is constituted by its interdependence with other histories, things other than itself. Precisely because monistic history does not recognize the conditions for the possibility of its own identity, it naively expands its specific values indefinitely and continues to insist upon the universal validity of those values: it misunderstands and misconstrues the moment according to which the necessity to claim its universality and the insistence upon its identity are simultaneously inaugurated. Thus the moment of otherness is deliberately transformed in order to maintain its putative centrality as the initiator of the universal and the commensurability of universal and particular values. This no doubt amounts to the annihilation of the Other in its otherness. Probably the mission which monistic history believes itself to take charge of is best summarized by the following statement: "They are just like us." Of course, it has to be remembered, this statement is definitely distinct from another statement—"We are just like them"—in which the centrality of *us* is not insured: that is, the inferiority in the power of *us* is instituted instead of the superiority, but these form a *supplementary* pair.

Monistic history has worked in the service of a certain historically specific domination, a form of domination which has not ceased to be turbulent in its effect even today. However, Kōyama saw and tried to seize a turning point in the development of monistic history. He insisted that another history, world history, which recognizes other histories, was about to emerge. And this emergence should mark a fundamental change in relationship between the subject of history and its others; it should indicate that the monistic history in which others were refused their own recognition was no longer possible. In this new history, the plurality of histories and the interaction among them would be the principle. Hence, spatial terms would of necessity be incorporated into a history that would have to be construed as a synthesis of time and space, and internationalized.

What Kōyama advocated may sound like a genuinely pluralistic history as opposed to a linear singular one, and, if one were to believe all that has been said, this transition from monistic history to world history should mark a radical historical change leading to a different power arrangement in which cultural, national, and historical particularities are fully respected. All the cultural worlds would then be mediated not by what Kōsaka Masaaki called the "ontological universals" (*yū-teki fuhen*) but by the "mu" universals (*mu-teki fuhen*).[14] And if this should be the case, one would then envisage the beyond of modern times, the other side of the historical break which would allow one to objectify the limits of the modern discourse—in short, a genuine postmodernity.

In this context, it is noteworthy that, for Kōyama as well as for

Kōsaka, the unity of the subject of history, of pluralistic history, is unequivocally equated to that of the nation-state. Yet they stress that the nation-state does not immediately correspond to a race (*jinshu*) or folk (*minzoku*). The state for them is a being-for-itself which is opposed to other states, and, in this regard, it exists in the "world." The state, therefore, is not likened to other "entities" such as race, nation, clan, or family precisely because it has to be mediated by its relationships with other states and consequently be self-reflective—that is, a subject. On the other hand, the nation designates a community rooted in nature, a community where people are born and die. The bondage that keeps its members together is that of blood, pro-creation, and land, and is natural in the sense that the tie between mother and child is natural.

Kōyama issues a warning disclaimer here: the nation as a natural community can never be the subject of history because it is not mediated by universals. The natural community (Kōsaka refers to it as "substance" [*kitai*]) is not a subject in itself, for it has yet to be rationalized. The natural community must be represented by the state; only through the state, the natural community is identified as the *nation for itself*. And only through this representation to itself does the nation become historical and generate its own culture, a historical world of its own. At this stage, a nation forms a history or historical world of its own with the state as its subject.

While rejecting Hegelian philosophy as an extension of monistic history, Kōyama rigorously follows Hegelian construction. Accepting all the "modern" premises, Kōyama attempts to change merely their historical view. By introducing pluralistic world history and thereby claiming to go beyond modernity (*kindai*), he endorses almost everything the Japanese state has acquired under the name of modernization. The critique of the West and of the modern expressed in his critique of monistic history seems to disclose the fact that the whole rhetoric of anti-modernity is in fact a cover for the unprincipled endorsement of anything modern when Kōsaka and Kōyama deal with the issues on which the critique of the West is most urgent—the issues related to the Sino-Japanese situations during the 1930s and early 1940s.

In a roundtable talk held in November 1941, Kōsaka, Kōyama, and others refer to the relationship between historical development and the morality of a nation.[15]

KŌYAMA: The subject [*shutai*] of moral energy should be the nation [*kokumin*]. . . . The nation is the key to every problem. Moral energy has nothing to do with individual or personal ethics, or the purity of blood. Both culturally and politically the nation is the center of moral energy.

KŌSAKA: That is right. The folk [*minzoku*] in itself is meaningless. When the folk gains subjectivity [*shutaisei*], it necessarily turns into a national folk [*kokka-teki minzoku*]. The folk without subjectivity or self-determination [*jiko gentei*], that is, the folk that has not transformed itself into a nation [*kokumin*] is powerless. For instance, a folk like the ainu could not gain independence, and has eventually been absorbed into other folk [that has been transformed into] a nation. I wonder if the Jews would follow the same fate. I think the Subject of World History must be a national folk in this sense.[16]

One can hardly discern any difference between this understanding of modern subjectivity and that of the Hegelian dialectic. First of all, the *modern* nation must be an embodiment of the will (*jiko-gentei sei*). That is to say, the subject of the nation is, at the same time, self-determination (the determination of the self as such) and the determining self (the self that determines itself). And the *modern* nation must externalize itself in order to be aware of itself and to realize its will. Hence, it is, without exception, a nation representing itself in the state; it is the synthesis of a folk (irrational) and the state (rational). The nation is the reason concretized in an individuality (*kobetsusei* = folk), so that the nation cannot coincide with the folk immediately. In order for the folk to transform itself into the nation, the folk must be negatively mediated by other folks. That is, the stronger folk must conquer and subjugate other weaker folks in order to form the nation.[17]

The fragility of their anti-modern rhetoric becomes all the more apparent when the pluralistic world history is discussed in the context of the contemporary historical situation. In another roundtable talk titled "Tōakyōeiken no rinrisei to rekishisei" ("Ethics and Historicality of Great East Asian Coprosperity Sphere") held about three months after the previous one with the same participants, they directly relate the issue of history to the Sino-Japanese relationship.[18]

KŌSAKA: The Sino-Japanese war [*shina jihen*] involves many things and is extremely complex. But the final factor which determines the outcome should be the question "which morality is superior, the Japanese or Chinese one?" Of course, political and cultural maneuvers are very important. Yet our moral attitude towards the Chinese is even more important, perhaps. We should consider measures like this: we should send many of our morally excellent people over there to show our moral energy so that the people over there would be persuaded to convince themselves [of our moral superiority]. The Sino-Japanese war is also a war of morality. Now that we have entered the Great East Asian War, the war is much larger in scale now, namely, a war between the Oriental morality and the Occidental morality. Let me put it differently, the question is which morality will play a more important role in the World History in the future.[19]

It is amazing that they could still talk not only about the Japanese nation's morality but also about its superiority over the Chinese one at that stage. Imagining the national atmosphere around that time in which these utterances were made, one would rather refrain from asking whether or not Kōsaka was joking. Nevertheless, it is at least worthwhile noting that the relationship between the Japanese and Chinese moralities is put in a sort of dialectic. Kōsaka seems confident that the superiority of Japanese morality would eventually be proven as if the whole thing had been guaranteed by Japanese military superiority.

For Kōsaka, historical process involves a series of inevitable conflicts in which the morality of one nation is judged against that of another. Thus the incident in China (the Sino-Japanese war) is a moral war, and the war over the Pacific is also a war which will decide the moral superiority of the East or the West in view of the ultimate morality of the totality—that is, all of humanity. In this sense, history as he conceives of it is the history of moral development toward the establishment of morality for humanity, toward the ultimate emancipation of human kind. Despite repeated denunciation of the term "humanism," Kōsaka is never able to resist the temptation of justifying the status quo in terms of humanism. In other words, his critique of humanism and modernity is, in fact, a thinly disguised celebration thereof.

Apart from an incredible conceit expressed in this passage, there is a theoretical formation which clearly contradicts the premises of *pluralistic* world history. To imagine the relationship between China and Japan in terms of the war of Chinese and Japanese moralities is to posit a dialectical relationship between the two moralities. This means that, in the optimistic imagination, Japanese morality will eventually prove its universality as well as the particularity of Chinese morality. This would necessarily be a process in which particularities would be subjugated to the domination of a universality. Kōyama said, "[The Chinese] have subjective sense of their Sinocentrism but do not have an objective consciousness of 'the World'. . . . While there is a moral in China, there is moral energy in Japan."[20]

What we see here is the ugliest aspect of universalism, and it should not be forgotten that this is, after all, the reality of Kōyama's "pluralism." Not only a Japanese victory over China was presumed and unquestioned, but also Japanese moral superiority was assumed; the temporary military superiority of Japan (which, after all, was faked by national mass media) was thought to guarantee the right to speak condescendingly. If this dialectic movement between universalistic and particularistic moralities had proceeded as it was imagined, it would eventually eliminate the pluralistic coexistence of many histories and traditions passionately advocated in the critique of *monistic history*. Within the scheme of the universalism-particularism pair, the plural subjects will gradually be organized as many particularities subjected to a single center of universalism.

How, then, can one possibly avoid the detested *monistic history*? For world history would be no different from the history of progress toward the complete dominion by one center. Kōyama and Kōsaka think they are entitled to accuse the Chinese for their lack of a world-historical sense, for their insolence, and finally for their particularism; they felt entitled to do so because they thought they were speaking from the position of universalism.

Pluralistic world history proves itself to be another version of monistic history. I do not know how one could possibly avoid this conclusion when the subjects of world history are equated to nations. How can one put forward an effective critique of modernity when one affirms and extols one's national identity as the sole base for historical praxis? And their critique of modernity is at best some guise of anti-imperialism under which Japanese modernity (including the inevitable consequences of its expansionist impulse) is openhandedly endorsed. What annoyed them in monistic history is not the fact that many were suppressed and deprived of the sense of self-respect in the world because of its Eurocentric arrangement. What they were opposed to was the fact that, in that Eurocentric arrangement of the world, the *putative* unity of the Japanese happened to be excluded from the center. And what they wished to realize was to change the world so that the Japanese would occupy the position of the center and of the subject which determines other particularities in its own universal terms. In order to achieve this goal, they would approve anything Western on condition that it conforms to the structure of the modern nation-state. Far from being an anti-Western determination, what motivated them was the will to pursue the path of modernization. In so far as centralization and homogenization is part and parcel of modernization, their philosophy of world history paradoxically illustrates the inevitability of war by showing the impossibility of the coexistence of many centers. And the disastrous failure of this philosophy indicates that Japan was already so far modernized that it would necessarily initiate the movement toward universalism and would never be able to rid itself of the impulse to universalize and totalize despite all the rhetoric of anti-modernism.

Perhaps the most crucial point the philosophers of world history did not realize was that Japan did not stand *outside* the West. Even in its particularism, Japan was already implicated in the ubiquitous West, so that neither historically nor geopolitically could Japan be seen as the *outside* of the West. This means that, in order to criticize the West in relation to Japan, one has necessarily to begin with a critique of Japan. Likewise, the critique of Japan necessarily entails the radical critique of the West. So it seems to me that, in so far as one tries to speak from the position of *us*, the putative unity of either the West or Japan, one would never be able to escape the dominion of the universalism-particularism pair: one would never be effective in criticism no matter how radical a posture one might put on.

═══════

After Japan's defeat in 1945, Takeuchi Yoshimi was one of those few intellectuals who engaged themselves in the serious examination of Japanese morality in relation to China, and openly admitted that the war Japan had just lost was a war between Chinese and Japanese moralities. Brilliantly he demonstrated the inevitability of Japan's defeat on both socioeconomic and moral grounds. Japan proved itself morally defeated on its own terms. However, Takeuchi was also one of the few who refused to ignore a certain legitimacy in what incited many, including the philosophers of world history, to a rhetoric of *pluralism*, despite the fact that, during the war, he was among those who despised and refused the idea of a "Great East Asian Coprosperity Sphere" advocated by people like the philosophers of world history. By every means he tried to sustain an intellectual concern about the problem of Western domination which, of course, did not disappear with Japan's defeat.

In a manner similar to Kōyama's definition of monistic history, Takeuchi draws attention to the involuntary nature of modernity for the non-West. Here, too, the term of modernity must signify not only a temporal or chronological but also a spatial concept in the sense that the significance of modernity for the non-West would never be grasped unless it is apprehended in the non-West's spatial relationship to the West. Modernity for the Orient, according to Takeuchi, is primarily its subjugation to the West's political, military, and economic control. The modern Orient was born only when it was invaded, defeated, and exploited by the West. This is to say that only when the Orient became an object for the West did it enter modern times. The truth of modernity for the non-West, therefore, is its reaction to the West: Takeuchi insists that it must be so precisely because of the way modernity is shaped with regard to the problematic concerning the subjective identity of the West.

Modernity is the self-recognition of Europe, the recognition of Europe's modern self as distinct from her feudal self, a recognition rendered possible only in a specific historical process in which Europe liberated itself from the feudalistic (with her liberation being marked by the emergence of free capital in economy, or the establishment of modern personality as an independent and equal individual in human relations). Europe is possible only in this history, and inversely it can be said that history is possible only in Europe. For history is not an empty form of time. It consists in an eternal instance at which one struggles to overcome difficulties in order thereby to be one's own self. Without this, the self would be lost; history would be lost.[21]

The West (Europe) cannot be the West unless it continually strives to transform itself; positively the West is not, but only reflectively it is. "Her [Europe] capital desires to expand her market; the missionaries are committed in the mandate to expand the kingdom of heaven. Through ceaseless tension, the Europeans endeavor to be their own selves. This ceaseless effort to be their own selves makes it impossible for them to remain what they are in themselves. They must take a risk of losing themselves in order to be their own selves."[22] The idea of progress or historicism would be unintelligible without reference to this continual search for the self, a ceaseless process of self-recentering.

Inevitably the self-liberation of the West resulted in its invasion into the Orient. In invading the Orient, "she [Europe] encountered the heterogeneous, posited her self in opposition to it." At the same time, Europe's invasion gave rise to capitalism in the Orient. No doubt, the establishment of capitalism there was taken as a consequence of the West's survival-expansion, and it was thought to testify to progress in the history of the world and the triumph of reason. Of course, the Orient reacted to the West's expansion and put up *resistance* to it. Yet in this very *resistance* it was integrated into the dominion of the West and served, as a moment, toward the completion of Eurocentric and monistic world history. In this scheme, the Orient was to play the role of self-consciousness that had failed in the continual dialectical reaffirmation and recentering of the West as a self-consciousness that was certain of itself; it also served as an object necessitated in the formation of the West as a knowing subject. Thus the Orient was expected to offer an endless series of strange and different things whereby the familiarity of *our* things was implicitly affirmed. The knowledge of Oriental things was shaped after the existing power relation between the West and its other-object, and, as shown in Edward Said's *Orientalism*, it continued to affirm and solidify that relation. But we must not forget that the Orient thus known cannot be represented to itself; it can be represented only to the West.

On the one hand, the West is delimited, opposed to that which is alien to it; it needs its other for its identity. On the other hand, the West is ubiquitous and invisible as it is assumed to be the condition of the possibility for the universal validity of knowledge. Only in a discursive formation called modernity is universality possible as essentially Western universality. But, Takeuchi says, "The Orient resists." He reiterates the term *resistance*.

The Orient resists; it disturbs the West's dominion. It is important to note that the modernization of the Orient was prompted by this resistance. Here, Takeuchi stresses that if the Orient had not resisted it would never have been modernized. Accordingly, the modernization of the Orient should not be thought of as a mere imitation of Western things, although there have been cases in which the will to resist was very weak, as in Japan's modernization. As is amply shown by the fact that the Orient had to modernize and adopt things from the West in order to resist it, the modernization of the Orient attests to an advance or success for the West, and, therefore, it is always Westernization or Europeanization. So it necessarily appears that, even in its resistance, the Orient is subjugated to the mode of representation dominated by the West. And its attempt to resist the West is doomed to fail; the Orient cannot occupy the position of a subject. Is it possible, then, to define the Orient as that which can never be a subject?

It goes without saying that neither the West nor the Orient are immediately referents. The unity of the West is totally dependent upon the manner in which resistance is dealt with in the gathering together of its subjective identity. At this juncture, Takeuchi's explanation of the term resistance seems to begin to oscillate between two different readings.

Meanwhile, Takeuchi points out, the Orient does not connote any internal commonality among the names subsumed under it; it ranges from regions in the Middle East to those in the Far East. One can hardly find anything religious, linguistic, or cultural that is common among those varied areas. The Orient is neither a cultural, religious, or linguistic unity, nor a unified world. The principle of its identity lies outside itself: what endows it with some vague sense of unity is that the Orient is that which is excluded and objectified by the West in the service of its historical progress. From the outset, the Orient is a shadow of the West. If the West did not exist, the Orient would not exist either. According to Takeuchi, this is the primary definition of modernity. For the non-West, modernity means, above all, the state of being deprived of its own subjectivity. Then does the non-West have to acquire its own subjectivity? His answer to this seems to harbor the kind of ambiguity so characteristic of his entire discourse. "For there is no *resistance*, that is, there is no wish to maintain the self (the self itself does not exist). The absence of resistance means that Japan is not Oriental. But at the same time, the absence of the self-maintenance wish (no self) means that Japan is not European. This is to say, Japan is nothing."[23]

Takeuchi says "Japan is nothing." But is Japan really nebulous and amorphous without any inclination toward self-recentering? Because Japan does not wish to be itself, to posit itself anew, he argues, it fails to be itself and also fails to be like the West. His denunciation of contemporary Japan makes it seem as if Japan had not had any representation of itself, or the self that was not concretized in various institutions: as if there had not been any state which imposed the sense of a nation upon those living in the region; as if those living in the region did not identify themselves with the nation; as if the nation called Japan had existed for thousands of years merely as a natural community.

Japan is a modern nation. Precisely in their effort to sustain itself, people in Japanese territories have organized themselves as a nation and represented themselves in the state of that nation. How could a nation without the sense of national identity possibly launch a war which lasted for more than fifteen years, resulting in an amazing amount of human and economic wreckage? It seems that Takeuchi is caught in the historico-geopolitical pairing of the premodern and the modern, according to which, since the West is modern, Japan should be premodern or at least non-modern. Instead of analyzing the pairing of the West and the non-West excluded by the West, Takeuchi assumes the validity of this pairing in talking about Japan. But his analytical device collapses upon the object of its analysis.

This sort of misapprehension seems to derive from Takeuchi's conviction that, in order to counteract the West's aggression, the non-West must form nations. Then what is heterogeneous to the West can be organized into a kind of monolithic *resistance* against the West. A nation can oppose heterogeneity against the West, but within the nation homogeneity must predominate. Without constructing what Hegel called the "universal homogeneous sphere," the nation would be impossible. So, whether you like it or not, the modernization process in the formation of the modern nation should entail the elimination of heterogeneity within. Exactly the same type of relationship as that between the West and the non-West will be reproduced between the nation as a whole and heterogeneous elements in it. In this context, the nation is always represented by the state so that it is a subject to which its members are subject, whereas heterogeneous elements remain deprived of their subjectivity so that they are not subject to the subject.

Insofar as he never loses faith in the universal emancipation of mankind, Takeuchi is certainly a modernist. Therefore, he believes that monistic world history is, after all things are considered, an inevitability and that, consequently, the universal emancipation will be realized not by the West but by the Orient. In history, he says, the true subject is the Orient. In the meantime, we must endure the elimination of heterogeneity in order to construct the nation, the subject of history. It is misleading to say that Takeuchi is antimodern; he rejects only limited aspects of modernization.

On the other hand, one can detect a thread suggesting a different reading of his term *resistance*. For the Orient, resistance is supposed never to contribute to the formation of its subjective identity. In other words, resistance is not negation by means of which a subject is posited in opposition to what it negates. Hence, resistance has to be likened to negativity, as distinct from negation, which continues to disturb a putative stasis in which the subject is made to be adequate to itself. Here, Takeuchi is concerned with something fundamental to the whole problem of modernity and the West.

> I do not know what resistance is. I cannot logically pursue the meaning of resistance. . . . I dread the rationalist belief that everything can be brought into presence. I am afraid of the pressure of an irrational will which underlies the rationalist belief. And to me that seems to be [the essence of] Europe. [Until recently] I have noticed that I have been haunted by this feeling of fear. When I realized that many thinkers and writers in Japan, except for a few poets, did not feel what I felt and were not afraid of rationalism, and when I noticed that what they had produced in the name of rationalism—including materialism—did not look like rationalism, I felt insecure. Then I came across Lu Xun. I saw Lu Xun enduring this kind of fear all by himself. . . . If I were asked "What is resistance?", the only answer I have is "It is what you find in Lu Xun."[24]

Resistance comes from a deeply rooted fear of the will to represent everything, the will essential for modern subjectivity. Lu Xun exemplifies a desperate effort to resist subjectivity, to resist subjection to subjectivity, and finally to resist subjection to the subject.

> For Lu Xun, it is impossible to assume an observational and indifferent attitude, that is, the attitude of humanism. For the fool [Lu Xun himself] would never be able to save the slave as humanism naively hopes. . . . The slave is a slave precisely because he seeks to be saved. Hence, when he is awakened, he will be put in the state of "no road to follow," of "the most painful moment in life." He will have to experience the state of self-awareness that he is a slave. And he has to endure the fear. As soon as he gives in and begs for help, he will lose the self-awareness of his own slave status. In other words, the state of "no road to follow" is the awakened state, so if he still believes that there is a road to march on, he must be dreaming.

And he continues,

> The slave must refuse his slave identity, but at the same time, he must refuse the dream of liberation as well. He must be a slave with the acutest sense of his miserable status, and remain in the "most painful awakened state in life." He must remain in the state that, because there is no road to follow, he must keep on trying to go. He rejects what he is, and at the same time he rejects any wish to be someone other than what he is. This is the meaning of despair which exists in Lu Xun and which makes Lu Xun possible. . . . There is no room for humanism here. . . .[25]

Here, above all, resistance is that which disturbs the possible representational relationship between the self and its image. It is something that resists the formation of those identities which subject people to various institutions. Yet this does not liberate them; this does not lead to emancipation because people are often subject to what they most fear through the words of emancipation. Possibly one should leave them in their sleep rather than "cry aloud to wake a few of the lighter sleepers, making those unfortunate few suffer the agony of irrevocable death." But if one is determined to be awake, one must at least resist one's hope to go beyond. What enabled Takeuchi to criticize modernity seems to come from this sense of resistance, although Takeuchi so often approves of modernism. This is what separated him from those who naively imagine the possibility of overcoming the modern. By the same gesture of emancipation, they all fall into the trap set up by modernity. As Takeuchi has given up an emancipatory ideology, he can be all the more effectively critical of modernity despite his commitment to certain modernist values.

The sense of uncertainty which the term postmodernity provokes may indicate the gradual spreading of this resistance. And I think I understand the term "play" best when I, unjustifiably perhaps, associate it with what Takeuchi saw in Lu Xun.[26] Only at this stage one could talk about hope, but rather hesitantly, just as Lu Xun did in his short story "My Old Home."

> The access of hope made me suddenly afraid. When Jun-tu had asked for the incense burner and candlesticks I had laughed up

my sleeve at him, to think that he was still worshipping idols and would never put them out of his mind. Yet what I now called hope was no more than an idol I had created myself. The only difference was that what he desired was close at hand, while what I desired was less easily realized.

As I dozed, a stretch of jade-green seashore spread itself before my eyes, and above a round golden moon hung from a deep blue sky. I thought: hope cannot be said to exist, nor can it be said not to exist. It is just like roads across the earth. For actually the earth had no roads to begin with, but when many men pass one way, a road is made.[27]

Notes

1 Jürgen Habermas, *The Theory of Communicative Action*, vol. 1, trans. Thomas McCarthy (Boston, 1984), 44.
2 Ibid.
3 See Richard Rorty, "Habermas and Lyotard on Postmodernity," in *Habermas and Modernity*, ed. Richard J. Bernstein (Cambridge, Mass., 1985), 167.
4 David Pollack, *The Fracture of Meaning* (Princeton, 1986), 4.
5 Ibid.
6 Following the critique of positivist linguistics put forth by Tokieda Motoki during the 1930s, one could assert three points—the unity of language is very much like the Kantian "ideal" or *constituting positivity* which makes the empirical study of language possible; the unity of language, therefore, is never given in "experience"; and, consequently, the idea of the universal essence of language would never be obtained through the induction of the accumulated empirical data on the increasing number of particular languages.
7 It is in the eighteenth century that the unities of the Japanese culture, language, and ethnicity as they are conceived of today were brought into existence. In this sense, the Japanese were born in the eighteenth century. See my dissertation, *Voices of the Past* (Chicago, 1983), 217–335.
8 Pollack, *Fracture of Meaning*, 4.
9 Ibid., 16.
10 Ibid., 3–4.
11 Ibid., 227.
12 Ibid.
13 Kōyama Iwao, "Sekaishi no rinen" ("The Idea of World History"), *Shisō* (April–May 1940).
14 Kōsaka Masaaki, "Rekishi-teki sekai" ("Historical World"), in *Kōsaka Masaaki chosakushū* (*Complete Works of Kōsaka Masaaki*), vol. 1 (Tokyo, 1964), 176–217.

15 Kōsaka Masaaki, Suzuki Shigetaka, Kōyama Iwao, and Nishitani Keiji, "Sekaishi-teki tachiba to Nihon" ("The Standpoint of World History and Japan"), *Chūō kōron* (January 1942).

16 Ibid., 185.

17 Kōsaka, "Rekishi-teki sekai," 192.

18 Kōsaka Masaaki, Suzuki Shigetaka, Kōyama Iwao, and Nishitani Keiji, "Tōakyōei-ken no rinrisei to rekishisei" ("Ethics and Historicality of Great East Asian Co-prosperity Sphere"), *Chūō kōron* (April 1942).

19 Ibid., 120–21.

20 Ibid., 129.

21 Takeuchi Yoshimi, "Kindai towa nanika" ("What Is Modernity?"), in *Takeuchi Yoshimi zenshū (Complete Works of Takeuchi Yoshimi)*, vol. 4 (Tokyo, 1980), 130.

22 Ibid., 131.

23 Ibid.

24 Ibid., 144.

25 Ibid., 155–57.

26 See Jacques Derrida, *Dissemination*, trans. Barbara Johnson (Chicago, 1981), 61–171.

27 Lu Xun, "My Old Home," in *Selected Stories of Lu Xun*, trans. Yang Hsien-ji and Gladya Yang (Peking, 1972), 63–64.

J. Victor Koschmann

Maruyama Masao and the Incomplete
Project of Modernity

> One cannot . . . provide a coherent account of
> postmodernity without a determinate concept of
> modernity; and such a concept cannot be devel-
> oped a priori, but is necessarily dependent on the
> theorization of long-term historical processes.
> —Peter Dews, *Autonomy and Solidarity* [1]

The philosopher Jean-François Lyotard has summed up postmodernism as "incredulity toward metanarratives." [2] He proposes that in the postmodern world none of the master narratives that the modern epistémè produced, such as those associated with Hegel, Marx, and Freud, retain any of their legitimating force. We can no longer appeal to them, implicitly or explicitly, as warrants to secure the truth-value or significance of the generalizations we make in the course of scientific or discursive practice. Also obsolescent, therefore, is our former confidence in the subjects, both individual and collective, that had been cast as the main agents of those metahistorical processes. In this disillusioned postmodern condition, according to Lyotard, we are able to confirm or disconfirm our claims to truth only according to a variety of strictly local forms of "customary knowledge" that are embedded in popular narratives.[3]

However, Jürgen Habermas, who is one of the main targets of Lyotard's argument, has risen to defend the continued plausibility of universal standards of legitimacy and truth. He argues that unless we retain at least one standard by which validity can be judged, we will have to give up the "rational criticism of existing institutions." That is, without any means of distinguishing between validity and power, truth and falsehood, we would lack an independent standpoint from which to demand reform, and all criticism would be rendered "context-dependent."[4] He admits that modern rationality has come under fire, but argues that it should not be rejected entirely:

> The 20th century has shattered this optimism [of the Enlightenment]. . . . But the problem won't go away: should we try to hold on to the intentions of the Enlightenment, feeble as they may be, or should we declare the entire project of modernity a lost cause?

Habermas's answer is to press on, since "the project of modernity has not yet been fulfilled."[5] In his view, the postmodernism of Lyotard, as well as the "anti-modernism" of Georges Bataille, Michel Foucault, and Jacques Derrida, signals the abandonment of reason, and is therefore not only philosophically retrograde but politically conservative.[6]

Postmodernism is also contentious in Japan.[7] Literary critic Karatani Kōjin has defined it as a movement which seeks the "deconstruction of modernism or, more fundamentally, of the framework of Western metaphysics." It involves the "disappearance of the subject, the decentering (or 'multicentering') of the [putative] center, and also the substitution of surface for depth, copies for originality and pastiche or collage for creativity." However, because modernity has not necessarily meant the same thing in Japan as it has in the West, postmodernism might have implications peculiar to the Japanese context. Karatani goes on to argue that,

> [a]lthough in Japan the words poststructuralism and postmodernism are used to refer to concepts originating in France, they are in fact also functioning in a self-sufficient space where the

"other" of the West is as yet unknown. . . . Of course, Japanese society is also enmeshed in the various institutions and epistemological mechanisms of modernity and is affected by the processes that present-day capitalism imposes on all countries. To that extent, we have the same problems as France or the United States. However, there is also a context unrelated to that which is peculiar to Japan. It was formed in the Edo period [1603–1868].[8]

Karatani's observation opens the question of whether in the Japanese context "modernism" might also differ somewhat in content, emphasis, and implication from that in the West. If so, the meaning and relevance of Japanese postmodernism would have to be reassessed.

One way to begin addressing such issues is to investigate more closely the concept of modernity that was put forward in the early post–World War II period, an era which, perhaps more than any other in Japan's history, was imbued with the values and program of a kind of modernism (*kindaishugi*).[9] I will seek to contribute to such an investigation by reinterpreting some of the major postwar texts by Maruyama Masao (1914–   ), perhaps the era's leading theorist and advocate of modernity. In addition to clarifying basic elements of Japanese modernist thought, such an investigation might cast light on the question of whether the ideal of modernity in the Japanese context has become entirely irrelevant, as Lyotard believes to be the case in the West, or whether, as Habermas has energetically argued, it might in some aspects still be considered an incomplete project.

≡≡≡≡

Japan surrendered on 15 August 1945, and in December 1945, soon after he was returned to civilian life from his post in Hiroshima, Maruyama Masao wrote a tiny essay entitled "Kindaiteki shii" ("Modern Thought") that begins by disparaging the wartime project of "overcoming modernity":

> Some of our honorable writers, critics, and scholars have argued that "modernity" completed its historical function in the past and that finally even in Japan—nay, uniquely in Japan—the only remaining problem was how to "overcome" it. When this atmosphere of the past few years is viewed from the perspective of

Japan today—as we learn the ABCs of modern civilization from General Douglas MacArthur—it is difficult to suppress a sense of misery mixed with absurdity.

It was Maruyama's view that, "far from 'overcoming' modern thought, we in Japan have *not yet succeeded in fully achieving it*." [10]

Written in the dark days of late-1945, this fragment established the incomplete project of modernity as the focal point of an intellectual agenda for the postwar era. It represented the commitment of Maruyama himself, and increasingly that of other progressive intellectuals, to modernity as a positive ideal. It also suggested a somewhat reductivist interpretation of that ideal, as consisting most meaningfully in a certain quality of personality or subjectivity. Maruyama approached this agenda not as a philosopher or theorist, like Habermas, but rather as an intellectual historian. It is no accident, therefore, that his historical works bear most provocatively on modernity and subjectivity. The most important of them is entitled "Fukuzawa Yukichi no tetsugaku" ("The Philosophy of Fukuzawa Yukichi"). [11]

Maruyama's study of the late nineteenth-century thought of the Meiji period publicist Fukuzawa Yukichi (1834–1901) is of interest as a monument in the development of postwar Japanese ideas of modernity for two reasons. First, since the bulk of Fukuzawa's work was not systematically philosophical, but consisted in timely commentary on political, economic, and social affairs, Maruyama's effort to delineate Fukuzawa's philosophy required that he "read between the lines" in order to glean the "method of thought and value consciousness" that lay beneath the surface of discourse. [12] This involved a particularly active, constructive process of interpretation which provided Maruyama with considerable scope for exercising his own judgment. Second, in 1972, Maruyama admitted that the essay represents his own thought. In an interview with Andō Jinbei, editor of *Gendai riron* (*Contemporary Theory*), there appears the following exchange:

MARUYAMA: Of course, I would not presume to say that my thought is completely the same as Fukuzawa's. We live in different eras so our concerns are naturally different. Nevertheless, I think this insight hits the mark, more precisely, at least, than would an equation between myself and [Ogyū] Sorai—that is, [there is] an

overlap between *a certain kind of relativism* in Fukuzawa and in
my own. . . .

ANDŌ: A certain kind . . . ?

MARUYAMA: Yes. One could call it political relativism.[13]

We are apparently justified in reading the essay as a guide to Maruyama's own early postwar political thought.

Maruyama begins by focusing on Fukuzawa's commitment to the
relativity of value judgments. He quotes Fukuzawa's own articulations, one of which comes near the beginning of that writer's only
philosophical work, *Bunmeiron no gairyaku* (*Outline of a Theory of
Civilization*, 1875):

> Light and heavy, long and short, good and bad, right and wrong
> are all relative terms. . . . Therefore, one cannot discuss the right
> and wrong, the merits and demerits of an issue without first
> establishing a *basis of argumentation*.[14]

According to Maruyama, Fukuzawa virtually never makes a value
judgment in the abstract, and never treats value as an entity or fixed
a priori. His perceptions, therefore, must always be understood to
be conditional. Maruyama expresses this by saying that Fukuzawa's
statements always need to be taken as if they were "in brackets"
(*kakkotsuki*).[15] That is, they are valid only within the limits of a
particular situation or point of view, and should not be taken as universally applicable or absolute.

At the same time, Maruyama argues that Fukuzawa was never
merely a thoroughgoing relativist. Fukuzawa emphasized that one
should always establish a "basis of argumentation"—take an autonomous position toward the world in order to grasp its significance.
Maruyama says that Fukuzawa was saved from "aimless opportunism" by an inner "truth principle" that provided the degree of detach-
ment sufficient to allow an independent judgment. Yet Fukuzawa
never grounded this principle in any metaphysical system. He:

> certainly did not reject the notion of objective truth; however, he
> denied that this "truth principle" confronts us as an already fixed
> and stationary existence. Rather, his basic way of thinking was
> that it assumed specific form only within a particular situation.

In Maruyama's view, Fukuzawa's orientation was similar to the pragmatism of James and Dewey in that Fukuzawa "argued for the determination of all perceptions by the practical goal (the 'basis of argumentation'). . . ." Value was never already there objectively; it emerged only as the function of an encounter between subjective purposefulness and a set of objective conditions. In order to make his point, Maruyama contrasts Fukuzawa's approach to nature against that of his contemporary, the social Darwinist Katō Hiroyuki. Whereas Katō viewed objective nature pessimistically, as an iron determinism, Fukuzawa saw it as raw material which was constantly being worked, and thus rendered technological, through the practical (*shutaiteki*) manipulations and experimentation of human beings.[16] Rather than the results of science, Fukuzawa emphasized the scientific spirit: that is, the experimental method. For him, knowledge was always linked to action: man had to intervene subjectively (*shutaiteki ni*) from a position of relative autonomy in order to render the world comprehensible.

According to Maruyama, "emphasis on the relativity of value judgments correlated with respect for the autonomous activism (*shutaiteki nōdōsei*) of the human spirit," and here Maruyama's emphasis shifts from the relativity of value judgments to the quality of the subjectivity that is capable of making such judgments. He says,

> [For Fukuzawa] only a tough, subjective [*shutaiteki*] spirit can resist treating values as fixed a priori, and instead constantly allow them to be fluid and relative to the concrete situation. While assessing each particular circumstance, and establishing an approach and a standard for action according to that assessment, it is also necessary to avoid becoming caught in a single perspective; one constantly has to maintain the spiritual composure necessary to rise above the existing conditions, and to adjust to the formation of a new situation. In contrast, a spirit poor in such subjectivity [*shutaisei*] becomes firmly rooted in a particular situation and set in one perspective, and as a result abstractly absolutizes a single value standard that is actually bound to a particular context [*ba*].[17]

I think we can take this as an initial statement of what Maruyama means by modern subjectivity. It is the capacity to make judgments according to standards that arise in relation to lived, historical situations. Accordingly, it implies the subject's tireless engagement with a historically changing environment. Its opposites are passive adaptation and rigid formalism, both of which are aspects of what Fukuzawa called *wakudeki* (irrational attachment, fetishism).[18] Modern subjectivity requires the flexibility and composure necessary to make appropriate value choices in historically relative situations.

Having delineated in a preliminary way the kind of subjective autonomy Fukuzawa espoused, Maruyama moves to the level of society as a whole to show how this quality relates to what Fukuzawa termed the social atmosphere (*kifū*). Not surprisingly, he finds that in a closed, fixed society consciousness tends toward fetishism while in an open society a more active, flexible subjectivity prevails. Not only do autonomous subjects act in ways that disrupt rigid social norms but, conversely, free and open social institutions play a crucial role in enabling and encouraging autonomous action; on the other hand, "absolutism in judgment goes along with absolutism in politics." That is, "there is a correlation between rigidity in social relations and centralization of power, and between centralization of power and turgidity in human thought and judgment."[19] In an open society,

> [o]ne cannot facilely depend today on the value standard that was appropriate yesterday . . . so one must constantly investigate the current situation in order to distinguish those elements that are *more* beneficial or *more* true. . . . Human judgment progresses only under the pressure of constant activity and tension. At the same time, since this progress demands from the subject the sort of spiritual preparation that will allow it always to transcend the contemporary situation, this judgment continuously *renders its own perspective fluid*. Because it is impossible, therefore, for political power to dominate standards of value, that power itself becomes relativistic and recognizes the plurality of values [in society]. Then, the spirit is freed from all forms of "superstition" [*wakudeki*].[20]

Maruyama's argument here has important political implications. He postulates that modern subjectivity is not merely an epistemological mechanism but also an antiauthoritarian political strategy. When the subject "renders its own perspective fluid"—and thus undergoes a continuous process of self-transformation (self-deconstruction?)—those in power lose control of values and have to recognize the legitimacy of pluralism. Maruyama illustrates this point by discussing Fukuzawa's conflict-oriented view of freedom. In Fukuzawa's view, freedom that rules uniformly is no longer freedom at all. In other words, "freedom is born in the midst of unfreedom." [21]

Maruyama points out that a fundamentally optimistic philosophy of history underlies Fukuzawa's belief in the promise of human emancipation through ever-increasing freedom and pluralism. Yet alongside Fukuzawa's optimism was an almost equally strong sense of modesty and awe. According to Maruyama, he "never forgot how powerless man was in the face of overwhelming domination by that part of nature which man had not yet explored and made into tools." [22] However, Maruyama argues that Fukuzawa's optimistic view of human potential always ultimately prevailed over his realization of man's impotence. In a fascinating passage, in which he introduced play as the behavior appropriate to man's powerless state, Fukuzawa wrote:

> Once born into the world, man is indeed a small fry [*ujimushi*]; but, on the other hand, man is not without a certain preparedness. What is that? While knowing that human life is but play [*tawamure*], *it is in the nature of a small fry to apply himself to this playing as if it were not play at all but serious . . . work.* Indeed, this is not really the way of small fry at all, but the pride of man alone as the very spirit of all things.

As Maruyama points out, Fukuzawa paradoxically portrayed man as powerless "small fry" even while urging him to act as if he were omnipotent. But Fukuzawa went on to turn this very paradox into a "method of securing tranquility" (*anshinhō*):

> Take the fleeting world lightly and consider man and all things as so much play. Throw yourself into that play with all your energy, without respite; indeed, you should not only strive tirelessly, but push yourself to the limits of truth and enthusiasm. Then, at a

certain moment, you will again remember that all is mere play in a fleeting world. Your ardor will cool and you will turn about. Now, you must again just let play be play. This is what I call the great, self-evident method of securing human tranquility.[23]

Of course, the effect of this willingness to play—the ludic dimension of practical action—is to free the human spirit from fetishism. Play provides the composure and open-mindedness that enable the subject to see beyond the immediate situation. Maruyama says that "Fukuzawa's humanism is so surprisingly tough that he is undaunted by the dwarfishness of human existence in the universe, and not only does he face it head on, but he converts the resulting sense of powerlessness into an opportunity for a stronger spiritual autonomy [*shutaisei*]."

Maruyama argues that if one were to adhere single-mindedly to the viewpoint that life is play, he would most likely turn eventually to religious escapism or nihilistic hedonism; if, on the other hand, he absolutized the serious dimension, the result would be fetishism and loss of autonomy. "It is only when the seriousness of life and the frivolity of life augment and functionalize each other that there can be a truly autonomous and independent spirit." A functionally productive alternation between these dimensions is possible only when one is able to act "as if"—*as if* life were play in order not to become immobilized by the gravity of it all, and *as if* life were serious in order to resist the temptations of escapism or opportunism.

In the conclusion to his essay, Maruyama both summarizes his overall analysis of Fukuzawa's philosophy and, in a fascinating reference to a 1910 piece by the German sociologist Georg Simmel, opens that analysis to new interpretive possibilities:

We have found that in Fukuzawa's work the main propositions are *conditional* and should be understood as in brackets. In that tendency, we see the characteristic of his thought, which is to shift perspective constantly. Moreover, his most inclusive "brackets" are around the proposition that life is play. As Simmel points out, play suspends all that is substantial in human activity and comes into being where that activity has become entirely formalized. It is, therefore, *fiction* in the purest sense, and fiction, above all, is

entirely the product of man, borrowing nothing from either god
or nature. By placing all of life in the brackets of 'as if,' and viewing it as fiction, Fukuzawa . . . pressed the logic of humanism to
its furthest extreme.[24]

Maruyama refers to Georg Simmel's "The Sociology of Sociability."[25] His evocation of Simmel's essay is not accompanied by
further explanation, but its contents obviously influenced him, and
are therefore worth a brief recounting. Simmel discusses play as a
pure form, which draws its themes from real life but suspends their
seriousness. But Simmel's main emphasis is rather on *sociability*,
which he defines as the social counterpart of play, as well as of art.
Just as play and art "draw their form from . . . realities but . . . leave
. . . reality behind them," sociability "makes up its substance from
numerous fundamental forms of serious relationships among men,
a substance, however, spared the frictional relations of real life."[26]
It is particularly significant that sociability, as the "sociological
play-form,"[27] has no purpose outside its own fulfillment. It is self-
sufficient, an end in itself. Simmel says, "sociability distils, as it
were, out of the realities of social life the pure essence of association,
of the associative process as a value and a satisfaction."[28]

Sociability provides, moreover, *an artificial space* in which both
objective interests and personal egos are suspended, and each participant acts "as if" all were equal, and "as though he especially
esteemed everyone." To pretend in this way is not duplicitous: "This
is just as far from being a lie as is play or art in all their departures
from reality. But the instant the intentions and events of practical
reality enter into the speech and behavior of sociability, it does become a lie—just as a painting does when it attempts, panorama fashion, to be taken for reality."[29]

Sociability "lies," therefore, when realities are allowed to penetrate
its space too directly and obtrusively—when they violate the autonomy of its world of forms: "as soon as the discussion gets business-
like, it is no longer sociable; it turns its compass point around as soon
as the verification of a truth becomes its purpose."[30] However, the
play of sociability also lies when it attempts to separate itself entirely
from seriousness. Simmel says, "If sociability cuts off completely the

threads which bind it to real life and out of which it spins its admittedly stylized web, it turns from play to empty farce, to a lifeless schematization proud of its woodenness."[31]

Maruyama's evocation of Simmel's concepts of play, art, and sociability contributes a great deal to his portrayal of Fukuzawa's philosophy, primarily by augmenting the weight and significance of his concept of play. As noted above, for Simmel, play in the form of sociability is the quintessence of the social—a symbolically rich and productive activity that relates to material interests and drives in the manner of form to content, but is nevertheless relatively autonomous from those forces and virtually their equivalent in value. By introducing Simmel's analysis of play, Maruyama seems to be implying that we need to take Fukuzawa fully at his word when he says "life is but play," and we need also to realize that play in this sense is hardly trivial—certainly no mere derivative, or ephemeral effluent, of material interests or hard realities—but rather their necessary counterpart.

How, then, should one sum up the position on modernity and subjectivity that is suggested by the seminal essay on Fukuzawa? On the one hand, the insistence on the relativity of value judgments that Maruyama inherits from Fukuzawa, and the ludic turn in his philosophy of life, tend to deprive the subject of the hypostatized position often assigned to it in modern thought. In order to understand the world, Fukuzawa's active subject must constantly step outside the secure refuge of inertia and attachment, deconstruct its view of the world, and "render its own perspective fluid." That is, subjectivity must repeatedly establish itself on a new basis of argumentation, which provides the modicum of autonomy necessary to make judgments. Moreover, its judgments are always enclosed in the bracketing of conditionality, since they can rely on no metaphysical grounding equivalent to the Cartesian guarantee. Indeed, serious subjectivity is unable to sustain itself indefinitely because the very condition of its existence is a ludic supplement which periodically replaces the logic of domination (content) with the self-absorbed ecstasy of play (form). Seriousness is always becoming play, and vice versa, just as man, lord of the universe, is always already the "small fry," dethroned by the irresistible forces of nature.

On the other hand, Maruyama's Fukuzawa remains anthropocen-

trically humanistic, devoted to the metanarrative of growth and progress through the domination of nature, and convinced of the need
for a "tough and resilient" subjectivity. Despite what seems to be its
unstable ontological basis, this subjectivity always recuperates and
grows stronger as, according to Maruyama, Fukuzawa "converts the
. . . sense of powerlessness into an opportunity for a stronger spiritual
autonomy." So despite Maruyama's implication that they are equal
and equivalent, the instrumentalist dimension of serious subjectivity
consistently prevails in the last instance over the ludic dimension.
Fukuzawa's de-emphasis of man is merely a temporary moment in
the recuperation and strengthening of a human presence that remains
the subject of consciousness and history.

In addition to adding significance to Fukuzawa's notion of play,
Maruyama's introduction of Simmel's essay provides a fruitful starting point for an interpretation of some more pointedly political works
which Maruyama produced in the early postwar era, particularly the
playful, yet serious, dialogue between "A" and "B" in his 1949 essay,
"Nikutai bungaku kara nikutai seiji made" ("From Carnal Literature
to Carnal Politics").[32]

The concept of sociability, which Maruyama drew from Simmel, also
plays a central role in the 1949 essay. As a way of approaching the
issue of how pornographic description differs from proper fiction, "B"
contrasts the weakness of sociability in Japan with its presumptive
vitality in Europe. He says, "To put it in exaggerated terms, I should
almost say that [in Europe] everyday life as such is already to a certain extent a 'literary creation,' that subject matter itself has already
been given form."[33] This hypothetical difference in the quality of
sociability is paralleled by a contrast in dominant literary form. In
Japan, ". . . the minds of our writers cling like leeches to natural,
sensual phenomena, and lack a really free flight of the imagination,
so in one sense all of our literature is 'carnal.' " This is because "the
mediating force of the spirit is weak. It fails to preserve the internal
unity of fiction itself and in the end it's dragged off in all directions
by separate, disjointed sensual experiences."[34] Just as, for Simmel,
sociability turns false when egocentric desires and interests intrude,

for Maruyama's interlocutor the fictional integrity of a literary work is destroyed when the author injects his or her real life into the narrative.

As the conversation proceeds, Maruyama converts the notion of fiction, as reality mediated by subjective spirit, into a model for modern society and politics. "B" asks, "Why does the modern spirit believe in the value and use of fiction, and why does this spirit keep turning out fiction?" He pursues an answer initially through etymology:

> Look up the word [fiction] in the dictionary and you'll see it comes from the Latin word *fingere*.[35] I'll tell you that it originally meant "to fashion" or "to invent." Then the connotation of the word changed, and it came to mean "to imagine" or "to pretend." In other words, it originally referred, in a broad sense, to a human being having some purpose in mind, and *producing* something in line with his idea.

Accordingly, the truly modern spirit "rates the product of intellectual activity much higher than natural realities." It also "sees 'mediated' reality as being on a higher level than 'immediate' reality."[36]

"B" then sketches a brief history of modern attitudes toward society, focusing on the emergence of "an awareness that the public order, institutions, *mores*, in short the whole social environment that encompasses mankind, is man-made, and can be changed by the force of man's intellect." He also contrasts Western humanism against Asian "humanism," arguing that in the latter, man is "not thought of as an independent entity, but as part and parcel of his own concrete environment," and "every act . . . is bound up in social proprieties and customs."[37]

"B" goes on to explain, in a manner vividly reminiscent of Fukuzawa, that institutions are also "fictions." They are always made by human beings "for the sake of some convenience or to carry out some kind of function," yet tend over time to become hypostatized as part of the natural environment. Therefore, "we have to keep on re-examining institutions and organizations in the light of their objectives and functions. If we don't keep re-examining them they solidify, so to speak, and end up simply as conventions." When that happens, "there's no mediation going on between ends and means, and so means quickly turn into ends in themselves." Fukuzawa would characterize this as fetishism (*wakudeki*).

For example, even the postwar parliamentary system could "turn into nothing but a body with enormous autocratic power."[38] Indeed, the premodern nature of Japanese social relations is such that,

> . . . in this country we have more to worry about than just the danger of modern organizations or institutions becoming hypostatized and no longer performing their original function.
>
> We've always had a vast arena in Japan where social coordination takes place without ever going through the channel of organizations. The things that go on in this arena are everything from naked violence, terror, and intimidation, down to the subtler pressures exerted by *oyabun* and other kinds of bosses. I suppose we can say that these are methods of solving the problem by means of *direct* human relations.[39]

"B" 's discourse, which we can take to represent Maruyama's views, implies that a democratic system ought to be fictional in the sense that it is produced and reproduced by human beings in accord with the purpose or idea (the fiction) of democracy itself. In contrast to the premodern form of social determinism he detects in Japan, where behavior is coerced by and through tradition and communal habit masquerading as natural forces, democracy as an idea and as a constructive process would require that human subjects continuously strive to establish their relative autonomy in a basis of argumentation and then make the value judgments that can be effective in bringing reality ever closer to an ideal state. Their attempts are always directed toward concrete situations, and thus in brackets; nevertheless, they flow from a firmly (if always conditionally) established position of modern autonomy, and thus are always more than mere passive adaptation.

Like sociability, a democratic political system should be relatively free of the *direct* clash of interests and drives, and especially of violence. Within its realm, interests and desires should be introduced systematically and then mediated and adjusted in a manner that preserves a high degree of integrity and autonomy: if the realm of the political is directly penetrated by raw economic interests, social obligations, and personal desires—or, conversely, completely cut off from the social world of interests and desires—then democratic politics will be a lie rather than a fiction.

≡≡≡

As Maruyama wrote the 1949 essay, Japan—still under Allied Occupation—was on the brink of a major political transition. In February 1949, American Secretary of the Army Kenneth Royall visited Japan to reopen the question of a Japanese peace treaty on terms, favored by the Joint Chiefs of Staff, which would make Japan into a forward military base against the Soviet Union.[40] Japanese intellectuals, including Maruyama, were in general firmly opposed to a one-sided peace treaty and the exclusive alignment with the West such a peace would entail, and many were committed to an international position of unarmed neutrality for Japan. In January 1949, the prestigious monthly *Sekai* (*The World*) had reprinted a UNESCO document on the causes of war. In March, soon after Royall's visit, the journal included a pacifist statement signed by sixty or so of Japan's leading intellectuals, and in April published a special collection of essays on "World Peace and the Treaty Issue." From this point on, *Sekai* pursued an editorial policy vigorously opposing any peace settlement that would exclude the Soviet Union, and the centerpiece of that policy was a December 1950 article signed by thirty-five members of the Peace Problems Discussion Circle (*Heiwa mondai danwakai*), entitled "On Peace: Our Third Statement." Between the two statements, of course, Mao Zedong had proclaimed establishment of the People's Republic of China in October 1949, and in June 1950 the Korean War broke out, contributing extra intensity to the confrontation between left and right in Japan.

This era was also apparently a time of transition in Maruyama's own political involvement. Whereas in the early postwar period he had adopted the stance of an independent and politically somewhat aloof gadfly (*amanojaku*), modeled on the role assumed by Fukuzawa in the early Meiji period, in 1949 he entered the fray and committed himself to the struggle for a peace treaty that would include all of

Japan's former enemies. He became a leading member of the Peace Problems Discussion Circle and played a central role in drafting the third statement on peace.[41]

Maruyama's new activism did not, however, disturb his philosophical orientation. The statement on peace clearly reflects the pragmatic approach to politics that Maruyama had elaborated in his Fukuzawa study. Fukuzawa's commitment to the relativity of value judgments, and his notion that one can understand the world only after first establishing a basis of argumentation, are clearly evident. The statement says that any view of international politics "contains volitional elements," making it "impossible to achieve any objective understanding which is unrelated to a subjective position." It also points out that "if we believe it possible to adjust relations without resort to arms, we will greatly increase such a likelihood."[42] Also apparent is resistance against fixed viewpoints established a priori, in this case represented by the rigid preconception that the two Cold War blocs are irreconcilably opposed.[43]

The statement did more than just outline a point of view on the problem of world peace. It also reflected and further sharpened a political and intellectual opposition that had emerged in the domestic Japanese context between "progressives," who aggressively opposed a one-sided peace treaty, and those calling themselves "realists," who accepted global confrontation as inevitable and supported Japan's alignment with the West in the Cold War. From Maruyama's point of view, Japanese "realism" was an inflexibly deductive form of fetishism that was blind to the fluid particularities of the Japanese and other situations.[44] A vigorous struggle against this kind of "realism" was the self-consistent political expression of the intellectual attitude that Maruyama had first articulated in his work on Fukuzawa and later politicized in the dialogue on carnal politics and other essays.

A review of Maruyama Masao's postwar essays suggests that, despite its metahistorical optimism and strong reliance on a concept of modern subjectivity, Japanese modernist thought in the postwar era was never strongly or unambiguously metaphysical in orientation. Nor did it posit an unduly hypostatized or essentialized subject. The postwar ideal of modernity was directed against the residues of feudalism and fascism in Japanese society (and of Stalinist objectivism in Marxism). Therefore, modernist critics emphasized the need to dissolve the direct, "carnal" social relations they associated with feudalism and fascism. They sought to open up society and ideology in order to provide sufficient space for free subjectivity and the intervention of pragmatic human will.

Surely Maruyama's pragmatic approach is not entirely out of date, either in Japan or the West. It is in some ways consistent with the current position of Richard Rorty, who argues for the possibility of "splitting the difference" between Habermas and Lyotard by concentrating on the modest, praxis-oriented form of social engineering he finds in the pragmatist tradition of Dewey.[45] It is also similar in some ways to Fred Dallmayr's proposal that the human subject should be "deflated" rather than abandoned altogether.[46] To the extent that Maruyama's postwar viewpoint can be taken as an index of major trends in Japanese modernist thought, we are led to question the relevance—and also the political implications—of a Japanese postmodernist criticism that would expend its energies on a critique of metaphysics and the hypostatized subject. If modern thought in Japan has succeeded in avoiding the extremes of subject-centeredness that modern metanarratives have nurtured in the West, perhaps it still can be viewed as a project that has not fully exhausted its potential.*

Notes

* The author gratefully acknowledges research support from the Social Science Research Council and the Japan-United States Education Commission (Fulbright Program).
1 Peter Dews, ed., *Habermas: Autonomy and Solidarity—Interviews with Jürgen Habermas* (London, 1986), 27.
2 Jean-François Lyotard, *The Postmodern Condition: A Report on Knowledge*, trans. Geoff Bennington and Brian Massumi (Minneapolis, 1984), xxiv.
3 Ibid., 19–23.
4 Jürgen Habermas, "The Entwinement of Myth and Enlightenment: Re-Reading *Dialectic of Enlightenment*," *New German Critique* 26 (1982); quoted by Richard Rorty, "Habermas and Lyotard on Postmodernity," in *Habermas and Modernity*, ed. Richard J. Bernstein (Cambridge, Mass., 1985), 162.
5 Jürgen Habermas, "Modernity—An Incomplete Project," in *The Anti-Aesthetic: Essays on Postmodern Culture*, ed. Hal Foster (Port Townsend, 1983), 9, 13.

6   Ibid., 14; also see Jürgen Habermas, "Neoconservative Criticism in the United States and West Germany: An Intellectual Movement in Two Political Cultures," in Bernstein, *Habermas and Modernity*, 78–94.

7   For a highly critical account by a Japanese philosopher, see Takeuchi Yoshirō, "Posto-modan ni okeru chi no kansei" ("Pitfalls for Knowledge in Postmodernism"), *Sekai* (November 1986): 92–114.

8   Karatani Kōjin, "Ri no hihan: shisō ni okeru puremodan to postomodan" ("The Critique of Confucian Principle: Premodern and Postmodern in Philosophy"), *Gendaishi techō* (May 1985): 40.

9   See Hidaka Rokurō, *Sengo shisō no shuppatsu* (*The Beginnings of Postwar Thought*) (Tokyo, 1968), 7–19; and Sakuta Keiichi, "The Controversy over Community and Autonomy," in *Authority and the Individual in Japan: Citizen Protest in Historical Perspective*, ed. J. Victor Koschmann (Tokyo, 1978), 220–49.

10   Maruyama Masao, "Kindaiteki shii" ("Modern Thought"), in *Senchū to sengo no aida, 1936–1957* (Tokyo, 1976), 188–90; emphasis mine.

11   Maruyama Masao, "Fukuzawa Yukichi no tetsugaku—toku ni sono jiji hihan to no kanren" ("The Philosophy of Fukuzawa Yukichi"), in *Kindaishugi*, ed. Hidaka Rokurō (Tokyo, 1964), 58–92.

12   Ibid., 58.

13   "Umemoto Katsumi no omoide," in Maruyama Masao, Satō Noboru, and Umemoto Katsumi, *Sengo Nihon no kakushin shisō* (*Progressive Thought in Postwar Japan*) (Tokyo, 1983), 396–97.

14   Maruyama, "Fukuzawa Yukichi no tetsugaku," 60–62; English translation from Fukuzawa Yukichi's *Outline of a Theory of Civilization*, trans. David A. Dilworth and G. Cameron Hurst (Tokyo, 1973), 5–6; emphasis mine.

15   Maruyama, "Fukuzawa Yukichi no tetsugaku," 63.

16   Ibid., 67–69.

17   Ibid., 69.

18   Fukuzawa developed his use of this word in the course of his readings of the British historian H. T. Buckle and other European writers, and sometimes meant it as the equivalent of their "prejudice," "superstition," or "credulity." For a detailed discussion of the various nuances of Fukuzawa's use of the term, see Maruyama Masao, "Fukuzawa in okeru 'wakudeki'" ("Fukuzawa's Use of the Term 'Wakudeki'"), in *Fukuzawa Yukichi nenkan* 13 (1986): 25–56.

19   Maruyama seems to find in Fukuzawa an idea comparable to the social interpellation of subjects that is postulated in Althusserian theories of ideology. See, for example, the account in Göran Therborn, *The Ideology of Power and the Power of Ideology* (London, 1980).

20   Maruyama, "Fukuzawa Yukichi no tetsugaku," 72; emphasis mine.

21   Ibid., 75.

22   Ibid., 85.

23   Ibid., 86; emphasis mine.

24   Ibid., 87–88; emphasis mine.

25 Georg Simmel, "The Sociology of Sociability," in J. H. Abraham, ed., *Origins and Growth of Sociology* (Harmondsworth, 1973).

26 Ibid., 290.

27 Ibid., 294.

28 Ibid., 290.

29 Ibid., 294.

30 Ibid., 296.

31 Ibid., 298.

32 Maruyama Masao, "From Carnal Literature to Carnal Politics," trans. Barbara Ruch, in *Thought and Behavior in Modern Japanese Politics*, ed. Ivan Morris (London, 1963), 245–67.

33 Ibid., 249.

34 Ibid., 251.

35 The word *fingere* seems to be the contribution of Maruyama's translator, Barbara Ruch. In the original Japanese text, Maruyama uses the term *fictio*. The point in both cases, of course, is to show an etymological root that means to fashion or invent.

36 Maruyama, "Carnal Literature," 253–54.

37 Ibid., 255–58.

38 Ibid., 260.

39 Ibid., 264.

40 Michael Schaller, *The American Occupation of Japan: The Origins of the Cold War in Asia* (New York, 1985), 164–65.

41 Maruyama offers his own account of this transition in "Fuhenteki genri no tachiba" ("The Standpoint of Universal Principle"), in *Kataritsugu sengoshi*, vol. 1, ed. Tsurumi Shunsuke (Tokyo, 1969), 83–87. On p. 87 he says that he wrote a draft of the first portion of the third statement.

42 See the summary translation of the first part of the statement by the Peace Problems Discussion Circle, "On Peace: Our Third Statement," *Journal of Social and Political Ideas in Japan* 1 (April 1963): 14.

43 Ibid., 15.

44 Maruyama continued his critique of "realism" in a number of essays. See Maruyama Masao, *Zōhoban gendai seiji no shisō to kōdō* (*Thought and Behavior in Modern Japanese Politics*) (Tokyo, 1964), 131–51, 171–86. For a brief English-language discussion, see Matsumoto Sannosuke, "Introduction," *Journal of Social and Political Ideas in Japan* 4 (August 1966): 11–16.

45 Rorty, "Habermas and Lyotard," 174; also see Rorty's *Consequences of Pragmatism* (Minneapolis, 1982). However, Maruyama would probably find it difficult to accept Rorty's resorting to "ethnocentrism" as a viable alternative to universal reason.

46 Dallmayr says: "The alternative to anthropocentrism may not be anti-humanism but a *deflated notion of man*." See Fred. R. Dallmayr, *Twilight of Subjectivity: Contributions to a Post-Individualist Theory of Politics* (Amherst, 1981), 9.

Masao Miyoshi

Against the Native Grain: The Japanese Novel and the "Postmodern" West[1]

Every experience of reading a marginal text is at least potentially upsetting. When a third world text is read in the first world, the sense of unfamiliarity is often marked, and the reader's discomfort is proportionately acute. To restore the accustomed equilibrium, the reader either domesticates or neutralizes the exoticism of the text. The strategy for domestication is to exaggerate the familiar aspects of the text and thereby disperse its discreteness in the hegemonic sphere of first world literature. Thematic reductivism always helps. Once human nature is invoked, people everywhere are bound to prove alike, eventually. Thus, the reader may safely insist that men and women the world over are born, copulate, die, and write about the "universal" cycle. In this age of global interdependence and management, no geographical area is allowed to remain unabsorbed and unintegrated. Third world texts will be tamed, with the hegemony of the first world conferring the needed authority. Should a particular sample happen to be intransigent, there is always a provision for rejecting it as an inferior product. The principle of canonicity never fails. The experience of reading a foreign text is nearly always transformed into an act of self-reaffirmation.

The plan for neutralization also operates by distancing the menacing source. A strange text is acknowledged to be strange, and this tautology, implicit in such a procedure, thrusts the text out of the reader's proximity. One opens a book in order to close it, as it were. Such pseudocomments as "delicate," "lyrical," or "suggestive," if not "illogical," "impenetrable," or "incoherent" seek to conceal the absence of an encounter by cluttering up the field of reading and distracting the reader from the text. Most foreign texts thus remain more or less readerless, despite repeated attempts at their capture, appropriation, and representation in the hand of cultural administrators.

To come closer to our topic at hand, Japanese prose fiction in the last hundred years appears fairly well represented among the American readers.[2] As Japanese economic power rises, interest in the literary products of the nation, too, grows a little in the United States. Thus in the last forty years, a good number of its literary products have been made available in English, with male writers' prose fiction prominent among them. Scores of monographs have been written on Japanese literature, and more and more colleges and universities offer courses on the literature as well as the language of the country. Despite such signs of increased familiarity, however, the first world reader continues to find Japanese fiction remote. Unlike its French or German counterparts, Japanese fiction seems to require the mediation of an expert's advice and commentary. There is no doubt, of course, that the cultural distance between Japan and the West remains great for now. Either for this reason, or for other reasons having something to do with general Western ethnocentricity, a sort of proprietorship is maintained among some Japanologists who impress outsiders with the difficulty of the Japanese language and the exceptionality of Japanese culture. It is also to be admitted that specialists in the United States often find themselves needing the cooperation of their Japanese colleagues, who in turn adhere to a system of export licensing. In these days of global cultural and economic exchange, then, the community of scholars is never free from the danger of becoming a multinational bureaucracy of learning that would keep the flow of traffic under careful control.

There is something very much like an official policy in the scholarship of Japanese literature in the United States, which seems consonant with vague but definable "national interest." As geopolitical hegemony is to the state, so is traditionalism to its culture. The first world "tradition" is to be the universal norm and the inevitable future of every culture in the world. There is also a generally accepted genealogy of knowledge in this field. At the risk of oversimplification, the following propositions must be noted and dealt with by anyone engaged in this enterprise. First, the lineage of the Japanologists in America descends from the religious and industrial missionaries who went to the Far East to civilize and democratize the barbarians. Second, the imperial evangelists of civilization took over the role of teachers and advisors on their return home around the turn of the century. Third, their godsons, who had been dormant for a while, were mobilized into a cadre of interpreters and administrators during World War II and the postwar years. Fourth, a noticeable advance was made in Japanology by this generation of Occupation-trained specialists, and their impact on the scholarship remains both powerful and intact. Fifth, because of the historical circumstances of missionary and conquest, this genealogy has no shortage of those uncritical (or even unaware) of their own ethnocentric and hegemonic impulses.[3] Sixth, throughout the history of Japanology, the input from Japanese Americans (*issei, nisei,* and *sansei*) has not been conspicuous (in contrast to their European counterparts where such infusion has provided an important and matter-of-fact propellant). Such an absence is cognate with the scarcity of oppositional readings of Japanese literature that might have provided a dialectic context for criticism. Seventh, the area specialists in the Japan field are likely to be inbred and ghettoized, conversing only on rare occasions with scholars in other areas and disciplines. Of course, the blame for such isolation does not necessarily fall on the Japanologists themselves, but on those outsiders who are supremely indifferent to non-Western civilizations. Finally, the Japan field under the circumstances has long been a sort of colony in the university, where extraterritoriality is still allowed to prevail.[4]

Given this context, it should not be wholly unexpected to run into a remark like the following by an established academic translator of Japanese literature: "I do not believe Japan has produced a great literary corpus, or that it can boast a single undisputed literary masterpiece, or that very many works of classical Japanese literature can stand up to sustained, intensive literary criticism."[5] Whatever such comments might suggest about the conditions of the Japanese literary field, one plainly sees here a discursive paradigm that is best called Orientalism. It seems appropriate, then, to reconsider the whole discourse of the modern Japanese novel as it is conducted in the United States, and to a lesser extent in Japan as well. We might begin by examining the words used to describe the body of prose narrative produced in Japan in the last two hundred years: "modern," "Japanese," and "novel."

First, the term "modern," which is most commonly used among the Japan specialists as well as the generalists in their designation of the corpus. The modernization theory, still viewed as authoritative in the United States, is of course wide open to inquiries and challenges. Since historical transformation and continuity are obviously not synchronous throughout the world, the universal application of a historical periodization based on one cultural system would be senseless as well as ethnocentric. The modern calendrical period in the first world may or may not be "modern" in other parts of the world. Both in its referent (post-Renaissance, post-1800, post-1900, just now) and in its interpretant (capitalism, urbanization, individualism, alienation, secularization, industrialization, bureaucratization, etc.), the signifier "modern" should be regarded as a regional term peculiar to the West.

The chronopolitical definition, however, is not always unilateral. Japanese historians and cultural theorists face the West-imposed definition and often choose to accept it. The majority who would view Japan as a part of the first world hegemony join the Western modernizationists and likewise deploy the Japanese counterpart, *kindai*. On this supposedly universal chronology—often of development and progress—some regard Japan as having already reached this "advanced" stage, while a few others believe the country to be still premodern.

Those who believe Japan to be a "modern" society are not unanimous in their response to the diagnosis: there are those who approve "progress" and embrace "Westernization," others who welcome "progress" but deplore "Westernization," still others who are attached to traditionalism but accept a version of "Westernization," and finally those who are both anti-progress and anti-West. Those who adhere to the view of Japan as premodern are similarly divided among the same types of pro- and anti-modernization. These different placements of Japan on the chronopolitical chart represent no mere academic factionalisms in historiography. Although the degrees of intensity in disagreement have varied, the discord has exploded from time to time into a violent intellectual and political confrontation. In prewar Japan, this "modernity" with its implications of "progress" and "Westernization" was a crucial concept, closely enmeshed with the idea of traditionalism, nationalism, and Asianism, profoundly dividing the ranks of intellectuals. In those years, the state forcibly intervened for the proper placement of Japan on the chart of progress as well as the preservation of "cultural purity." Even in these post-postwar days, however, the disagreement persists. While a vast majority seems to accept Japan as having "achieved" the modern status by now, Mishima Yukio and Maruyama Masao, for example, insist on finding "premodern" elements in the fabric of Japanese society, although the two are opposed in rejoicing and lamenting in such discovery.

While the presence of premodernity is still very much talked about, there has been in recent years an increasing interest in the traits of "postmodernism." First came the sense of the end of the postwar era. The urgent postwar programs for catching up with the West— economic recovery, political reorganization, and institutional rationalization as well as the atonement for war guilt—were felt to be sufficiently completed. And as the postwar "democratization" agenda were replaced by a far more aggressive economic expansionism, the targets of modernization that had loomed so remote only a few years ago began to appear in close range. The so-called decline of the West —in terms of the political and military follies and the general loss of leadership and confidence—has helped a great deal here. And as the West displayed revulsion at its own *modern* past and faced up to its "postmodern" possibilities, some Japanese intellectuals seem to have regained a quasi-prewar self-assurance. Far from being premodern, they are now postmodern! As a matter of fact, the description of postmodernism began to fit the Japanese conditions remarkably well, as if the term were coined specifically for Japanese society. The dispersal and demise of modern subjectivity, as talked about by Barthes, Foucault, and many others, have long been evident in Japan, where intellectuals have chronically complained in fact about the absence of selfhood. The postmodern erasure of historicity—as Jean-François Lyotard reflects—is the stuff of Japanese nativist religion (*shintoism*) in which ritual bathing is intended to cleanse the whole past alongside the evil residues from the past. Anti-traditionalism has been a prominent counterforce to the official traditionalism, and parody and pastiche have constituted one of the two main streams—together with imported "realism"—for the last two centuries. Modularity has been conspicuous in Japan's architectural and literary productions. Visualization is the country's specialty, as evidenced in overabundant artworks, designs, and graphics. Japanese hostility to logic and rationalism has long been a clichéd source of embarrassment to the native philosophers. Logocentricity appears to be one crime Japan is scarcely guilty of: so much so that Karatani Kōjin and Asada Akira could boast to Derrida that there is no need for deconstruction as there has never been a construct in Japan. Japan's packaging and image-making are world renowned, especially in these days of superproduction and reproduction on the global scale. Even Baudrillard might find Japan's devotion to simulacra a little frightening. And finally, so desubjectified and decentralized, citizens simply live—produce and consume, buy and sell—in late stage capitalism, and politics (that is, a critical examination and intervention in interpersonal and intertypological relationships) has been practically abolished.[6]

This is a caricature, of course. On the surface at least, however, these are indisputable traits of what's generally described as postmodern. The surface, furthermore, is hardly to be taken lightly in this context. Is postmodernism a historical period or a cultural system? In the context of Japanese society, it is clearly not a periodic term:

these same traits seem to have been around much too long—under different economic and political circumstances. And if it is a cultural event, it should be localized and so treated, without essentializing it. Besides, all these different assessments of today's Japan—premodern, modern, and postmodern—seem largely dependent on the end one wishes to serve. There is no neutral or innocent reading; nor does any particular reading hold ascendancy over others at present. Japan's "modern" novel, in this sense, should merely signify the body of prose fiction produced in Japan in the last two centuries without involving the customary referents or interpretants of the modern/postmodern West or its novel, of which more later on.

As for the signifier "Japanese," the referent ought not to present any problem, since the territorial or linguistic definition is not an issue here (with the possible exceptions of Ainu and Okinawa productions). The only question seems to be in the interpretant: whether recent Japanese prose fiction is exceptional in the sense that it defies comparison with any other literature, or is only a variant among many literatures and is unique only as any other literature is. A priori logic points to the latter. For exclusivism and essentialism are ethnocentric and fantastic, and as such both inappropriate and groundless. If exclusivism and essentialism are merely forms asserting variance and particularity, then they should be so reformulated. Japanese literature, like any other national or regional product, is definable only in its relation to temporal and spatial constraints. It might be particularly and conspicuously "Japanese"; but there is nothing ontologically sacred or absolute in its makeup. This aspect is important to keep in mind inasmuch as the need to de-universalize and particularize the Western norm remains foremost on our new critical agenda.

Lucien Goldmann's tripartite scheme in "The Revolt of Arts and Letters" might serve as a model for reading the history of the Japanese prose narrative form—insofar as one refuses to surrender the particular to a universalist paradigm and remains wary about Goldmann's concept of homology. He proposes classical capitalism, imperialism, and organizational capitalism as three periods.[7]

The lineage of Japan's modern prose fiction must be traced back at least to the Edo period. One does note toward the end of this age signs of a monetary economy and a rising bourgeoisie that might be characterized as constituting "a commercial revolution" despite the central feudal regime of the shogunate.[8] The city of Edo was the world's most populous city by 1800, and was the administrative nerve center of the nation with a large bureaucracy and a service industry. Rapid expansion, as well as the Tokugawa House's hostage system, produced a transient and migrant population alienated from its home villages. Transportation throughout Japan increased, and literacy spread across all classes. Publishing also grew to a degree readily comparable with that in contemporary Europe, accompanied by an expanded information network. In short, there were several elements in the life of the Japanese that might be recognized as constituents of proto-capitalism.

Edo ur-capitalist feudalism found its literary forms in kabuki drama and the prose *gesaku* ("playful writing"). *Gesaku* fiction is parodic, episodic, and self-referential. Further, it is torn between the acceptance of formal restrictions and the energy for contesting them. On the one hand, there is an attempt to circumscribe the field of an individual's mind and action in the framework of a biography, while the style and tone, ranging freely from the colloquial to the formulaic, from the ironic/parodic to the tragic/sentimental, and from the ordinary to the fantastic, prevent it from constructing anecdotes and episodes into a narrative whole. The *gesaku* is engrossed in the thick texture of verbal surface, and thus it is inhospitable to characterization and employment. It refuses to be introspective or egalitarian and disallows a discrete narrative outline to correspond to the contours of the gradually emerging individual. Likewise, it is organized by a chronometric sense of time that is aggregative rather than causal. If the earlier Edo prose (such as Saikaku's) celebrated the Tokugawa order that had finally arrived after the long chaos of the civil wars, the *gesaku* seems to sense the coming of an end to the order, and it exhibits growing irritations at its realization of the conflict between feudal restriction and bourgeois liberality. *Gesaku*, often taken to be a literature of decadence, is at the same time an expression of resistance and criticism, however modest its scale and impact. Its playful sophistication contains at least potential traits of postmodernity.

The second stage in the history of the *shōsetsu* (i.e., telling tales) is from the mid-Meiji era (around 1890) to the 1970s, including Japan's invasion of China and its war with the United States. At the beginning, Japan was about to regain its confidence after what had been a nearly colonial encounter with the West. Whatever political and economic success the Meiji restoration had produced was now to be tested abroad in the form of homegrown imperialism. At the end of this second stage, Japan was recovering from the death and destruction occasioned by its military defeat and from the humiliation of foreign occupation. During these turbulent years, Japan's state-controlled capitalism expanded steadily and survived the total annihilation of production systems. It even endured the massive leftist opposition of the 1950s and 1960s. In this age of nationalist capitalism the individual was quite free to develop his entrepreneurial skills. At the same time, the confines of state-imposed stricture were ultimately nearly absolute. The individual was expected to be cooperative and congruent with society and state, and though eccentricity was tolerated, neither defiance nor revolt was permitted.

The fiction of this period has thus some resemblance to Goldmann's "novel of the problematic character," though it is also distinct from it. Futabatei's *Ukigumo*, Sōseki's *Kokoro*, or Dazai's *The Setting Sun* each presents a character in a claustrophobically confined space (in contrast to the panoramic expanse in which Edo fiction typically unfolds). The protagonist is a superfluous man, alienated and introspective. Further, unlike the hero in Edo fiction, the later hero is not just a name, but an interior space that reflects on itself. Yet he is no Pip, Julien Sorel, or Oblomov. Bunzo, Sensei, or Naoji (of the three works just mentioned) is always aware of the ensemble of his society in the sense that his problematic is not so much one of character as of role. Consistently, characterization is turned into an elaborate and refined social arbitration, as in a book of manners and morals. Preserving the traditional formal energy, the mode and style of narration range widely and freely in a given work. Transcending the boundaries of the individual's consciousness is the narrator, who is both inside and outside the character. This narrator, however, is not so much an omniscient god as an all-knowing pater familias. All such features match the ambiguity surrounding the individual in state-dominated capitalism up to the very eve of the economic miracle of the 1960s.

In a long period such as this, there obviously will be more or less clearly identifiable subperiods. The *shōsetsu* of the Meiji era, with Ōgai, Tōson, and Sōseki charting the course, received the direct "influence" of Western fiction, which means that Meiji writers acknowledged and valorized certain elements in Japan's narrative possibilities while ignoring and minimizing others. In their works, the problematic character is more pronounced at the center of the stage. Thus Ōgai, Tōson, and Sōseki are the apologists—critical though they may be—for the Meiji bourgeoisie.

There were, on the other hand, a few who tried to present the life of the poor. In proletarian literature the wretched and the undifferentiated seemed to suggest a new possibility for characterization, a collective hero. The revolt, however, did not come from the lower depths of society. With the coming of the Asian and Pacific War, therefore, the resistance was easily neutralized and absorbed into the mainstream bourgeoisie, as individual writers underwent ritual conversions (*tenko*) whereby they abandoned their critical opposition and adapted themselves to the imperial programs. Some writers continued their passive noncooperation by remaining silent, while others collaborated actively. None were guiltless, since nearly all writers were at least acquiescent. None of them were, however, wholly guilty either, since they were all under coercion. In this grey mix of guilt and innocence, the contours of the individual were blurred into the background of the state totality.

This dialectic of the self and the Other changed very little after the catastrophic defeat in 1945. Swiftly moving away from the rightist position of the war years, writers renamed themselves "humanists" and "modernists," "democrats" and "internationalists." There was an ironic repeat performance of "conversion": in proclaiming their *shutaisei* ("individuality") in unison, the writers were unwittingly reaffirming state collectivism. The oaths of readaptation were chorally orchestrated. In fact, as the cold war commenced in the mid-

1940s, there was still another need for a turning back, totaling three zigzag reversions for some writers: from the left to the right in the 1930s, from the right to the left after the war, and from the left back to the right in the 1950s. The Japanese state seems to have remained unaltered throughout these gyrations; with or without the emperor as its symbol, it has animated the people and loomed ever larger in the common mind every waking moment.

Obviously, the theme and mood of the *shōsetsu* continued to change during this second period lasting three quarters of a century. Yet there are some formal constants that would justify this treatment of the duration as one period. In *Writing Degree Zero*, Roland Barthes suggests two ideas to characterize the type of novel that would correspond roughly to Goldmann's liberal capitalist novel of the problematic character: the preterit and the third person. According to Barthes, the preterit, or the past tense, signifies the "presence of Art" because the past tense abstracts a pure verbal act from the multiplicity of experiences. It connects one act with another, constructing a hierarchy in the realm of facts. "Allowing as it does an ambiguity between temporality and causality, it calls for a sequence of events, that is, for an intelligible Narrative. This is why it is the ideal instrument for every construction of a world; it is the unreal time of cosmogonies, myths, History and Novels."[9] Barthes thus sees a "demiurge, a God, or a reciter" lurking behind the past tense. The deity is the author, the inaugurator, the creator present in the Western novel.

Now the Japanese language, which lacks a past tense and depends for temporal notation on the perfect and imperfect aspects, provides a possibility for art in a clearly different fashion. In the *shōsetsu*, events occur without being conscripted into the unreal time of cosmogony. Unlike Barthes's—and Aristotle's—model, the *shōsetsu* rejects the interpretive beginning, middle, and end. Doing away with the tension of a beginning that potentially and inherently contains the destination and closure of the narrative, it also rejects the acceleration of counterforce that will brake the narrative movement to a stillness of an end. The *shōsetsu* is more similar to the annals than to narrativized history.[10] Paratactic rather than syntactic, arithmetic rather than algebraic, the *shōsetsu* is the expression not of order and suppression, as the novel is, but of space, decentralization, and dispersal. There is no creator; there is a shamanic priestess who articulates the tribal spirit by harkening to it.

To put it another way, the novel expresses the problematic of the individual in the contradiction between formal constraints and the ideological characterization of the individual as a free agent. The *shōsetsu* is the reverse: while the character is always defined in the close texture of society, thus imparting to him an approximation of a role, the plot is open-ended and spacious, as if man's true existence is irrelevant to the actual details of living, the acts and events of actuality. Politically and psychologically deprived of liberty and freedom, *shōsetsu* characters seem to inhabit a space unbothered by life's constraints.

Barthes also points to the importance of the third person in the novel:

> The "he" is a typical novelistic convention; like the narrative tense, it signifies and carries through the action of the novel; if the third person is absent, the novel is powerless to come into being, and even wills its own destruction. The "he" is a formal manifestation of the myth, and we have just seen that, in the West at least, there is no art which does not point to its own mask. The third person, like the preterite, therefore performs this service for the art of the novel, and supplies its consumers with the security born of a credible fabrication which is yet constantly held up as false.

The "third person" is a mask the Western novel dons without an exception. The convention demands the distance of the "he" from the author. As man and author gradually work up to be the third person, his "soliloquy becomes a novel."[11]

Against such a victory of the "he" over the "I" in the novel, the defeat of the "he" at the hands of the "I" characterizes the *shōsetsu*. The *shōsetsu* is so overwhelmingly marked by the dominance of the "I" form that the *shi-shōsetsu* ("I-fiction") is the orthodoxy of the convention. Instead of man and author attempting to transform themselves into the third person, they aim at discarding—or at least, concealing—the narrator. The man will speak and write directly. He will not wear a mask, but insists on the first person even to the extent of aggressively reporting his own daily routine (that excludes any formal and artistic intention) and presenting it as an emplottable event. It is the reverse of the novel: rather than a "credible fabrication which is yet constantly held up as false," the *shōsetsu* is an incredible fabrication that is nonetheless constantly held up as truthful. Art is hidden, while honesty and sincerity are displayed. Distance is removed, while immediacy is ostensive. The rejection of individualism in Japan is thus compensated for by the dominance of the first person. What makes the *shōsetsu* fascinating is this complex negotiation between the formal insistence on the "I" and the ideological suppression of the self. In other words, if "the preterite and the third person in the Novel are nothing but the fateful gesture with which the writer draws attention to the mask which he is wearing,"[12] the aspects and the first person in the *shōsetsu* are nothing but the fateful gesture with which the writer draws attention to his own naked face, which, whether he is aware or not, is no more than a mask.

The *shōsetsu* is thus an art that refuses to acknowledge art. Signs of Western high modernist art are conspicuously absent. The author's will is directed to allowing order to emerge between himself, his work, and his reader, rather than within the work itself. It refuses to abstract; it keeps the multiplicity of movement and experience concrete; and without organizing these into a shape, it lets the narrative run on. It disperses and decentralizes art so that the reader as well as the author may become aware of the space outside the work. It refuses to interrupt life with the willed discipline of art at the smithies of verbal form. Instead, it seeks to ignite flashes of beauty that lie unmarked at the rims of language. Thus, typically, the *shōsetsu* is published in a serialized form. Unplanned at the beginning, the progression of the narrative is a coordinate of outside time. As the narrative unfolds, its shape is constantly altered. There is no real conclusion until the author's death makes its ending unresumable. Relevance is always to the world outside the work, not to the work's autonomous unity.[13] In writing and reading a *shōsetsu*, the individual is expected to merge with others, to harken back to the voice of his tribe. Contextuality is all important.

The third period begins at the end of the unrest of the 1950s and

1960s and the outset of Japan's unprecedented economic growth. The organization of this new Japan is incomparably powerful. The new Japan trains its citizens as well-adapted functionaries in its corporate program, mobilizing them far more efficiently than any militarist regime ever has. It is centrally planned and painlessly enforced. Of course, Japan's economic and technological advance is spectacular, and the pride and confidence the Japanese feel about it are understandable. Yet in this national celebration, consumerism is pervasive, eating deeply into the fabric of life. The privatized experience that once was legitimate among intellectuals is now being emptied of self-contemplation. Thus critical oppositions are now virtually nonexistent. Periodically, people may protest against rearmament and pollution, but such movements are both specific and sporadic. The overall sense of affluence dominates, and occasional signs of unease about the harried pace of life are put aside unacknowledged.

The mark of an individual is his purchases and possessions; likewise, time passes as he labors and daydreams about advertised goods. Books, too, are consumed; that is, they are bought, enjoyed, discarded, and forgotten. No longer authors, manufacturers of books dash off two or even three *shōsetsu* a year, in addition to such lucrative media fragments as *kanso* ("impressions"), *rondan* ("op-ed articles"), assembly-line nonproducts, *taidan* ("dialogue"), and *zandankai* ("round-table conversations"). The journals of opinion, once the arena of intellectual and ideological combats, are now congenial to those in the seat of power and authority. Many journals have simply disappeared, while few have emerged. Literary magazines are notoriously in decline. Books are prompted by large publishers by means of widely publicized awards and prizes that presumably certify quality and confer prestige, but work to increase sales.[14] While more and more people are getting bored with printed words, literature has been redefined as a serious industry and a form of entertainment in which the writers' membership in the collective enterprise is taken for granted.[15] All three leading national newspapers have huge circulations and compete in safe reporting and conformist analyses. Paralleling the holy alliance of capital, labor, and bureaucracy is a powerful consortium of writers (*sakka*), scholars (*gakusha*), reviewers/commentators in the media (*hyoronka*), and publishers (*honya*), all supporting one another in a unified effort to advance their economic interests and power bases. Such a quadrilateral cooperative, often made closer by a shared college or publishing background, grows into an unchallenged monopoly. When several such alliances form a still larger cartel of literature, the nation's culture is ill served indeed.[16]

The *shōsetsu* produced under such conditions is no longer characterized by the perfect/imperfect aspects and "I-ness." As a consumer, the "I" is even less distinguished from the others, while the sense of time, too, is robbed of its experiential discreteness. Thus, most typical of the *shōsetsu* in this period is Tanaka Yasuo's *Nantonaku, kurisutaru (Somehow, Crystal,* 1980), which presents disembodied adolescent voices, or mildly erotic daydreams, whose only existential testimonies are store names, miscellaneous foreign words, and trade names that are carefully annotated in the book's 442 footnotes. Hardly gathered into sentences, nouns—especially names like "Dior" and "Jaeger"—echo in the hollows of dead narrative possibilities. Presented in a succession of slick commercials, these names are meant to guide the reader in the glossy world of buying and consuming. *Nantonaku, kurisutaru* tries to look ironic and sophisticated, but barely manages to conceal its crude apologia for affluence. Through such disintegration of narrative art, high-tech Japan reduces human intercourse to a commercial transaction and man's existence to a commercial potential.

Under the circumstances, the literature of critical opposition is nearly invisible. There are a few determined modernists, of course. Ōe Kenzaburō seems the most outstanding of those consistent intellectuals who continue their critical examination of self and society with relentless thoroughness. Several feminist writers—Tsushima Yūko, Tomioka Taeko, and Takahashi Takako, for example—are also strikingly oppositional. One of the most fascinating works of these few exceptions is Inoue Hisashi's *Kirikirijin (The Kirikiri People,* 1981). Totalling 834 pages, the book is massive. A satiric utopian fantasy, it traces the winning by a northern village of its independence from the state of Japan through a revolution lasting a mere forty hours from its happy beginning to its sad end. To narrate an event of forty hours' duration in more than eight hundred pages means a dense surface and texture; as Inoue explains it, the book is also meant to be read in forty hours, with the reader—if he so wishes—matching his reading time hour by hour to the chronology of the revolution.[17]

In the tradition of the Edo *gesaku*, *Kirikirijin* is obsessed with the verbality of the text. The village revolutionists insist on speaking in their local dialect, which happens to be the generally despised northeastern drawl. What is important is the work's rejection of standard bureaucratic Japanese that serves merely as a transmitter of messages. The marginal and deformational "zu-zu drawl" deflects the reader from the neutral flow of communication to the language of writing itself. The content must always be tested by the form.

Inoue's presence—like Ōe's and Tsushima's—indeed looms in the cultural erasure of today's Japan. His exceptionality also suggests, however, that Japan's economic miracle has finally neutralized the country's long insularity. In its single-minded devotion to productionism and consumerism, Japan is no longer distinct or isolated. As one of the most industrialized nations, Japan is in some ways comfortable with the so-called advanced nations. Fulfilling Fukuzawa Yukichi's slogan, "Escape from Asia, and Join Europe," Japan seems now a full-fledged member of the global organizational capitalist alliance. As such, a significant part of its cultural life has merged with the international mass phenomena. Does it make sense to call this situation postmodern? Possibly. Yet, as we have noted, Japan's "postmodern" traits precede earlier in history, thus denying a temporal specificity. They have been there all over for so long. In fact, as to the fashionable appellation *postomodanizumu*, there are rumors in very recent days that it has already lost its glamour. Just like existentialism, phenomenology, poststructuralism, and Frankfurt School Marxism, postmodernism, too, seems fast turning into a theoretical has-been. It has fulfilled its own prediction and has effectively self-destructed. At least the book market of Tokyo seems to have delivered the sentence with its customary incontrovertible authority.

═══

This examination of the Japanese prose narrative has been conducted within close proximity to the genealogy and context of the Western novel. This West-based procedure is unavoidable for two reasons.

One, my concern is mainly with the reading of Japanese fiction in the United States, and hence references must be made to the native ground. Two, and perhaps more importantly, Japanese hermeneutics is such that critics and scholars in Japan are accustomed to regarding the *shōsetsu*—erroneously, I believe—as a species of novel. With a few exceptions, most Japanese readers treat the form of *shōsetsu* as a transparent container within which they see a social and psychological allegory. The result is the native concurrence and confirmation of the first world hegemonic interpretation, often accompanied by the Orientalist verdict that the Japanese novel is underdeveloped.

This strategy of situating the discourse in the context of first world literature is thus clearly unsatisfactory, and some other frame of reference is surely called for. Although this paper is not intended to be a full exploration of an alternative methodology for reading the *shōsetsu*, some suggestions must be made toward that end. Thus what follows is a description of a few forms that are indigenous to Japan and are not conformable to Western expectations. The *shōsetsu* could be viewed as a confluence of narrative possibilities as inherited by the Edo period and later writers whose perception and response, dream and realization, were guided and defined by the constraints of their times. Just as the novel form took its shape from an ensemble of epic, Renaissance drama, folklore, and ballad, so does the *shōsetsu* range over the *monogatari* and *utamonogatari*, *noh*, *nikki* and *tabinikki*, Buddhist sermons, *renga*, *kabuki*, and so forth. I shall consider a few of these forms here as examples of the matrices of *shōsetsu* components.

First, the tenth-century *Ise monogatari* (*Tales of Ise*). One of the earliest prose tales in Japan, or in the world for that matter, it is hardly narrativized. Its 125 sections together suggest the life of a historical Don Juan courtier whose poems had appeared in earlier anthologies. Despite the biographical drift, the man's name is seldom mentioned in *Ise*. If some sections refer to the events historically associated with his supposed career, there are many others that are irrelevant to it. *Ise*'s sequence, in fact, only loosely resembles the chronology of a man's life. The modules follow one another paratactically, with the sole constant factor being the formulaic opening phrase in every section, "Long ago there was a man," or simply, "Long ago." We have here, then, a narrative that is segmented into separate vignettes that together would hint at the vague outline of a man's life. The shadowy contours of a life, made barely visible by rejection of a tight syntax of motivations, causes, and consequences, and by adoption of a sequence of unrelated episodes, are a feature that we might well remember as we read Japanese narratives of later days.

Each of *Ise*'s 125 sections has at least one *waka*. Out of the two hundred poems, only about thirty are actually attributed to the central figure, the rest coming from various sources of the eighth, ninth, and tenth centuries. Some of these sections are no more than a poem plus a few introductory words on the circumstances of its composition, the whole passage often having been lifted verbatim from an earlier poetic collection. There are, however, many sections in which the preexisting poems are adopted into the narrative situation furnished by *Ise* as a whole. That is, a *waka* or group of *waka* seems to have encouraged the writer or writers to generate a narrative context around it. A poem, in other words, extends to a narrative, which by continually referring back to its source poem makes a circular, reflexive movement between poetry and prose. We see here, then, a singular instance of creative cooperation and imaginative fusion between poetry and prose, *waka* poet and prose-narrativist, writer and reader, a historically identifiable person and a transparent referentially empty everyman ("the man who lived long ago"), all of them together composing this remarkably segmented and unplotted, and yet contiguous and related, story. There is no single author, nor is there a discrete central persona. There is not even a fully integrated narrative that insists on representation. Further, the *waka* poems, the imaginative pivots of the narrative sections, are in no meaningful sense lyrical; they operate through most intricate networks of conventions, both verbal and topical. If there is any expressive urge on the part of the poet, it is totally submerged in public conventions and practiced art. In a poetry that emerged in a perceptual scheme not yet sundered into subject and object, the term "lyric" which presupposes "the author's turning his back on his audience" simply does not apply.[18]

Perhaps more interestingly, all of these sectionalized tales barely describe exterior events or episodes. Many are mere poetic commentaries. Even in more narrativized sections, the miniature tales present the process and circumstances of poetic composition, and thus they are subordinate to poetry and art, as if an imitation of life were not as worthy as a reflection on art. *Waka* was generated by an artifice, certainly not by the poet's raw experience. Thus, the poetry seems at least twice removed from reality or essence, and it would have no doubt invited Plato's contempt. Despite its famed closeness to nature, Japanese poetry is artificial, self-enclosed in art. The *Tales of Ise* thus seems to invite its reader to deconstruct the notions of biography, fiction, authorship, nature, lyric, originality, poetry, and prose all at once.

To move on to the fourteenth- and fifteenth-century *noh*. The *noh* is often called the *noh-play* in English, which is quite inaccurate. Of course, the *noh* is staged, performed by those who talk, act, and dance, has a chorus that chants with a small orchestra of flutes and drums, and even has a few props. Yet the *noh* is not dramatic; neither tragic nor comic, neither mimetic nor symbolic, it is not even emplotted.

The typical *noh* opens with the entrance of an actor identifying himself in such vague terms as "I am a traveling priest called such and such" (no specific name is given). He says he is journeying for a purpose, say, a visit to a fallen warrior's or a poet's grave. In a few sentences, and after taking a few steps, he declares that he has arrived at his destination. The *noh* space is obviously a poetic space not at all coextensive with any physical dimensions. The actor then encounters the main actor (*shite*), who usually appears as a humble woodsman or fisherman. A short dialogue ensues in which the first actor repeats his intention, and the main actor supplies him with some information. The main actor disappears and then reenters, this time in the shape of the dead warrior or poet whom the initial actor seeks to mourn. The ghostly incarnation then reenacts a crucial scene, as that of his death, in an emphatically stylized dance. All this time, the initial actor remains on stage, but midway his unmasked expression turns utterly blank, as if he were simply absent. On the *noh* stage, presence is not indicated by the appearance of a figure, nor absence by the disappearance of a figure.[19]

The story line, if this is a story line, varies from *noh* to *noh*, but the fact remains that the main interest of the *noh* is not in its unfolding of an unexpected event. Most of the events and characters are borrowed either from such well-known works as *Ise* or *Genji* or from public events via *Heike*, and the audience is presumably familiar with what happens in the play.

The performers, too, are not actors in the ordinary sense. The main actor sometimes performs two characters in one scene: in the case of a *noh* called *Tadanori*, the main actor impersonates both the defeated warrior-poet Tadanori and the person who kills him in the murder scene itself. This denial of a one-to-one correspondence between the actor and the character is even more conspicuously demonstrated by the chorus that often speaks for one character and then for another, as if distinctions among characters were trivial. Unlike the Greek chorus, which sings in its own voice, the *noh* chorus presents several points of view, often even sharing a line with the main actor. Thus the *noh* seems indifferent to dramatic representation of human acts. It is set on presenting a being or doing, a "concrete abstraction," through a complex interrelationship of actors, their masks and costumes (or the absence thereof), music, chorus, stage design, and theater space.[20]

There are many other features that point to the radical differences between the *noh* and the Western theater, ancient, medieval, or bourgeois modern. The nature of the audience, the operation of the actors' companies, the mode of training and rehearsal, the masks and costumes, the audio and visual effects, including elocution—all such contributive factors seem to minimize what Brecht calls "hysteria" and maximize his notion of the "alienation effect."[21] The audience is never deceived into believing that they are spying on a slice of life; theirs is an experience of sheer art, far removed from life. *Noh* has no dialectic of clashing agons. The protagonist/antagonist opposition, where such exists, is not resolved by one party accepting or vanquishing the other, but simply by dissolving the barrier that has separated the warring parties. Finally, the surface of the text is so dense with puns, associations, epithets, and allusions as to make it nearly impenetrable. In the case of *Tadanori*, the verbal play of the warrior's name, the scene of a full-bloom cherry tree, and the name of the *Lotus Sutra* leads to the breathtaking last lines, "The flowers return to their roots," and "The flower is the master." This Yeatsian passage (I have in mind the closing stanza of "Among School Children") asserts the sheer mastery of the flower, the central sign of the Buddhist *Lotus Sutra* principle and the *noh* principle often enunciated by the fifteenth-century master Zeami. Like *Ise*, *Tadanori* is preoccupied with the nature of art. It is not about anything unless it is about art, about itself. Defying as it does the Western category of drama, the *noh* seems to require a different epistemology for its elucidation.

Linked poetry, as practiced by Basho in the seventeenth century, continues the long tradition of poetic exchange that began as greetings, love messages, etc. As such, it is typically an art by more than one person. In Basho's case, the unit of *renga* (linked poetry) was a 36-line version that alternates between the 5-7-5-syllable lines and the 7-7-syllable lines. Usually four poets participate in a session, composing their lines one at a time in a complex, predetermined order. Certain rules obtain as to the thematic pattern. The motifs of seasons, love, journey, and religious devotion are also regulated. A vast number of objects and events are assigned to one of the seasons. The rules can be ignored, of course, as all rules are. Yet a tight nexus of rules paradoxically frees the poet from the restriction of his inner space. The participant poets seem to follow gladly the leadership of the master such as Basho, and they obey the rulings of the scribe-referee who decides on the propriety of each composition.

Of the thirty-six lines, each of which can be considered a whole poem, the opening poem is the only independent one; the poet who offers it is not bound by preceding compositions. At the same time, his freedom is not unlimited, for he must respond with sensitivity to the mood of the group, which in turn likely reflects the season, weather, time, and place of the session. He also watches his master as he sets the circle of poetic creators-transmitters in motion, assessing the potentials his work will provide for them. The second poet takes over, often filling the empty space left by the first line. This second man is already a reader and a poet at the same time: he reads, that is, interprets and answers and shifts and continues what is given (as well as what is *not* given) in the first verse. The brevity of each line must be maximally utilized to amplify the power of silence and clarify the contours of the "concrete abstractions" contained in the preceding line. The third poet typically transforms the context set by the second, and his shift may be a dramatic one. If the previous scene is set in contemporary life, in a colloquial diction with a familiar object, the third poet might change it into a scene out of an ancient romance by adding an elegant and quaint phrase or a mere reference. If an old man was suggested earlier on, the third poet might magically transform him into a young woman by the subtlest qualification. Once the motion is set, the subsequent lines continue the process of metamorphosis, although the design of change itself must be also altered. Monotony must be avoided, and the principle of the three tempos —slow introduction, moderate development, and fast climax—that guides the movement of the *noh* operates as well in *renga*.

Renga, then, is first of all a miniature serialization in which what has already been composed is ineradicably there, determining what is to come and gradually narrowing the range of the future so far as the total length is predetermined. *Renga* also requires a joint effort. In Basho's *kasen*, four poets both complete and cooperate with one another. Obviously, they all remember their *renga* as a whole, and yet the integrity of a work, as Western literature traditionally understands it, is totally irrelevant. Despite a certain discernible drift in the thirty-six lines as a whole, the main effect of linked poetry is that of a succession of metamorphoses that maintains a constant level of awareness about the possibilities and the limits of the form.

The language of *renga* is once again characterized by polysemy, allusion, epithet, and association. Poems involve the whole literary tradition, which they both recall and parody. As a *renga* ranges over the various modes of humor, pathos, solemnity, intimacy, sentiment, eroticism, dramaticity, contemplativeness, and so forth, the language remains totally unsymbolic. The poetry prevents meaning from invading the image; it forbids interpretation to separate the form from the content. The meaning of *renga* is what it is. There is no separation between the signifier and the signified. *Renga* lines continue to remain empty of meaning as they shape images and echo sounds. None of these properties belongs to the speaker; as they manifest themselves, they enter the public domain of meaning that everyone—the poet and the reader or the poet-hyphen-reader—shares with everyone else.

The modular line—the line that is a stanza that is a whole poem

—thus depends on the sense of joint identity that *renga* poets build around their revered master. The final poem, all thirty-six of these lines, is neither narrative, nor lyrical, nor odic, nor ceremonial, nor occasional, nor accidental. The way of *renga* poets seems to harmonize with the other poets in the act of uttering words. As Beckett would say, and Michel Foucault would endorse, "What matter who's speaking?"

≡≡≡

Ise, the *noh*, and linked poetry are not marginal elements in Japanese writing. In fact, their salient features are evident in such other genres as prose tales, essays, and diaries, and they are conspicuous in the *shōsetsu*. In all of these forms, textuality is perceived of not in terms of autonomy, but of interrelation. Authorship is seen as more public and communal than private and individual. The modality of art tends to be not representational and mimetic, but presentational and linguistic; not "realistic," but reflexive. Less emphasis is placed on the acute sense of separation between the inside and outside, subjectivity and objectivity, artistic space and life space, than on the intense experience of fusion and collapse of such isolations. Taxonomical perception, too, seems focused on the rejection of separation and discreteness rather than the insistent detection of differences.

Once born, Japanese forms tenaciously live on. The 31-syllable *waka* has remained virtually unchanged for twelve or thirteen centuries, in contrast to Western forms that typically evolve at a quicker pace. Other forms, too, are adjacently or atavistically sighted in newly generated forms. If the emergence of the *shōsetsu* is historically determined, the same historical forces keep these older forms very much alive in it. To return to Goldmann's terms, our imminent task is to reexamine the historical circumstances that have allowed these forms of self-referentiality and parataxis, and of intertextuality and communality, to emerge and persist. The longevity of the forms is indisputable, the secrets of their survival still untold.

We might also recall here the earlier assertion that Japanese literature does not conform to Western critical terms even though it is not ontologically exceptional. One must pursue a step further: if it is not an exception, in what context should it be placed? In what direction should the critic turn next? One might begin with the obvious, what lies closest to Japan's tradition—that is, Korean and Chinese literatures. Many qualities of Japanese prose fiction suggested here are recognizable in Korean and Chinese forms, and renewed efforts at formal reexaminations are bound to result in new discoveries. One might then turn to farther peripheries, the oral cultures of the third world as suggested by many anthropologists and literary theorists. To call Japanese literature "oral" rather than "literate" might seem odd, but such Japanese forms as *monogatari, nikki, noh,* and *renga* as well as *shōsetsu* could be best described as imbued with interiorized or residual orality. So considered, the *shōsetsu* form might be found quite at home alongside the oral tales of the third world rather than the Western novel. It is unwise not to remember the Western novel in the examination of the *shōsetsu* form. However, not to recognize the form's native visage and lineage might be an even worse blunder. One might find some consolation, however, in making these difficult efforts—of reading the *shōsetsu* against the native grain in America —since one might not only be suggesting an alternative reading of Japanese fiction, but more generally of fiction as a whole for its reader of whatever origin. And finally, such an alternative reading might throw some light on the chronopolitical aspect of the postmodernism controversy.

Notes

1 A version of this paper was published in *Critical Issues in East Asian Literature: Report on International Conference on East Asian Literature, 13–20 June 1983* (Seoul, 1983), 221–47.

2 Japan is by now an economic superpower that cannot be easily placed among third world nations. There is, however, a gap between the economic statistics and the cultural perception of a nation. Although it is more than conceivable that Japan will gain "cultural hegemony" before too many years as it has "economic hegemony," the Japanese intellectuals' self-perception at this point vis-à-vis the West is hardly "first world." When Japanese critics complain that they are not being treated seriously in the West, they are both wishful and plaintive—so much so that one wishes that they embraced third world oppositionism to first world "universalism," rather than coveting an honorary membership in the West. After all, a mere three decades ago, Japan was one of the twenty-nine participants in the Bandung Conference, and Western racism has not even begun to alter its overall

scheme for the sake of the Japanese. In so many respects, Japan's culture remains utterly "exotic" to the first world.

3 See John W. Dower's "E. H. Norman, Japan and the Uses of History," in his edition of *Origins of the Modern Japanese State: Selected Writings of E. H. Norman* (New York, 1975), 3–101, especially 31. For the remoter history of American-Japanese exchange, see my *As We Saw Them: The First Japanese Embassy to the United States (1860)* (Berkeley, 1979).

4 Obviously there are exceptions, as is always the case with any generalization. One need not list here the names of those scholars with serious intellectual commitment in the field, although their presence is of particular significance in the context of Japanology.

5 This sentence appears in a letter from the translator, Professor Helen C. McCullough, University of California, Berkeley, to one of her students dated 12 July 1978. Though she wrote the letter as a semi-personal, semi-official one at first, she released it, together with the rest of her correspondence with the student, to the campus newspaper for publication. Thus it properly belongs to the public domain.

6 For the recent debate on Japan and modernity, see Fujita Shozo, *Seishinshi teki kosatsu (Consideration of Intellectual History)* (Tokyo, 1982); and Takabatake Michitoshi, *Toron: Sengo Nihon no seiji shiso (Postwar Japanese Political Ideology)* (Tokyo, 1977). On postmodernism of Japan, see works by Karatani Kōjin and Asada Akira, and articles in *Gendai shiso*.

7 Lucien Goldmann, "The Revolt of Arts and Letters in Advanced Civilization," in *Cultural Creation*, trans. Bart Grahl (St. Louis, 1976), 52.

8 Daniel Lloyd Spencer, "Japan's Pre-Perry Preparation for Economic Growth," *American Journal of Economics and Sociology* 17, no. 2 (January 1958): 197. See also Charles David Sheldon, *The Rise of the Merchant Class in Tokugawa Japan* (Locust Valley, 1958); Nobutaka Ike, *The Beginnings of Political Democracy in Japan* (Baltimore, 1950); and Sumiya Mikio and Taira Koji, eds., *The Outline of Japanese Economic History, 1603–1946: Major Works and Research Findings* (Tokyo, 1979).

9 Roland Barthes, *Writing Degree Zero*, trans. Annette Lavers and Colin Smith (New York, 1968), 30.

10 See Hayden White, "The Value of Narrativity in the Representation of Reality," *Critical Inquiry* 7, no. 1 (Autumn 1980): 5–27.

11 Barthes, *Writing Degree Zero*, 35–37.

12 Ibid., 40.

13 Serialization, the standard form for novel publishing in the nineteenth century, is still prevalent in Japan. For example, Kojima Nobuo completed a work in 1981 that he had serialized for fourteen years. Toward its end, the work makes many references to the real world, radically altering what the novel had been in its earlier sections.

14 There have been numerous discussions of literary prizes and awards. See, for example, Domeki Kyosaburo's *Asahi shimbun* articles (3 March and 5 October 1981)

on the degradation of the award system. See also Honda Katsuichi's attack on the prizes offered by the Bungei Shunju Publishing Company in "Bunshun-kei hankaku bungakusha tachi no shie o kou," *Ushio* (November 1982): 148–51.

15 This, too, is a perennial topic in the press. See, for example, a statistical survey published in *Mainichi shimbun*, 27 October 1981.

16 Of course, such interdependence in the literary enterprise is evident in any society. The degree of Japanese protectionism, however, is rather extreme. One never sees in Japan, for instance, an equivalent of the devastating review by Benjamin De Mott of Norman Mailer's *Ancient Evenings* (published by Little Brown) that appeared in the *New York Times* (10 April 1983).

17 Tsurumi Shunsuke and Inoue Hisashi, "*Kirikirikoku* wa dokoni aruka" ("Where Is the State of Kirikiri?"), *Umi* (March 1982): 165. This dialogue (140–66) is one of the most helpful documents for reading Inoue's masterpiece.

18 Northrop Frye, *Anatomy of Criticism* (Princeton, 1957), 250.

19 This description applies more appropriately to the *mugen* (ghostly) type, the more dominant of the two major *noh* types.

20 Roland Barthes, "Lesson in Writing," *Image-Music-Text*, trans. Stephen Heath (New York, 1977), 172.

21 "Alienation Effects in Chinese Acting," *Brecht on Theatre*, trans. John Willet (New York, 1978), 91–99.

Norma Field

Somehow: The Postmodern
as Atmosphere

This essay examines the 1980 Japanese novel
Somehow, Crystal (a title hardly less peculiar
in Japanese—*Nantonaku, kurisutaru*—than in
English) in an effort to respond to the
question posed by Fredric Jameson at the
end of his lecture titled "Postmodernism and
Consumer Society": namely, whether postmodernism, in addition to reproducing the
logic of consumer capitalism, can as well
acquire the "critical, negative, contestatory,
subversive, and oppositional" capabilities
often attributed to modernism.[1] Affirmative
responses are in the air, productively es-
chatological ("the *end* of art theory *now* is
identical with the objectives of *theories of
representations* in general . . .") and seemingly unnostalgic (the postmodern is "that
which searches for new presentations, not
in order to enjoy them but in order to impart a stronger sense of the unpresentable").[2]
This spectacle of heroic austerity is at the
very least confounding when juxtaposed with
the insouciant proliferation of simulacra and
pastiches in the marketplace today. As often

happens, the identification of a phenomenon (e.g., the age of the simulacrum) is imprudently conflated with its celebration.[3]

Before going any further, I should acknowledge that any attempt to answer Jameson's question, not to say the question itself, is at least incongruous and probably incompatible with the object of inquiry— postmodernism. This is because of postmodernism's hostility to, or rather, studied indifference to hierarchical distinctions of the sort exemplified in America by Clement Greenberg's formulations of avant-garde and kitsch, or Dwight MacDonald's masscult and midcult.[4] The transcendence of evaluative distinctions suggests the suspension of categorical distinctions such as, most crudely but crucially, those of art and life. Such leveling *seems* spiritually incompatible not only with Habermas's vision of a modern reunification of the realms of art, science, and morality separated since the Enlightenment, but perhaps as well with its critical alternative, Lyotard's notion of proliferating language games.[5] I underscore *seems* because efforts to demystify, to dismantle barriers in the name of revitalization, and even to atomize in the name of emancipatory difference often overlap with each other as well as with their common enemy, the cynical reduction of the world to units of equivalence, the familiar manifestation of which is of course commodity culture. This is to reword Jameson's question so as to emphasize the burden posed by postmodernism's susceptibility to, indeed, structural kinship with, commodity culture in any attempt to argue its emancipatory effects. It follows that it should be difficult to appeal from within postmodernism to the reflexive (read *redemptive*) character of art. This last, however, is an issue I wish to explore through the example of *Somehow, Crystal*.

As the eighties approach their end, Tanaka Yasuo's *Somehow, Crystal* invites designation as the exemplary phenomenon of the decade in Japan. After its appearance as a prize-winning first novel in the monthly journal *The Arts* (*Bungei*) in December of 1980, it sold approximately eight hundred thousand copies in book form. Nevertheless, it is hardly self-evident that this work, which met with virtually complete critical dismissal, should merit reconsideration. At the time of its selection in 1980, *Somehow* captivated only the literary critic Etō Jun among the four judges. Etō's enchantment was in turn noticed by the critic Katō Norihiro in his essay, "In the Shadow of 'America': Literature in the Age of High-Growth Economics."[6]

The book's cataloging of brand-name goods favored by the affluent young was simultaneously the source of its popularity and its critical rejection. Etō, who for some time has been identified with the political right, detects (a) an appealingly old-fashioned sentiment emanating from the "nowy" heroine and (b) appreciates the commercial information as a didactive gesture by the author to reach beyond a regional and generational subculture.[7] I infer that (b) is more fundamentally situated in the presumption that the novel, by being widely accessible, becomes an agent for the preservation and promotion of Japanese community. Katō, drawing on Etō's other writings on the Occupation and the postwar constitution, argues convincingly that (a) appeals to Etō as a symbol of his own reluctant acceptance of Japanese dependency on the United States. Let us take the hint: only when the two strands of commodity culture and national/individual identity are juxtaposed does this novel become interesting. My discussion will focus on these two concerns and a third issue, inseparable but occupying a different plane from the first two: namely, the language in which the questions of commodity and identity are represented in this novel. The challenge, as always, lies in analytically joining what was analytically sundered.

The narrative, divided into ten sections unobtrusively marked by a pair of small triangles, spans a two-week period during which the heroine, a college girl, is separated from her musician boyfriend Jun'ichi who is away on tour. She has a casual encounter with Masataka, a boy (there being only boys and girls in this world) encountered at a disco. When Jun'ichi returns, she learns that he, too, has had a flirtation. Perhaps this sketch makes *Somehow, Crystal* seem a hopelessly exiguous piece of writing. It is not. It manipulates simple material with extraordinary calculation. Its vacuousness as plot, which verges on nonexistence, is an important part of its effect. There is, moreover, a parallel text of notes accompanying, indeed contending with the primary narrative. The significance of the notes may be gauged by the author's extensive revisions as well as their increase in number from 274 to 442 in the interval between magazine appearance and publication in book form.

Both the book's wildly popular success and its critical condemnation can be partially attributed to these notes. Readers delighted in the information, critics fumed, no doubt because it was an unabashed instance of consumerism, and not only undignified as such but an instrumental affront to aestheticist purity. Here is a glimpse at the pleasures of the crystal life:

> If you feel like cake in the middle of the night, the place to go is Chianti's* in Aoyama 3-chome,* where you can have your cake with a glass of white wine. Afterwards, go for ice cream at Swensen's,* a shop with San Francisco flavors on "Killer" Avenue.* It's not bad, walking home, wondering if you're going to get a stomachache from that huge ice-cream cone.[8]

The asterisks mark those terms accorded notes. It is the last sentence that clinches the character of these passages, for it is precisely such pronouncements that elevate the merely pleasurable or even the aesthetic to the plane of the moral—that is to say, pose a prescription for the conduct of life. This passage is peculiarly reminiscent of the tenth-century classic, *The Pillow Book* of Sei Shōnagon, particularly those passages structured in the form of "In spring it is the dawn. . . . In summer the nights," where the dawn is asserted to be the essence of the spring.[9] I don't mean to suggest that *Somehow, Crystal* in any way approximates the range of subject matter or passion for experience conveyed by *The Pillow Book*. Indeed, in juxtaposing the two, one immediately feels the impoverishment of the crystal book, not to mention the crystal life, as the twentieth century draws to a close.[10] Still, the comparison is useful in pointing to the didacticism of the 1980 guidebook, which exceeds the sum of the information offered.

In his study of contemporary images, the poet-philosopher Yoshimoto Ryūmei argues for a process whereby the images of television commercials transcend (transgress) their original function, that of augmenting the exchange value of commodities, to become objects in their own right, more compelling than the commodities they supposedly represent, until finally they escape the administration of "capital or the system." Or, if that is too optimistic, he continues, one can at least assume that commercials will depict the desirable future of "capital and the system" more vividly than any hitherto imaged world. Whether that vision of the future "has the bright hues of life or the dark hues of death," he adds characteristically, "is a matter of comparatively little importance. All that matters is whether, unconsciously, commercials come to deny the effectiveness of commercials."[11] Can the crystal syndrome be analogously assessed?

Somehow, Crystal is in part a study of the brand name syndrome. As such, it is sensitive to linguistic differences, particularly in their graphic manifestations. The great majority of items in the book are foreign-made or licensed by foreign firms and therefore conspicuously represented in the syllabary reserved for foreign loan words. Additionally, in the notes, many of these items are not only defined but reproduced in the precious materiality of the Roman alphabet: thus, "tight," "smoggy grey," or "Liberty Print."[12] Conservatively put, the entries for at least 80 percent of the notes designate a foreign artifact, graphically signaled as such.

The remaining 20 percent, in Chinese characters, look peculiarly dense and therefore foreign in their own right. The effect here, to borrow a term from Harry Harootunian, is one of re-exoticization. This is detectable not in the gossipy, thinly veiled speculations about the identity of one or another school, but in those entries consisting of old Japanese stores, and especially place names familiar from fictional and other accounts from earlier in the century such as Mita, Mukōjima, Sendagi, Yanaka, or Nippori. Inserted amidst the names of American singers, tennis players, European furnishings, and imported delicacies, these Japanese names, which normally bear the patina of age, acquire a glossy novelty—much as do scenes from Kyoto or Kamakura when they are featured on the pages of magazines bearing such names as *An-an* or *Non-non*. Thus is Japan rebaptized, at the price exacted whenever the principles of commodity culture are embraced. Baudrillard calls the brand name "not a proper name, but a sort of *generic Christian* name."[13] Whether this loving attention to graphic representation achieves the transcendence suggested by Yoshimoto whereby the images of television commercials acquire the status of use value, the characters of *Somehow, Crystal* at any rate seek their identities in the consumption of brand-name goods.

Not surprisingly, the most provocative discussions of identity are juxtaposed with questions of money. Of a fellow model named Nao, a "Japanese" (quotes in the original) who is a quarter Russian and a quarter Belgian, the heroine observes that

Modeling as a profession suits her. . . . That's because if you work
as a model, you don't need to worry about your identity. She's
got to be completely different from me and Naomi. We got into
this because we wanted the money, we wanted to "live a life that
somehow felt good."[14]

Modeling is empty: Nao can model only her nonidentity, which in
this case refers to non-Japaneseness. Naomi and the heroine, by contrast, who are secure in their Japaneseness, model merely in order to
acquire money to ensure their freedom—in this case, freedom to purchase the commodities that produce the "atmosphere" defining their
identities. Nao's situation, by comparison, is simpler and, one might
say, purer:

Nao = non-Japanese = nonidentity = model

· · · ·

Nao[mi] and heroine = Japanese = identity = model =
freedom-to-buy = atmosphere = identity

What is the fit between identity defined as Japaneseness and identity
defined by the atmosphere produced by the freedom-to-buy? Do they
represent two incompatible systems? Or does the anteriority of the
former guarantee the secondary and therefore playful nature of the
latter, the playfulness in turn enabling an unfixed but satisfactory
identity? Or does the addition of terms in the second series merely
obscure the dependence of Japanese identity on the freedom to buy
foreign luxury goods, thereby compelling recognition as very special
members of the prosperous white West—or perhaps as the founding
fathers of the nonwhite West?[15]

A modified version of the last interpretation is suggested by the
heroine herself with the help of the handsome Masataka. Although
she has seen plenty of "whites" in Tokyo with poor table manners,
she cannot help deploring with Masataka the spectacle of misguided
Japanese proudly managing their spaghetti with spoons as well as
forks. It is Masataka who takes the discussion a step further by connecting manners to fashion and thence to national identity: " 'I guess
in the end you have to say that we have no resistance to brand names.

Our generation. Maybe it's not just our generation, maybe it's all Japanese.' "[16]

Such conversations and musings on modeling and table manners bring together the motifs of body, race, and commodity with those of knowledge and identity, both national and individual. The issue is highlighted in the two sex scenes of the novel. The first, with Masataka, takes place over some seven pages, with nine noted items. The second, with the returned Jun'ichi, takes a scant three pages and has only one noted item. The first is high-tech sex between a fashionable young man and a fashionable young woman. This is not to suggest that it is unfeeling: the fashionable young woman finds the fashionable young man not only technically superb, but exceedingly considerate. As one might expect from the relentless presence of notes, the narration of the process, however, is much like the preceding discussion of good food, music, and clothing. As skilled as Masataka is, he cannot induce in the heroine the waves of "high voltage current" that Jun'ichi, and Jun'ichi alone, is capable of. Jun'ichi, at least upon his return from tour, is hardly careful or considerate. The heroine is not interested in technical details; indeed, visited as she is by the "high voltage current," she has no leisure for such detail.

The moral, we conclude, is that orgasm has no brand name. For a woman it comes only from a man to whom she is "firmly, spiritually bound."[17] It is described as an experience in which the female body "loses its freedom," according to the idiom. Is this loss symmetrical to the freedom-to-buy that money (acquired, for instance, by modeling—possibly another form of loss of freedom by the body) confers? Other forms of sexual gratification—masturbation, for instance—easily find commodified comparison—"as disappointing as when you're made to eat French cooking where the rabbit's been stewed in white wine instead of red." That physical loss of freedom singly experienced in sexual surrender to the man to whom one is spiritually bound is priceless and therefore threatens to overwhelm the values guaranteed by the freedom-to-buy. If the earlier set of equations can be simplified to produce triangle A below, then the heroine's attachment to Jun'ichi results in the supplanting of the third angle of triangle A to produce triangle B:

A

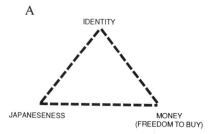

B

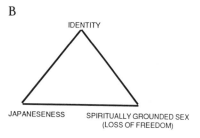

The heroine struggles to reconcile the two third terms and at the same time to keep triangle A from collapsing into triangle B:

> I've ended up affiliated with the controller named Jun'ichi.
>
> . . . .
>
> Now that I know the joy that only Jun'ichi can give me, I suppose the only reason I'm still "affiliated" with him instead of dependent on him is that I've got my work as a model.[18]

The Eurasian Nao needs to model because she has no identity. The Japanese heroine models merely for the money, which buys the commodities guaranteeing her autonomy. But this autonomy is crucially circumscribed by her recognition that only one man can satisfy her, a man who, though he may resemble Al Pacino in the midst of lovemaking, seems unpreoccupied with the foreign brand-name garments adorning his person. The admitted weakness of Japanese for foreign commodities is apparently redeemed by this powerful recognition. Amidst the incantatory magic of brand names, orgasm is crowned with the epithet of electricity, scientific offspring of thunder, which perhaps serves as a metonymic bridge to the transcendence postulated by Yoshimoto for the television commercial image. The high-voltage current attests to the propriety of relationship prevailing between man and woman, itself a mirror of the well-being of the state. Thus does the emancipatory rhetoric of commodity culture yield to the most orthodox of unities.

Of course, it may be that these unities are bogus, and that they are moreover exposed as such in the crystal text. That is to say, the security of identity as Japaneseness may be contaminated, even guaranteed, by the identity produced by the atmosphere emanating from foreign goods: perhaps, as suggested earlier, Japanese identity is nothing other than the ability to purchase Western commodities. The heroine's reflections on her lover's resemblance to Al Pacino are characteristically frivolous but threatening, for she risks turning him into a brand name—which also holds the possibility for recovering a modicum of autonomy: for without the mediating presence of money, the heroine (and Japan as well?) are secured in metaphysical identity.

I should make explicit that thus far I have been discussing material presented by the heroine-narrator of the primary text. The importance of the sex scenes, however, is emphasized by the marked difference in their treatment by a second narrator, the narrator of the notes. Retrospectively, one realizes that this narrator is always dominant, that his contributions never function merely to dispense the information so enthusiastically received by the great majority of readers. This becomes particularly apparent from the revisions made between magazine and book publication. All the ironic comments —such as "when you think you're writing on a writing desk, you feel like you're coming up with better ideas than if you're writing on a *tsukue*" (Japanese for *desk*)—were introduced at that stage.[19] The persistence of the mocking tone transforms the narrator of the notes into a controlling presence, so much so that even the heroine's name (a properly insipid Yuri) is introduced in the notes.[20] Taking this into account, we retrospectively feel the second narrator's voyeuristic presence from the moment Yuri wakes up to the objects in her room.

This narrator's gaze ranges well beyond the nubile Yuri. In a note to Masataka's speculation that not only his generation but all Japanese might be susceptible to brand names, the narrator observes,

> Those "arts" critics who say that the characters in this book are only mannequins are people who fuss about brand names in the form of educational pedigree and titles. As for those "arts" reporters who complain that there is no life in this novel, they would only be ordinary people once they took off their press badges—more brand labels.[21]

This narrator perilously resembles the author, contrasting, for instance, the novels of "Mr. Kataoka Yoshio and Mr. Tanaka Yasuo [the author]" with those being scorned in the main text.[22] Here, self-reference, at once instrument and proof of modernist virtue (the transcendence of naive illusion) and respectable still in postmodernism, is used to argue the congruence between word and world: there is no difference between valuing a Cacharel blouse and a Tokyo University degree, and our author-like narrator is certainly free of such delusions. Why, then, the bantering intrusions in the first sex scene and the clichéd if eloquent silence in the second?

Putting aside this question for a moment, I would like to investigate the mechanisms by which the notes acquire their persuasive force. I believe one factor is their narrator's use of the polite *desu* (copula) and *masu* (verb) endings in contrast to the neutral *ru/ta* endings of the heroine's text. The significance of this contrast is underscored by its absence in the original magazine version, where the notes also appear in *ru/ta* form. Provisionally, we might guess that it is the apparently personal touch of the notes in *desu/masu* form, with their politeness ironically reinforcing the mocking, sophisticated tone, that gives their narrator primacy over the narrator of the primary text. The picture is complicated, however, by an internal opposition between *ru* and *ta*, and it is this opposition I will explore first before returning to the larger one of *desu/masu* and *ru/ta*. To take an example:

> If you're going to buy *chiyogami* [printed rice paper], it seems to me you've got to make the gesture of getting on the Chiyoda Line and going to Isetatsu in Sendagi. If it's Mickey Mouse postcards you want, you might try going to a funny little card shop in Aoyama that's supposed to be open only on weekends, called On Sundays.* But if it's Edo *chiyogami*, you can't help thinking of Bunkyō-ku or Taitō-ku. If you just got it in Shibuya, you might feel as if you'd bought cardboard instead of *chiyogami*.
>
> . . . .
>
> It wasn't just a question of loyalty* to the brand or to the shop.* [T]
>
> . . . .
>
> Going to Sendagi for one sheet of *chiyogami*: it's the spirit of the thing I wanted to cherish. [T]
>
> . . . .

Buying a Courrèges summer sweater and carrying it off in a Courrèges shopping bag: it's the snobbery* I wanted to cherish. [T]

. . . .

It's o.k. to have espresso with cake, but once in a while, you want to have it in the French style, with white wine: it's the affectation I wanted to cherish. [T]²³

The sentences marked [T] all end in *ta*; all the others have *ru* endings. Translation into the simple English past is of course inadequate and is intended only as a convenience for distinguishing sentence types. Even in this short passage, the distinction in usage between *ru* and *ta* seems so deliberate as to command our attention, whether we cast it as a question of tense or one of aspect.²⁴ In other words, in addition to being neutral where *desu/masu* is polite, *ru/ta* (signifying "nonpast" and "past" according to one terminology) explicitly poses problems commonly known by the terms of tense and aspect. Here, without wishing to diminish the importance of the relation between the temporality of narrated events and the temporality of their narration or of distinctions between duration and completion, and without ceasing to regret the morphological losses (and attendant reduction of semantic possibilities) in the course of the evolution of modern Japanese, I would argue that determinations of tense and aspect cannot take us far enough.²⁵ Even if one decides that a given verbal form indicates tense or aspect, or perhaps more radically that there is no such thing as tense, there still remain to be investigated presumptions of value associated with pastness or presentness, completion or continuation.

But, first, we must begin by acknowledging the apparent existence of two opposed verb systems, one centered on *ru*, the other on *ta*. A comparable dichotomy is recognized by Emile Benveniste and Harald Weinrich, to name but two whose work seems especially pertinent.²⁶ Benveniste's well-known distinction between historical utterance and discourse precludes the use of the present tense and the first and second persons (the locus of subjectivity, he argues elsewhere) in the former and presumes the presence of speaker and hearer, as well as intent by the one to influence the other, in the latter.²⁷ Weinrich distinguishes between narrative, centered on the preterit and inviting relaxed reception, and discourse, centered on the present and demanding the contrary because the "situation touches upon our own existence."[28] The crucial difference between the two verb groups may be summarized as the exposure of the conditions of enunciation in the former ("discourse" for both Benveniste and Weinrich) and their concealment in the latter ("history" for Benveniste, "narrative" for Weinrich).[29]

Although their distinctions are invaluable, neither Benveniste's nor Weinrich's discussions account for certain other discourses pertinent to a discussion of *Somehow, Crystal*. I have in mind informational discourses of various sorts, as presented in textbooks, tourist guides, government pamphlets, commercials, etc. These predominantly employ the present tense and therefore fall into the category of "discourse" according to both Benveniste and Weinrich. However, although there is an undeniable attempt to influence the reader in these cases, and a corresponding tension (because our existence is involved), it is surely inappropriate to suggest that the conditions of enunciation are disclosed—in which case, they fall into the equally inappropriate category of "history" or "narrative." What is happening here? We must return to the presumptions of value underlying tense/aspect determinations.

The language of information has a special investment in the present. This language prides itself on the most comprehensive (because incorporating the most recent) presentation of truth. In this case, the logic of the present tense is the logic of truth that is knowable because of its synchronicity with the living—namely, we who occupy the present, situated at the forward edge of time. If we bring in the language of fiction, the picture becomes still more complicated. A writer may choose the present tense precisely because, as is often argued, it affords greater immediacy in the form of the knowably true (analogous to the reasoning of science and information); or, on the other hand, the present tense may be valued for the subjective truth of uncertainty (which counts as absence of established truth for information and is analogous to Benveniste's and Weinrich's discourse).

All of this is schematic, and one must remember that actual language-use variously combines these possibilities. Still, let us pursue this exercise with the past tense. The logic of the past tense may also be the logic of the knowably true, i.e., the past and therefore the complete (Benveniste's history and Weinrich's narrative: relaxation may seem an odd notion here but what is incontestably known may indeed be contemplated in relaxation). On the other hand, the past may suggest uncertainty precisely because it is completed and not synchronous and therefore unknowable—in which case it is hardly beyond debate and not at all relaxing. The logic of fiction can evaluate this in at least two ways: either that pastness is a guarantee of truth such that fiction cannot be deemed false; or that pastness precludes knowable truth and accordingly guarantees instead a distinctive realm for fiction, the realm of subjective truth, or finally, the truth of rhetoric. What I am trying to show is that the association of the present with discourse and the past with narrative need not be as fixed as one might think. Moreover, we need to recognize that the values accorded a given tense or aspect can only be context specific.

To return at last to the *ru/ta* opposition. *Ru* serves to indicate the present, the future, the habitual, the necessarily recurring, or the denomination of attributes. These are also the features of what I have called the language of information. *Ta* spans the range of tense, aspect, and mood, and can indicate the past, past recurrences, or even discovery or recognition.[30] Noguchi Takehiko, in investigating the reason why the great majority of Japanese novels are grounded in *ta*, concludes that it is because *ta* is felt to be the marker of fiction, and as such should be distinguished from the preterit *ta*, though they are morphologically the same.[31] The great grammarian Tokieda Motoki notes that "Rather than being an expression of an objective situation, *ta*, as the expression of the speaker's position, often signifies recollection or confirmation. . . . Of course, since the speaker's position is often based on an objective situation, the two are intimately related."[32] *Ta* in Tokieda's grammar is an important example of that category of words known as *ji* that offer direct (without conceptual mediation) expression to the subject of enunciation. Every statement, in order to qualify as such, is governed by a *ji*, and where it is missing, it must be assumed, producing the curious and controversial notion of the "zero marker," or less literally, the "absent marker" (*rei kigō*).[33]

The latter notion is useful to the present discussion in two ways, one loosely in keeping with Tokieda's views, the other as a misappropriation. The first has to do with the apparently inextricable involvement of subjectivity in the production of linguistic coherence; this I take to be pertinent to the preceding discussion on the diverging values assigned to the various tenses and aspects—there being no inherent truth value to either the past or the present, the complete or the incomplete, it is not surprising that conflicting claims are made for the one or the other. The drama of suppression and disclosure suggested by Benveniste's categories of history and discourse is subtly muted in Tokieda's scheme, where the subject of enunciation is always present, either explicitly or implicitly. Every instance of language use, to put a Lacanian cast on it, subjects one to subjectivity. The second implication of Tokieda's analysis, more immediately useful for us, lies in its perhaps inadvertent demonstration of the differing effects of the explicit or implicit presence of the subject marker. *Ta*, in other words, can make the subject of enunciation strongly felt, whereas *ru* must be supplemented by a zero marker in order for the statement which it terminates to achieve subjective unification.

One more general observation, and we are ready to return to *Somehow*: as suggested above, modern Japanese novels are grounded in *ta*, whether because it is perceived as a past tense, an aspect marker of completion, or the sign of fiction. When *ru* sentences intervene, they are commonly construed as instances of the historical present, serving "to draw the reader into the situation, to draw him into a vividly drawn situation, or to avoid monotony in sentence endings." A series of *ru* sentences framed by *ta* sentences (*ta, ru, . . . ta*) constitutes a typical pattern in Japanese fiction.[34]

What is striking about the primary text of *Somehow, Crystal* is the predominance of *ru* sentences—*ru* sentences which are not, moreover, framed by *ta* sentences. In fact there is a pervasive asymmetry, as in the example above where a series of *ru* sentences is terminated by the refrain of "It's x that I wanted to cherish." In the opening of the novel, a series of *ru* sentences continues for a full two pages before the first *ta* sentence appears: "Today was the day for French class in the afternoon"—a classic example of the *ta* of recognition.[35]

What is the effect of the predominance of the *ru* sentence in the heroine's text? It presents the ideology of the brand name, of consumer culture, as quasi-scientific information, resistant to discussion. By masking its impersonality in the heroine's chattiness, this discourse augments its potency. Against the preponderance of the *ru* sentences, the *ta* sentences of subjective recognition, acknowledgment, and affirmation are reduced to the trivial ("today was the day for French class") or the tautological ("the snobbery I wanted to cherish," "the affectation I wanted to cherish"). In other words, the heroine's expression of personality is but a linguistically passive rendition and confirmation of commodity culture.

The manipulation of *ru/ta* becomes particularly acute in the two sex scenes discussed earlier. Indeed, the high-tech effect of the encounter with Masataka derives from the insistent use of *ru* sentences as well as from the intrusiveness of the notes. As the scene approaches its climax, there is a dramatic shift to *ta*, reinforced by the use of *watashi*, the first-person pronoun.[36] Although "I" and "he" appeared earlier, the *ru* endings had depersonalized them, and the narrative to this point had the effect of a mechanical description by the heroine watching the manipulation of her body. So the conjunction of the "I" with *ta* is dramatic—and yet it is immediately undercut by a note on "I": " 'I' means 'I.' "[37] Accordingly, what might have been a recounting of the heroine's exhilarating entry into her own body becomes instead the description of anticlimax, punctuated by cool observations about how well her partner is doing given that this is his first time with her. The ideology of *ru* overwhelms the possibilities of *ta*, and their opposition crumbles.

When Yuri is reunited with Jun'ichi, however, the narrative falls into the orthodox *ta, ru*, . . . *ta* pattern.[38] The world falls into place when one's man comes home. Does this resurrection of *ta*—equally ideological, of course, as the predominance of *ru*—reverse the impersonal sway of foreign gadgets, fashions, manners? Can Yuri's desire for the "crystal atmosphere" guaranteed by the freedom-to-buy be reconciled with her need for meaning conferred by sexual loss of freedom to Jun'ichi? Can Japan's daunting wealth and corresponding freedom-to-buy accommodate the persistent desire for a fixed national identity? Presumably, the only satisfactory form that such accommodation could take would be the instrumental subordination of the former to the latter, such that the wealth ensuring freedom-to-buy would serve to eternally bind Yuri to Jun'ichi, would serve to reinforce, indeed to reinvent, Japanese as opposed to alien values. To revert to the triangles, the dotted sides of triangle A would merge to reinforce the sides of triangle B.

The prognosis for such reconciliation as expressed in *Somehow* is suitably ambiguous. At the end of her text, the heroine, jogging uphill on Omote Sandō, observes: "As I wiped the sweat off my brow with my palm, the refreshing scent of the Diorissimo* I'd put on at the clubhouse mingled with the smell of sweat." [39] The ersatz lyricism invokes a note on Diorissimo: "The floral-toned Diorissimo, concocted from the combination of lilies-of-the-valley and jasmine, is thought to be well-suited to chaste wives and pure young ladies." [40] This statement is cast in the notes' narrator's habitual *desu/masu* form, which belongs to Tokieda's category of *ji*, verbal material allowing for direct expression by the subject of enunciation. It is worth noting how this category cuts across the category of discourse in Benveniste: here, it allows us to hold in our minds both the forms for politeness—*desu/masu*, indicating explicit awareness of the addressee by the subject—and the marker for pastness, *ta*. [41] The impersonal tyranny of science, information, and fashion easily assumes the insidiously soft tones of the commercial: the neutral and therefore persuasive discourse of *ru* can be masked by the personal and therefore persuasive discourse of *desu/masu;* or, the *ru* of the text is *ta*-ized by the *desu/masu* of the notes.

Just as the opposition between *ru* and *ta* collapses variously, so does that between *desu/masu* and *ru/ta*. We might grasp the shifting configurations schematically as follows: [42]

Temporality:	Nonpast	Past
	desu/masu, ru	*ta*
Level of Usage:	Neutral	Polite
	ru, ta	*desu/masu*
Mode of Expression:	Shi (objective)	Ji (subjective)
	ru	*ta, desu/masu*
Narrative Use:	Primary Text	Notes
	ru, ta	*desu/masu*

The narrator of the notes addresses us with a flattering intimacy, inviting us to share his bantering superiority to the heroine and her text. This is a spurious invitation, as we have seen, for the narrator himself suggests that the heroine is no more superficial than those who would criticize either her values or her delineation by the author. Generally, the discourse of *desu/masu* not only deceptively reinforces that of *ru* (giving it the aura of *ta*), but suggests that there are no alternatives, there being nothing beyond the world of *ru*.[43] In the case of the second sex scene, however, the discourse of *desu/masu* overtly sides with that of *ta* (and national and individual chastity) through abstinence—making it seem as if unmediated *ta*-ness were possible.

Where does this leave us? Reverting to the schema of the triangles, I suggest that they are neither the same nor different. Between triangles A and B there is no desirable choice, but their collapse into one signals the foreclosure of choice. Perhaps, in the end, the crystal atmosphere is at once an analogue of the novel and the veil that protects both reader and narrators from having to confront the ambiguities in all their powerful tension.

The veil *seems* to be torn asunder at the very end, however, for the last word in *Somehow* belongs to neither the narrator of the text nor the narrator of the notes. There is a final entry, again an addition postdating magazine publication. It consists of excerpts from government reports. The first is from a report issued by the Committee for the Study of Population Problems predicting an irreversible decline in population growth in the last years of the twentieth century, with the possibility of stabilization at the zero population growth level in 2025 if certain conditions hold. The second excerpt is from a Health Ministry white paper documenting the aging of the population. The third lists projected increases in contributions to the social security fund. This passage is entirely in *ru* form, especially severe given the format of the list and the statistics-filled content. The implied comment presumably concerns the twin fates of the desire for the crystal life and the desire for identity in the twenty-first century. But the brute use of *ru*, as with most last words, notoriously does not invite response. Is the crystal atmosphere decisively dispelled at last? Or do we cower in the shadow of postmodern Malthusianism and seek the comforting regions of the *Somehow*?

Notes

1 Fredric Jameson, "Postmodernism and Consumer Society," in *The Anti-Aesthetic: Essays on Postmodern Culture*, ed. Hal Foster (Port Townsend, 1983), 125.

2 Victor Burgin, *The End of Theory* (Atlantic Highlands, N.J., 1986), 204. The virtually classic description of postmodernism comes from Jean-François Lyotard's "What is Postmodernism?" in *The Postmodern Condition: A Report on Knowledge*, trans. Geoff Bennington and Brian Massumi (Minneapolis, 1984), 81.

3 See Jean Baudrillard, *Simulations*, trans. Paul Foss, Paul Patton, and Philip Beitchman (New York, 1983).

4 Clement Greenberg, "Avant-Garde and Kitsch," in *Art and Culture: Critical Essays* (Boston, 1961), 3–21; Dwight MacDonald, "Masscult and Midcult," in *Against the American Grain* (New York, 1983), 3–78.

5 Habermas's views on the subject are succinctly presented in his "Modernity—An Incomplete Project," in Foster, *Anti-Aesthetic*, 3–15. Lyotard's position is argued throughout his *Postmodern Condition*.

6 Katō Norihiro, " 'Amerika' no kage: Kōdo seichōka no bungaku" ("In the Shadow of 'America': Literature in the Age of High-Growth Economics"), in *Amerika no kage (In the Shadow of America)* (Tokyo, 1985), 7–129.

7 Etō Jun, "Sansaku o dōji ni osu" ("I Vote for All Three Works"), *Bungei* 19 (December 1980): 268–69.

8 Tanaka Yasuo, *Nantonaku, kurisutaru (Somehow, Crystal)* (Tokyo, 1980), 31. All translations are my own.

9 Sei Shōnagon, *Makura no sōshi (The Pillow Book)*, trans. Ivan Morris (Harmondsworth, 1967), 21.

10 As for the insistent repetition of "crystal" in this book: Katō Norihiro refers to Georges Perec's *Les choses: Une histoire des années soixante* ([Paris, 1965], 13, 298) as a "French version" of *Somehow, Crystal* and cites the passage from Malcolm Lowry's *Under the Volcano* used by Perec as an epigraph to *Les choses*: "Incalculable are the benefits civilization has brought us . . . without parallel the crystalline and fecund fountains of the new life which still remains closed to the thirsty lips of the people who follow in their griping and bestial tasks" ([New York, 1984], 324). The evocation of people to whom the "crystalline and fecund fountains" are closed absolutely separates Lowry's world (and, by implication, Perec's) from that developed in Tanaka's "crystal atmosphere." Katō suggests that the question of choosing between freedom and material well-being had already been "stolen" at the start of *Somehow, Crystal*.

11 Yoshimoto Ryūmei, "Gazōron" ("On Images"), in *Masu Imējiron (On Mass Images)* (Tokyo, 1984), 241. The sort of praise that Yoshimoto has been dealing late capitalism (its emancipatory effects, particularly through technological advances) is effectively countered by Tessa Morris-Suzuki in "Robots and Capitalism," *New Left Review* 147 (September/October 1984): 109–21, and "Capitalism in the Computer Age," *New Left Review* 160 (November/December 1986): 81–91. The "perpetual innovation economy" hardly invites optimism.

12 Tanaka, *Somehow, Crystal*, 150.
13 Jean Baudrillard, *For a Critique of the Political Economy of the Sign*, trans. Charles Levin (St. Louis, 1981), 69; emphasis mine.
14 Tanaka, *Somehow, Crystal*, 48.
15 To avoid confusing the reader imbued with the image of the refusing Japanese consumer that has been projected by the foolish and dangerous rhetoric of the current trade hostilities, I should perhaps emphasize that "freedom-to-buy" here means "freedom-to-buy-brand-name-goods." Whether the luxury items cataloged in this novel could play a significant role in the trade balance I cannot say. Common sense might argue against it, but the oppressive ubiquity of Louis Vuiton bags a decade ago provides counterevidence.
16 Tanaka, *Somehow, Crystal*, 55.
17 Ibid., 143.
18 Ibid., 143–44.
19 Ibid., 14 n. 6.
20 Ibid., 150 n. 18.
21 Ibid., 171–72 n. 248.
22 Ibid., 176 n. 304, 85.
23 Ibid., 37–38.
24 The question of tense and aspect in Japanese was memorably aired in English by Roy Andrew Miller, "Do the Japanese Know How to Tell Time?" *Journal of the Association of Teachers of Japanese* 10 (March 1975): 1–18, and by Masao Miyoshi, who responded in the same journal ([September 1975]: 209–16) with "Do the Americans Know How to Tell Time?: Some Do, Some Don't."
25 See Mitani Kuniaki, "Kindai shōsetsu no gensetsu, joshō: Shōsetsu no 'jikan' to gabuntai aruiwa Kamei Hideo no *Kansei no henkaku* o yomu" ("Prefatory Study of Discourse in the Modern Japanese Novel: 'Time' in the Novel and Elegant Language, or A Reading of Kamei Hideo's *Transformation of Sensibility*"), in *Kindai bungaku no seiritsu: Shisō to buntai no mosaku* (*The Formation of Modern Literature: Groping for Thought and Style*) (Tokyo, 1986), 118–28.
26 See Emile Benveniste, *Problems in General Linguistics*, trans. Mary Elizabeth Meek (Coral Gables, 1971), and Harald Weinrich, "Tense and Time," *Archivum Linguisticum*, n.s., 1 (1970): 31–44. My thanks to Earl Miner for sharing this article.
27 Benveniste, *General Linguistics*, 206–7.
28 Weinrich, "Tense and Time," 35.
29 See Oswald Ducrot and Tzvetan Todorov, "Temps du discours," in *Dictionnaire encyclopédique des sciences du langage* (Paris, 1972), 398–400.
30 Nitta Yoshio, "Jisei/Tense," in *Nihon bumpō jiten* (*A Dictionary of Japanese Grammar*), ed. Kitahara Yasuo et al. (Tokyo, 1981), 108.
31 Noguchi Takehiko, *Shōsetsu no Nihongo* (*The Japanese Language of the Novel*) (Tokyo, 1980), 38.
32 Tokieda Motoki, *Nihon bumpō: Kōgohen* (*Japanese Grammar: The Spoken Language*) (Tokyo, 1978), 170–71.
33 These matters are pursued throughout Tokieda Motoki's *Kokugogaku genron* (*A

Theory of Japanese Language) (Tokyo, 1941), but see especially chap. 3, pt. 2. The ghostly zero marker has been much criticized; with reference to *ta*, see Kitahara Yasuo, *Nihongo no bumpō (Japanese Grammar)* (Tokyo, 1981), 154. An exposition in English on *shi* and *ji* in historical context may be found in Naoki Sakai, *Voices of the Past: The Discourse on Language in Eighteenth-Century Japan* (Ph.D. diss., University of Chicago, 1983), 288–92.

34 The source of the quotation, as well as many examples of the *ta, ru, . . . ta* pattern, is Saeki Umetomo and Suzuki Yasunori, *Bungaku no tame no Nihongo bumpō (Japanese Grammar for* [the study of] *Literature)* (Tokyo, 1986), 28, 33–49.

35 Tanaka, *Somehow, Crystal,* 10.

36 Ibid., 68.

37 Ibid., 174 n. 283.

38 Ibid., 125–27.

39 Ibid., 148.

40 Ibid., 188 n. 442.

41 Courtesy language not directed to the addressee falls out of *ji* into the objective category of *shi*. Tokieda's *Theory of Japanese Language,* in part a critique of Saussure, was published in 1941. In calling attention to it here, I am hoping that linguists might undertake comparisons of his idiosyncratic but provocative work with Benveniste's conceptualizations, or J. L. Austin's speech act theory, or Shoshanna Felman's critique of Austin in *The Literary Speech Act: Don Juan with J. L. Austin, or Seduction in Two Languages,* trans. Catherine Porter (Ithaca, 1983).

42 See Ann Wehmeyer, *Variation in a Japanese Dialect: A Study of Verbal Morphology* (Ph.D. diss., University of Michigan, 1987). Drawing on the terminology of Samuel E. Martin (*Language in Culture and Society* [New York, 1964]) and Roy Andrew Miller (*The Japanese Language* [Chicago, 1967]), Wehmeyer illustrates a different categorization scheme whereby *desu/masu* belongs to the "axis of address" and *ru* to the "axis of reference" constituting the honorifics system in Japanese. See chap. 5, "Honorifics," especially 108–13, for an overview. I wish to record my thanks for her help on several points in this essay.

43 Again, a comparison with *Les choses* is in order: Perec's distinctly third-person narration affords the reader a distance that is unavailable within the seductively claustrophobic first-person narratives of both the text and the notes in *Somehow, Crystal*. More precisely, by raising only to dismiss the possibility of other modes of life, the narrator of the notes exempts us from pursuing such meager reservations as we might harbor.

Ōe Kenzaburō

Japan's Dual Identity: A Writer's Dilemma

As one Japanese writer, I stand before you harboring not unfounded suspicions that Japanese literature is decaying. A confession such as this from a writer from the third world should undoubtedly disappoint an audience that is expecting a genuine "challenge" given the context of our discussion. There are reasons, however, why I have willingly accepted to act the part of the disappointing clown. There is an element in the Japanese nation and among Japanese that makes us unwilling to accept the fact that we are members of the third world and reluctant to play our role accordingly. Japan appeared on the international scene clearly as a third world nation from about the time of the Meiji restoration (1868). In her process of modernization ever since, she has been a nation blatantly hostile to her fellow third world nations in Asia, as evidenced by her annexation of Korea and by her war of aggression against China. Her hostility toward her neighbors continues even today.

The destruction we wrought upon China

during the invasion is so great that what has been destroyed can never be restored or compensated for. However, even now, more than forty years after the end of the war, I do not think that we Japanese have done enough to compensate for what we *can* compensate for— either economically or culturally. The annexation of Korea in 1910 is no bygone matter when we consider the discriminatory status that some six hundred thousand Korean residents in Japan are now suffering. Furthermore, when we see our government supporting a South Korean government which oppresses aspirers to democracy in that nation, we see clearly that Japan is indeed one of the powers that oppresses the third world. Such must also be the national image of Japan not only to seekers of democracy in South Korea but to democratic forces throughout Asia as well.

I must listen with undivided attention to the criticisms of my colleagues, and especially to our participant from the Philippines, Kidlat Tahimik. Japan and the Japanese betray democratic aspirants in third world countries. We are often aggressors toward nations of the third world, of which we ourselves are in fact a member. The burden of that image weighs heavily on my back.

What, then, is the image of Japan and the Japanese in the eyes of the industrialized nations? If I, during my stay here in the United States, am welcomed by neutral smiles, that is because I am a Japanese whose job is to produce Japanese novels and not automobiles, TV sets, or audio equipment—which are highly competitive in the international market. I am free from the hearty welcomes of the happy users of Japanese products. At the same time, I am free from the overt antagonisms of workers engaging in the manufacture of products that must compete with Japanese ones. Nevertheless, when I compare this visit with my first one to this country twenty years ago, by the mere fact of my being Japanese I cannot help but feel a strong sense of crisis. Although I have always sensed that crisis in Japan, coming here has made me feel the crisis more acutely.

The crisis that I feel is the crisis of living in a country which, though an economic giant with its huge trade surplus, is dependent on imports for most of its food and resources. It is a nation where the livelihood of its people will be devastated if the balance of imports and exports is disrupted. I feel the crisis of living in a country which, in its process of rising to the status of a technically advanced nation, has spread pollution everywhere and is unable to find a solution to it. I feel the danger of living in a country which, though having experienced the Hiroshima and Nagasaki bombings, is now run by a government that can only support the United States SDI program, thereby helping spread the nuclear-deterrence myth in the Far East.

Because of her wealth, Japan is now a member of the advanced nations, but, to be sure, she is not an independent nation which implements plans of her own to establish world peace. I feel the crisis of being a citizen of a nation of self-satisfied people—as evidenced in the recent national election (1986) by the landslide victory of the party led by Prime Minister Nakasone, President Reagan's good friend and colleague. As one Japanese intellectual, I have come to sense the crisis stronger than ever through my visit here. I shrink back in fear when I think that the people on those four islands in the Far East are heading for destruction without knowing it, but in a few weeks I will have to go back to those islands and become lost in the crowd there.

≡≡≡

Such is my frame of reference. I therefore must admit that my presentation may be confusing, because I speak from a standpoint of twofold or perhaps threefold ambiguities. Nonetheless, I wish for myself that I will be able to overcome those ambiguities. I also hope to envisage for myself an idea of Japanese culture that could perhaps play a unique role among the cultures of the third world. In order to accomplish these wishes, I will present to you the ambiguities as ambiguities and would like to ask my fellow panelists to guide me out of them.

As I mentioned to you in the beginning, I suspect that Japanese literature is decaying. That is to say, I suspect with good reason that the Japanese are losing their power to create an active model for the contemporary age and for the future. I suspect that modern Japanese culture is losing its vital force and that we are seeing, as its outcrop, the waning of Japanese literature. In recent years it is said that the one realm of intellectual activity which has seen the sharpest decline is literature. To the younger generation that responds so sensitively to new cultural developments, literature no longer seems to be within their focus of attention. This, I believe, is already an established theory in cultural journalism. I fear that this is an ominous phenomenon foreboding the total destruction of Japanese culture, let alone cultural journalism.

It is not unusual for Kurt Vonnegut to draw figures of Japanese in his tender, pathos-filled, but infernolike paintings of the future world. One such piece is a painting of a city destroyed by a neutron bomb: a city in which human life has been terminated but where the machinery of the highly mechanized Matsushita and Honda factories are still in motion. The roof of one of the buildings is painted with a sharp semblance of Mount Fuji, and the apparently midwestern American city is the Japanese archipelago in metaphor. I cannot deny the possibility wherein Japanese culture, after losing its strength to create a human model to direct its culture toward a new future, shatters and crumbles, only to leave behind in motion such products as automobiles, TV sets, and microcomputers—and the younger generation taking no notice of the oddity of the situation. I would like to examine the present situation of Japanese literature by delving into the foreboding elements of these phenomena.

A characteristic lexical item employed among the writers of Japanese literature is the term *junbungaku*, which in English would translate as "sincere or polite literature" or in French as "belles lettres." It was only after the Meiji restoration that modern literature, with strong European influences, was established in our country. The precursory treatise that provided the rationale for literature in Japan was Tsubouchi Shōyō *Shōsetsu shinzui* (*The Essence of the Novel*), published in 1885—seventeen years after the Meiji restoration. By then, Kitamura Tōkoku, the pioneer in modern Japanese romanticism, who was keenly aware of the goings-on of the society of that period, had already started to use the term *junbungaku*. He wrote that man, "with his iron hammer named 'Historical Treatise,' preaches that 'junbungaku' needs to be crushed and thus endeavors to assail its realm." The term *junbungaku*, as employed by Kitamura Tōkoku, was used as an antithesis to the sciences of philosophy and history with which the Japanese of the early and mid-Meiji era strived to establish the spirit of modernization by borrowing European ideas. Therefore, the term *junbungaku*, when used nowadays, does not denote what it once did. It is used today to refer to, as it were, literature that has passively secluded itself from the literature of the mass media; that is, it is used to denote literature that is not "popular" or "mundane."

My presentation on what is "sincere" literature and what is not may ring strange in the ears of a non-Japanese audience, but I, as a Japanese writer, would like to elaborate on it for the purpose of confirming my identity. Although the term *junbungaku* is now used to differentiate the writer's passive withdrawal from mass-media literature, to Tōkoku, the young poet of romanticism and the rationalist of literature who, during the Meiji period, took the matter of the quest for his identity so seriously, even to the point of suicide, *junbungaku* constituted the antithesis to philosophy and history and was an active intellectual genre that he hoped would help create a spirit of modernization among the Japanese. I feel that it is now necessary for us to reevaluate the term *junbungaku* in light of its two definitions.

The role of literature—insofar as man is obviously a historical being—is to create a model of a contemporary age which envelops past and future and a human model that lives in that age. In Japan, where the history of modern and contemporary literature spans a period of over a hundred years, there have been a few men of letters who, as individuals, have created works which surpassed their times. However, it is only for a short period in the history of modern Japanese literature, a period which we refer to as the postwar era, that a group of writers, as a definite literary current, have clearly provided a contemporary age and a human model which inhabited that age. It was a new literary phenomenon that started immediately after the defeat in the Pacific War, in which Japan, in 1945, experienced the bombings at Hiroshima and Nagasaki. This postwar literature was a vital force, especially during the first ten years after the war. Although it is hard to say exactly when it ended, I believe it continued to thrive while postwar writers vigorously continued to produce their works, even amid various other literary currents.

Were we to look at specific examples, such as Ōoka Shōhei's novelistic account "The Battle of Leyte" (1969) and Takeda Taijun's "Mount Fuji Sanitarium," the year 1970 seems to serve as a fair guideline. That was also the year Mishima Yukio committed suicide after calling for a coup d'état by members of the Self-Defense Forces—the de facto armed forces of Japan. A comprehensive analysis of the post-war writers brings to light a contemporary age and a human model they created, and it is to that age and model that Mishima tried to produce a counterpart. Mishima too, however, from a broader per-spective, can be counted as one of the postwar literati.

With this chronology, we find that postwar literature was, in the history of modern and contemporary Japanese literature, a literature that strived to provide a total, comprehensive contemporary age and a human model that lived it. It was literature that endeavored to grapple squarely with the needs of intellectuals, and in fact "postwar literature" did win firm support from intellectuals in various fields. *Junbungaku*, which Tōkoku had proclaimed in defiance of philosophy and history in order to assert his raison d'être, was still in its embryo stage in the middle of the Meiji era. Tōkoku, calling out desperately for the protection of *junbungaku*, built a fence around a lot next to the edifices erected by the philosophy-and-history architects who had imported know-how and material from Europe, so that he and his compatriots would at least later have something on which to build their house. It can rightly be said that Tōkoku's toil and labor bore fruit in the form of postwar literature.

How was it possible for postwar literature to accomplish this? The feat can be attributed to historical pressures. The postwar literati started to publish their works within two or three years after Japan's defeat. Haniya Yutaka's "Ghosts," Noma Hiroshi's "Dark Pictures," Mishima Yukio's "Cigarette," Takeda Taijun's *Saishi kajin*, and Ume-zaki Haruo's *Sakurajima* are works which appeared only a year after the war. (For Mishima, however, *Confessions of a Mask*, published in 1949, is more characteristic of postwar literature than "Cigarette.") The year 1947 saw the publication of Shiina Rinzō's "Midnight Feast." A year after that came Shimao Toshio's "Island's End," Ōoka Shōhei's "Prisoner of War," and Abe Kōbō's "Road Sign at the End of the Street"—and here already we have the whole array of the postwar literati. These are writers who had to endure silence while fascism prevailed prior to and during the war years. Their pent-up frustrations became the springboard for forming their identity as intellectuals. On Japan's day of defeat their ages ranged from twenty to thirty-six; Mishima was the youngest and Ōoka Shōhei the oldest.

During the years of intellectual suppression—that is, during the immediate prewar period and the war itself—Haniya experienced Marxism through the peasant movement, Noma through the liberation movement of the *buraku*, a socially disadvantaged class of people. Takeda and Shiina suffered oppression for having participated in leftist activities while a student and laborer respectively. Ōoka had been taken prisoner by the United States forces. Noma, Takeda, and Umezaki had been drafted. When report of defeat reached Shimao, he was a Kamikaze pilot awaiting orders for a suicide attack. Neither Abe nor Mishima—the youngest of the writers—was free from the turmoil of the colonies or from the effects of student mobilization.

Over and beyond their experiences of harsh reality, these writers were either researchers in some special field of interest or, at the least, very careful readers. Haniya and Shiina studied Dostoyevski. Takeda read Lu Xun, Noma immersed himself in French symbolism, and Ōoka read Stendhal. In fact, all the postwar writers were young intellectuals who had endeavored to establish their identities by absorbing the literary impact from Europe. Unable to give vent to self-expression during the war years, these intellectuals honed their intellectualism and lived reality with a spirit of defiance against the battlefields and the fascist government that ruled them. Postwar literature was, in other words, a literary activity which these intellectuals had started simultaneously, once given the freedom to express themselves.

The defeat in the Pacific War, which brought about a decisive period of transition among the postwar writers, was, needless to say, the most important of events that ever took place in Japan's history of modernization since the Meiji restoration. For Japan, which had pursued modernization all the while and had dared to compete with the imperialist nations of the West, the defeat was nothing less than the revelation of a multifarious impasse for an imperialistically underdeveloped nation. The surrender also led to an examination of askew elements in Japanese culture and tradition of premodernization days. Moreover, the defeat spurred a reform which supplied momentum to third world–oriented liberation opportunities both within and outside the nation.

Were we to search for a metaphor for this situation in literature,

I would suggest Dickens's novels, which are studded with "units" that convey diverse meanings. As we read on, the "units" progress along the path Dickens plots for each of them. When the novel is completed, he affixes to each of the units a retrospective light by means of which each comes to bear full meaning. The individual units are alive already and have significant import in themselves within the story as it progresses, yet the light which emanates from the denouement reveals to us not a contradiction but a new import; and because of the fact that the final light imparts a new significance to the individual units in addition to the one they bore amid the progress of the story, the units take on twofold meanings, thus giving the story itself a new significance.

The diverse units which modernization bore ever since the Meiji restoration came to reveal twofold meanings upon surrender, that light which shone retrospectively from the finale. That is to say, the Japanese, through defeat in the Pacific War, saw for the first time the entire picture of the modernization of a nation called Japan. At that time it was postwar literature which depicted most sensitively and most sincerely that very picture of Japan and the Japanese.

At the international level Japanese modernization took the form of annexation of Korea, invasion of China, and wars of aggression in other regions of Asia. However, the intellectuals who had had to participate in these incidents and who witnessed the utter downfall of such imperialistic expansion, wrote of what they saw in various ways. Takeda Taijun and Hotta Yoshie wrote about what they saw in China. Noma Hiroshi and Ōoka Shōhei wrote of what they witnessed in the Philippines. The literary activities among Korean nationals in Japan correspond to those by Japanese writers who wrote from the standpoint of Japan as an aggressor nation. Korean writers in Japan wrote in Japanese and delved into the matter of Japan's colonial rule over the Korean peninsula, a matter which has ramifications and legacies even today. Okinawa, under the Ryukyu Empire, long maintained its own political system and a culture with strong cosmological features. After being taken over by Japan, however, Okinawa was victimized in the process of Japan's modernization to an extent incomparable to that of any other prefecture. The fact that Okinawa became the sole battlefield on Japanese soil speaks for itself. The

Pacific War culminated in the battles at Okinawa and left the islands in a state of total devastation. Even after the signing of the peace treaty, Okinawa remained under the dominion of the United States forces for years to come, but all the while she strived and managed to accomplish her own reconstruction. Because of this experience, Okinawa has a self-expression of her own.

The self-expression of the people of Okinawa is a product of their realistic ideas, efforts, and cultural tradition. We can find, in their expression, direct and important clues by which Japanese can search for a life-style which does not pose a threat to any of the nations in Asia. The writers who start by asking how to recover from the experiences of the Hiroshima and Nagasaki bombings bear in mind the movement which seeks the enactment of the A-Bomb Victims' Relief Law. The movement is also one which is making a continuous effort for the eradication of all nuclear weapons. Those writers gaze squarely at the destructive impasse to which Japan's modernization from the Meiji restoration brought us. It is here that we can discover for ourselves a principle as to how Japan and the Japanese should live in Asia in this new nuclear age. An examination of whether or not this principle has become a general one among the Japanese in the past forty years should be the basis for criticism of Japan and the Japanese today.

If we were to add to the list of postwar writers the name of Hara Tamiki, who wrote of his experiences as an A-bomb victim in Hiroshima and who chose to commit suicide as soon as a new conflict —the Korean War—broke out, it will become all that much clearer that the major preoccupation of postwar writers was to examine, with the force of their imagination, what, in pursuit of modernization, Japan and the Japanese had done to Asia and to the vulnerable elements within the nation, how the impasse foreboded defeat, and what means of resuscitation were possible for the nation after it died a national death.

We should also examine how the postwar writers dealt with the problem of the emperor system, for this was the cultural and political axle upon which Japan's modernization revolved. One of the conditions necessary for the nation's modernization was national unity. Thus, the emperor was made the absolute figurehead, and modernization was pursued under the pretext of his inviolable authority. What this actually meant was the deification of the emperor. At the beginning of the new year following the defeat, the emperor issued a proclamation that he was no deity, a proclamation to which Mac-Arthur expressed satisfaction. The fact that soon afterward another "emperor," a certain "Emperor Kumazawa," appeared, claiming to be the descendant of an emperor in the Middle Ages, is an indication of one of the diversities and the astounding amount of total energy which the deified emperor had been suppressing.

The Great Japanese Imperial Army which invaded all regions of Asia was nothing but the emperor's armed forces. In Okinawa, the only Japanese soil on which any battle was fought, many citizens died. Analysts claim that the tragedy the Okinawans had had to suffer was exacerbated by their sense of loyalty to the emperor, a loyalty stronger than that embraced by Japanese on the mainland, for they took greater pride in the fact that they, after the Meiji restoration, were admitted as children of the emperor for the first time in their history.

The aims of the postwar writers were to "relativize" the value of the emperor, who had had absolute power, and to liberate the Japanese from the curse of the emperor system which haunted their minds, even at the subconscious level. Were we to view the emperor system as positioned at the peak of the structural hierarchy, Noma Hiroshi depicted the lowest, the social outcasts for whom he had been working since before the war. Noma continued to write even after it was common knowledge within journalistic circles that the period of postwar literature was over. *Ring of Youth*, a novel on which he spent many years, was completed a year after Mishima's suicide. The work depicts a scene in which the outcasts demonstrate a show of force in a mass movement and emerge victorious. The victory is a short-lived one, but the mere fact that Noma depicted a victory by those who had been most oppressed is in itself very meaningful.

Mishima's call for a coup d'état in the compounds of the Self-Defense Forces in Ichigaya and his subsequent suicide constituted essentially a theatrical performance. In his later years Mishima's political, ethical, and aesthetic principles centered on his deep lamentation for the emperor, who had proclaimed he was not a deity but a human being. Mishima's suicide is an incident which can never be effaced from our memory, for he supposedly had prepared a baleful ghost to appear time and time again whenever Japan encountered a political crisis. This is one of the reasons why I have set 1970 as the year in which the curtain fell for postwar literature—literature which, through Japan's defeat in 1945, was begun as a means of giving vent to cultural energies that had been suppressed since the prewar days. What I mean now by the portents of the decay of Japanese literature is nothing other than the loss of the unique status which postwar literature had established in the realm of Japanese culture. In other words, the literary force which postwar literature had once possessed to enlighten Japan and the Japanese to reality and culture is now being lost.

What, then, is the situation of *junbungaku* in the latter half of the 1980s? Young intellectuals who respond quickly to intellectual fads say that *junbungaku* is already dead, or that it is about to breathe its last. They believe that although there still may be some literary activity shoved away in some bleak corner of journalism where the survivors are barely making a living, the latter will sooner or later fade away in the natural course of events. This group of young intellectuals is composed of critics, playwrights, screenwriters, and introducers of new and diverse literary theories from America and Europe. It even includes writers whose works are not considered to be in the realm of *junbungaku* as well as journalists in various fields and a group who nowadays in our country enjoy the greatest popularity among the younger generation: the copywriters of commercial messages. One might also add almost all the "cultural heroes" of today's grotesquely bloated consumer society in Japan. Lack of activity in the realm of *junbungaku* can be substantiated objectively when we compare the volume of its publication with that of other literature, such as popular historical novels, science fiction, mysteries, and various nonfiction categories. Although, obviously, the prewar period and the war years provide no basis for comparison, never have there been so many publications in Japan as in the past forty years. The number of *junbungaku* publications, however, is inversely proportional to the increase in the amount of the other publications. Moreover, there is not one work of *junbungaku* to be found in the 1985 list of the ten best-selling Japanese books in either fiction or nonfiction.

Amidst such a trend, Murakami Haruki, a writer born after the war, is said to be attracting new readers to *junbungaku*. It is clear, however, that Murakami's target lies outside the sphere of *junbungaku*, and that is exactly where he is trying to establish his place. It is generally believed that there is nothing that directly links Murakami with postwar literature of the 1946–1970 period. (As a hasty aside here, I believe that any future resuscitation of *junbungaku* will be possible only if ways are found to fill in the wide gap that exists between Murakami and pre-1970 postwar literature.)

Another indicator of the long downward path that *junbungaku* is taking can be seen by the long business slump for literary monthlies peculiar to Japan, those magazines which had helped nurture and develop short stories unique to Japanese literature. I am sure that those literary magazines are periodicals of least concern to the young intellectuals who now are the vanguard of Japan's consumer society. However, looking back on the first ten years after the war, such magazines, together with numerous general-interest publications, played an important role in maintaining high cultural standards. Almost all the representative literary works—the ones I have mentioned above —were, as was common practice in the publishing system of our nation, first published in literary magazines. It can be said that the slumping literary magazines are eliciting derisive criticism among the young intellectuals who have no direct means of recalling the glory and grandeur of those magazines, except as myth.

I must also mention the season of rationality which started to flourish from the latter half of the 1970s and lasted through the first half of the 1980s, a period which coincides with the decline of *junbungaku*. So strong was its force that it overwhelmed intellectual journalism. Rationality was the fad among new cultural theories, all of which were imported from Europe and the United States. Here we must not forget that the intellectuals who established postwar literature were those who had been educated before or during the war years and had acquired a certain cultural sophistication. Almost all of them had been greatly influenced by cultural theories of Western Europe or of Russia, whose thoughts reached Japan via Western Europe. The eyes and ears of Japanese intellectuals after the Meiji restoration had always been directed toward the West. Rare specimens among the postwar writers were Shiina Rinzō and Takeda Taijun. Instead of pursuing higher education, Shiina spent his youth as a laborer. What prepared him for literature was his involvement in the Marxist socialist movement, but what converted him from Marxism was his encounter with Dostoyevski. Takeda studied Chinese classical literature while Japanese imperialism was quickly preparing to invade China. Takeda was greatly influenced by Lu Xun, but Dostoyevski too was a thinker without whom he would not have been able to establish his identity.

It is from these writers, and from others who had been influenced by Western literature and thought, that postwar literature was born. Their methodology for delving deep into Japanese traditional thought and culture was also, first of all, Western. The same fact is evident when we examine the manner in which Maruyama Masao established his school of Japanese political thought. Maruyama was a salient contemporary of the postwar writers. By studying those writers, Maruyama in turn opened new horizons for them. The predilection for Western culture which prevailed among the intellectuals who were the vanguard of Japanese modernization carried over to the generation that came after them and continued to characterize their culture.

The Mexican thinker Octavio Paz marks 1968 as an extremely significant year and calls our attention to the series of protest movements and riots that occurred in Prague, Chicago, Paris, Tokyo, Belgrade, Rome, Mexico City, and Santiago. Student riots raged everywhere like a medieval plague, affecting the populace regardless of religious denomination or social class, only on a broader scale. Because the riots were spontaneous, they were all the more universal, and Paz analyzed their significance in light of the situation in which all technological societies, East or West, found themselves. In Japan it was the time when the United Red Army, formed three years after the Tokyo riots, trod the path toward annihilation. The bodies of numerous Red Army members executed in cold blood by their colleagues were dug up after the Asama Mountain Villa incident of 1972, a year which happens to coincide with the approximate time when postwar literature came to a close. As if in reaction to the political years, the new generation's cultural trend of the 1970s and 1980s swung toward antipolitics. What Paz had pointed out about identical subcultural trends having global horizontal ties had become apparent also in Tokyo.

It must be borne in mind that it was these events which prepared the way for the advent of the season of rationality, a trend for new cultural ideas imported from the United States and from Europe. Speaking for myself, as one writer, I evaluate very highly the diversified cultural thoughts springing forth from structuralism, for they provide a strong and vital incentive in the field of literature. Later I shall elaborate on one example of the effectiveness of its introduction. So strong has been its influence that I am even tempted to offer a comparison of the diverse influences of the structuralism-based cultural ideas of the 1970s and 1980s with the strong galvanizing influence Marxism had exercised on the Japanese mentality when it flourished for a short time before the war.

So great was the influx of new cultural theories following the advent of structuralism that it appeared they were going to permeate the whole of the nation's intellectual climate. An excellent summary of the new cultural theories of the West, *Structure and Power* by a young scholar named Asada Akira was read everywhere on university campuses. The book sold equally well outside academe and became the most widely read work by any of the postwar writers. *Structure and Power* was by no means easy reading; however, no work of *jun-bungaku* published during that period was able to generate as much intellectual interest among the younger generation. There followed a time in which many new French cultural ideas—some of which came via the United States—were introduced and translated, including poststructuralism and postmodernism, particularly the work of Barthes, Foucault, Derrida, Lacan, Kristeva, and the Yale School of deconstructionists. As far as translations are concerned, aside from those works of mere journalistic faddishness, works of sincere toil and labor started to appear in the latter half of the 1980s. Despite this fact, however, by then intellectual enthusiasm among the younger generation for these new cultural thoughts had come to an end, as it had within the realm of intellectual journalism which had staged, directed, and reflected that enthusiasm. I was by that time no longer a young writer and had never been part of that boom; but as I stand amid the wrack and ruin of the voluminous introductory works and translations and look back upon that age, I notice several interesting characteristics.

First, the young Japanese intellectuals, true to our national character, analyzed and systematized diachronically the various structuralism-based theories and also the criticisms thereof in order to "accept" and—to use an antonym not quite appropriate for this word—"discharge" those theories. For acceptance of Foucault, Barthes had to be discharged. Only after Lacan was dismissed could Derrida be accepted—but only to await the next new thinker. The shuttling of new cultural theories was, up to a point, an easy task for the introducers and translators who advocated their influx. Cultural heroes came and went. However, the curtain dropped on new cultural trends in our country as soon as these advocates found there was no one thinker or cultural theory for them to shuttle on the American and European conveyor belt.

At the height of the ongoing process of accepting and discharging new cultural theories, very often such phrases as "the performance of ideas" or "the frolicking with texts" came to be used. Without having to refer to any authority on words, I believe that those expressions were indeed very appropriate ones for those who could involve themselves only passively in coping with the kaleidoscope of ideas, for they were, by using those expressions, providing a definition of their identities. Also, amid this cultural trend, a very Japanese connotation was added to the usage of the prefix *post-*. By speaking of "poststructuralism" or "postmodernism," or even of cultural thoughts that were yet to come and for which they were unable to envisage any positive ideas (although obviously we could never expect them to do so, since all they did was passively accept and then discharge), the young Japanese intellectuals conjectured optimistically that, insofar as some cultural theory was in existence, a new one would follow if they simply added the prefix *post-* to the existing one. I am sure that there were not a few young intellectuals who were stricken by a series of self-destructive impulses when they learned that the concept of "post-such-and-such" was in fact insubstantial and when, in turn, they learned that the "such-and-such" thoughts in themselves meant very little, if anything at all.

Second, despite this remarkable trend for absorbing new cultural theories, almost no effort was made to interpret them meticulously in view of specific situations in which Japan found itself. Why then did the new cultural theories from Europe and the United States become so popular among the young intellectuals and in the realm of intellectual journalism? This is indeed the strange part of the story. However, I believe the phenomenon can be attributed mostly to the special characteristic which our nation's intellectual journalism had nurtured ever since the Meiji restoration. To put it very bluntly, there was an inclination for people to think that an intellectual effort had been accomplished merely by transplanting or translating the new American and European cultural thoughts into Japanese; and both the translators and those who read the translations were inclined to think in the same manner. Such a tendency exists even today.

Since the most important skills required in the task of introducing new cultural ideas were the abilities to read the foreign language in which those thoughts were presented and to translate the works into Japanese, the spokesmen for those ideas were often specialists in literature or languages. Even when cultural theories were replaced in rapid succession, the replacement did not apply to the spokesmen, because they were not necessarily advocates—or critics, for that matter—of what they spoke for. This fact brought about the lukewarm situation whereby a handful of literature and language specialists became the importers of new cultural theories. Obviously, the responsibility does not rest solely with these specialists. If the readers had read their introductions and translations in a way that would have enabled them to apply the new cultural theories in interpreting Japan's reality, their understanding of these theories would have been raised to a higher level. Such an understanding would have fostered the ability even to offer feedback to the sources of those ideas. It would then not have been possible for each new cultural theory itself and for those who had had a hand in introducing it in Japan to remain free from criticism. However, such was not the case. As soon as an introduction or translation was made, the one-way flow from Europe and America to Japan was completed. That is to say, its "acceptance" and "discharge" was over. That is how the continual expectation of new trends in theory became a convention.

This tendency has produced another characteristic phenomenon in today's Japanese cultural climate: namely, the absence of any and all effort to accept a variety of cultural thoughts synchronically. Never have we witnessed, in intellectual journalism in our country, the synchronic existence of two opposing new schools of thought—for example, structuralism and deconstructionism—and the resulting combination of antagonism and complementarity which can lead, in turn, to a mutual deepening of the two schools. That is why—with the exception of the architect Isozaki Arata, who in his works substantiated his criticism of postmodernism—the cultural anthropologist Yamaguchi Masao, the forerunner among introducers of new cultural theories, stands out as unique and is now being subjected to a reappraisal. Going against the general trend, Yamaguchi, in his work *Periphery and Center*, employed a structuralistic methodology and provided substantiation for his unique cultural interpretation of Japan's reality. In his discussion of postwar literature and its importance, his theory, together with its diverse implications, was extremely effective in clarifying the significance of the emperor system. Yamaguchi had been originally a specialist in monarchism, with field-study experience in Nigeria.

Criticism arose claiming that, in any examination of Japanese reality, placing importance on peripheral cultures and energizing them will not lead to the reversal of the relationship between those peripheral cultures and the central one. In other words, Yamaguchi's ideas were attacked as being nonrevolutionary. Critics of his theory asserted that stimulating the periphery would function effectively only in establishing a more solid central authority and that therefore the ideas in Yamaguchi's *Periphery and Center* were reactionary. A political short circuit was the pith and the marrow of their critiques. Their charges overlooked the fact that Yamaguchi's structuralism was one scrupulously calculated—that is to say, that he had something prepared for later which a methodology based on deconstructionism would reveal. Because Yamaguchi's ideas in *Periphery and Center* were based on structuralist methodology but from the outset coexisted synchronically with criticism based on deconstructive methodology, these ideas were made even more profound, thus allowing them to bear more realistic validity. In fact, Yamaguchi proved, by citing from Japanese mythology and from literature of the Middle Ages various examples of ways in which, despite the dichotomy between those who were driven away from society into the periphery and the chosen ones in the center (the imperial family), that the two often "blended together like fresh ink spots on blotting paper."

Although Yamaguchi's political thought overlaps with that of Mishima Yukio, the two point at diametrically opposite poles. To be sure, Mishima, who lamented the fact that the emperor made his "Human Proclamation" after the defeat and who called for the Self-Defense Forces to rise up in a coup d'état as the emperor's forces, sought to absolutize the emperor system in the context of a cultural principle and in it to seek a paradigm of political unity among the Japanese. In short, if Yamaguchi's ideas as expounded in *Periphery and Center* were to activate the peripheral aspects of Japanese culture and that, in turn, were to result in the strengthening of the center—namely, the emperor system—the resulting system would be totally different from the one Mishima advocated. What is more, Yamaguchi's emperor system would never be the kind which might serve as a guiding principle for the Self-Defense Forces to carry out a coup d'état. When we reread Yamaguchi's cultural theory in light of contemporary reality, we find that there is no room in his thought that would allow for a political short circuit or a political reaction. With its truly free laws of behavior, Yamaguchi's ideas on culture, as evidenced also in his unique "trickster" theory, left no room whatsoever for short-circuited criticism stemming from uncompromising political ideologies. However, Yamaguchi's precursory work leading to the rise in new cultural theories was not followed up well by the introducers of these theories—in other words, the cultural heroes of the late 1970s and early 1980s. It is precisely here that we can find the means to illuminate the full scope of the question I have raised.

———

I began my presentation by stating that Japanese literature is decaying and referred specifically to postwar literature, which represents the highest level of literary achievement since the Meiji restoration and the onset of Japan's modernization. I also noted the evident decline of Japanese literature at that highest level—termed *junbungaku* in Japanese—and how various cultural theories and critical isms, which replaced *junbungaku* in capturing the minds of young intellectuals, came to be accepted and discharged in a manner quite peculiar to our nation. I believe what these phenomena pointed to as a natural course of events was the following situation: young intellectuals during the late 1970s and early 1980s felt the decline of Japanese literature most keenly and fell head over heels for new cultural theories from Europe and America. In fact, so great was the number of introductory books and translations that these seemed to outnumber each year's new literary works. However, enthusiasm for new cultural theories was short-lived, coming and going after only a short craze.

In the context of the cultural climate of Japan, the new cultural theories, as one organic part of literature's decline, fell prey to the general flow toward decay faster than literature. I believe that the two phenomena—literature and its readers on the one hand, and, on the other, new cultural theories and the young intellectuals who accepted them—should be viewed not as dichotomous adversaries but as one entity "blended together like fresh ink spots on blotting paper."

In a broader perspective, one can say that the young intellectuals were not truly intellectuals as such, but merely young Japanese living a subcultural fad in an urbanized, average consumer culture. Moreover, if one were to extrapolate from the analyses of sociologists which point to the fact that the prevalent middle-class consciousness, though filled with disparities when seen in light of the actual lives of the Japanese on the whole, is shared far and wide in Japan, one could say that such a phenomenon attests to the fact that, in comparison to the days of the student riots, young Japanese have indeed become conservative. Political scientists have attested to the fact that the conservative trend among the younger generation in the large urban areas has played an important role in the recent landslide victory of the ruling conservative party. What this means is that signs of a conservative trend have begun to emerge quite noticeably in the big cities, where the bulk of the younger generation dwells; and such signs will soon start to appear in small cities as well, since the younger generation is conjoined by an urbanized culture that spans the nation.

Now, the problem, in the context of our discussion, is that this younger generation, so closely conjoined subculturally on a nationwide level, is abandoning literature. Moreover, this is the same younger generation which promptly interred, as things of the past, the trend toward new cultural theories which in many respects over-lapped with the subcultural fad they embraced. Asada Akira's trea-tise *Structure and Power* at one time became a fad on university cam-puses and occasionally was referred to as the "Asada phenomenon." I cannot simply dismiss this as a mere fad, because it is possible for such a trend among the younger generation to merge with the new cultural theories and then bear positive fruit. When we look back on the various cultural phenomena, that is what actually occurred in many countries after World War II. However, as mentioned earlier, that is not how things turned out in Japan.

The postwar writers and those who created cultural theory for their contemporaries were people who had gone through the hard-ships of war. Their being one with the younger generation enabled their works to effect a positive influence upon the younger genera-tion, who sought a means of resuscitation at a difficult time in a society that had recently suffered defeat. It is thus that they were able to educate the youth of a generation which followed their own. Speaking for myself, as far as literature is concerned, it is the post-war writers who laid the foundations for my own writing. As far as politics goes, the conservative party has been monopolizing the political scene for a long time. However, I believe that the genera-tion which overlapped with the readers of postwar literature dem-onstrated its strength by casting enough votes for opposition-party members so that the latter won enough seats to keep the ruling party in check. The people's movement in 1960 to protest the ratification of the new Japan–United States Security Treaty was a movement which had actively incorporated the opinions of the postwar writers and those of the cultural theorists. It was a movement which was equally as powerful as, and more animated than, the opposition progressive parties and the labor unions. A comparison of the political and cul-tural situation of those years—twenty years ago—with that of today sheds light on what it is exactly that has been lost and how we lost it. The light shines upon the road along which twenty years have taken us and also upon a very symbolic phenomenon: literature treading its path to wrack and ruin.

So, what is to be done? I, as a writer, think of what the critical path has been and what it should be for Japan and the Japanese from the standpoint of literature. I believe that by reflecting on the cultural climate of Japan in the latter half of the 1970s and the first half of the 1980s, we can see therein glimpses of what course of action we should take. What occurred during that period was the recurrence of short cycles of introductions of new cultural theories from America and Europe. It seemed that the acceptance and discharge of those theories was gradually accelerated, but in the end all enthusiasm for cultural theories died out. Although the diachronic, one-dimensional acceptance and discharge of new cultural theories continued, no effort had been made to interpret those theories in light of Japan's reality and culture. This sort of situation can never occur in societies that produce cultural theories; it can only occur in a country where the vast ocean separates it from the country that produces those theories, where the introduction of theories follows the overcoming of linguistic barriers, where there exists a fad-sensitive intellectual journalism that transmits those ideas, and where there are receivers of what such journalism transmits. In other words, with only a few exceptions, the Japanese were not able to establish a cultural theory of their own —something which could have been realized if they had examined the theories they imported in light of Japan's reality and culture. If that had been done, the resulting feedback from such an examination would have enabled the Japanese to establish a new cultural theory of their own. Though Japan experienced a period of great enthusiasm for new cultural theories, the theories essentially had nothing to do with Japan's reality and culture, and today we have as a result a situation in which those theories have become as remote an existence as they had been from the very outset.

In light of this situation, we see clearly what is lacking in terms of cultural work that is being done by Japanese today. Japan's modernization beginning with the Meiji restoration ran into a fatal impasse —namely, the Pacific War—and culminated in defeat. Upon very sincere reflection, the Japanese searched for various principles to guide them in making a fresh, new start, and the aim of the postwar writers was to provide literary conviction and expression of such principles. However, the intellectuals of the new generation, those of the 1970s and 1980s, have not followed up on these principles, nor have they taken a critical stance toward them. They had no intention of developing such principles in the first place. There is indeed a wide gap between the postwar intellectuals and those of the younger generation, as is clear when we look at how the younger intellectuals of the 1970s and 1980s, by not probing into the various accomplishments of the postwar writers or what they tried to achieve, severed any continuity with the postwar intellectuals.

Many of the postwar writers even went through the bitter experience of fighting in the war as soldiers, and, following defeat, they delved into the matter of Japan's new direction, a direction contrary to that which Japan had taken in her process of modernization. In other words, they envisaged a way for Japan to live as one nation in Asia, as one of the third world nations in Asia. The path Japan had taken prior to the defeat was one in which she had set up the central nations of the world—the United States and the European countries—as paradigms to follow. The postwar writers, however, envisaged a path quite the contrary and aimed at establishing an awareness of a principle in which Japan's place in the world would be not in the center but on the periphery. What the Japanese had abandoned in pursuing a center-oriented modernization, the postwar writers endeavored to revive by also learning domestically from Okinawa, which had a cultural tradition of its own, and internationally from Korea, which was instilling a typically Asian prosperity and diversity.

I would add that, as a writer who has engaged in literary activities with the awareness that I carry on the heritage of the postwar writers, I have while writing always borne in mind the island of Okinawa, a peripheral region of Japan, and South Korea, a peripheral nation of the world—and in the latter case especially the works of the modern Korean poet Kim Chi Ha. Also, I have employed in my writing the image system of grotesque realism as my weapon. I would note as well that by considering the cultural characteristics of the peripheral regions of Japan and those of Asia, I have trod a path lead-ing to the "relativization" of an emperor-centered culture. In that regard, I have chosen a course exactly the opposite of that taken by Mishima, who strove to absolutize the emperor system. My novel *Contemporary Games*, which I completed at the end of the 1970s, is a work in which I aimed at creating a model regarding reality and culture for the kind of Japan I envisage.

I believe that the problem Japanese literature faces today lies in the fact that the attitude toward reality and culture which the postwar writers had nurtured and which was followed up by the writers who came after them was severed completely by the young intellectuals of the 1970s and 1980s. It was amid such discontinuity in attitude toward reality and culture that the fad for new cultural ideas flourished.

Japan as a third world nation has an ambiguous place in the world and an ambiguous role to play. The young Japanese intellectuals had a still more ambiguous place in Japan and an equally ambiguous role to play. An examination of these ambiguities in light of the new cul-tural theories and the providing of an interpretation for them would have been a difficult task but one well worth undertaking, for I be-lieve it would have resulted in the development of a cultural theory unique to Japan; if not, at least it would have taken us beyond the realm of the almost automatic process of "accepting" and "discharg-ing" imported theories.

Among intellectuals of the present new generation, there are some who are taking an increased interest in the singularity of the Okina-wan culture, and their interests correspond with the self-expression of the new generation on Okinawa. Many young Japanese who par-ticipated in the protest movement for the release of the poet Kim Chi Ha still empathize with the grass-roots movements for the de-mocratization of South Korea. There is also a movement to keep a close watch on Japan's economic aggression against the Philippines and other Asian nations. The youths involved in that movement are now seeking an alliance on a grass-roots level with the younger gen-eration of other nations. A joining of hands with such youths by the young intellectuals who had played a part in introducing new cul-tural theories can be readily realized, if the latter make an effort to determine how the theories ought to be interpreted in light of Japan's reality and culture, and also if they seek to learn how to plan for the reconstruction of that very reality and culture. Such a merger could bring about direct, concrete results in energizing Japanese literature of the new generation.

═════

The topic of our discussion raises the very relevant question of whether Japanese culture can find a clue for saving itself from the downward path to decline that is so ominously portended by the decline in literature. I can think of no people or nation as much in need of a clue for self-recovery as the Japanese, neither among first nor third world nations; no other people but the Japanese, whose culture evidences a strange blending of first and third world cultures; no other people but the Japanese, who live that reality.

I would like to close by offering as a hint to the Japanese intellectuals of the new generation a positive directive for embarking upon their self-examination vis-à-vis our topic of our discussion. One reason I decided to participate in this symposium is the fact that I myself want to learn, for what I have talked to you about is a bigger question for me than for the young intellectuals. There was in Japan a poet and writer of children's stories, Miyazawa Kenji, who had been assigned a peripheral place in contemporary literature and modern history but whose importance is being recognized slowly but steadily. Miyazawa was born in Tōhoku, a peripheral district of Japan. Being an agronomist, he worked for the Tōhoku farmers, who tilled the soil under adverse conditions. He was a believer in the Saddharma Pundarika Sutra. Under the influence of contemporary Western poetry he established a world of his own expression and imagination. He wrote prolifically while continuing to work as an agronomist, a profession he pursued until his death in 1933 at the age of thirty-seven. His audience was not limited to readers of literature as such and posthumously he has won—and is winning—an even wider spectrum of readers. Very recently, his epic children's story *The Night of the Galaxy Railway* was made into an excellent animated movie, increasing his popularity even more. The question of what is genuine people's literature has been a topic of debate throughout modern and contemporary Japanese literature, but now people have started to realize that it is Miyazawa who deserves to the fullest degree the title "Writer of People's Literature." Sixty years ago, at the dawn of the Shōwa era (1926–), Miyazawa wrote a treatise titled *Outline of the Essentials of Peasant Art*, which epitomizes his ideas both as an agronomist and as a writer. I shall close by quoting its opening paragraph:

> We are all farmers—we are so busy and our work is tough.
>
> We want to find a way to live a more lively and cheerful life.
>
> There were not a few among our very ancient fore-fathers who did live that way.
>
> I wish to hold discussion where there is communion among the facts of modern science, the experiments of the seekers of truth, and our intuition.
>
> One person's happiness cannot be realized unless all the world is happy.
>
> The awareness of the ego starts with the individual and gradually evolves to that of the group, the society, and then the universe. Isn't this the path the saints of yore trod and taught us?
>
> The new age is headed in a direction in which the world shall be one and will become a living entity.
>
> To live strong and true is to become aware of the galaxy within ourselves and to live according to its dictates.
>
> Let us search for true happiness of the world—the search for the path is in itself the path.*

Note

* This paper was delivered at the "Challenge of Third World Culture" Conference at Duke University on 25 September 1986. It was published in *World Literature Today*, 62, No. 3 (Summer 1988), 359–369, with the author's permission.

Alan Wolfe

Suicide and the Japanese Postmodern:
A Postnarrative Paradigm?

Postmodernity has as one of its distinguishing characteristics the capacity and inclination to juxtapose polar opposites: the inhabitant of contemporary modern society accepts as a given the ready proximity of past and present, West and East, rich and poor, high and low culture, public and private, death and life. For some of us, the coexistence of unlimited possibilities with the confining realities of power, language, mechanization, alienation, or nuclear mass destruction renders this modernity a baffling dilemma.

A similar state of affairs was already apparent in high modernism,[1] yet one senses important differences with the postmodern context, differences which are perhaps elucidated by Jean-François Lyotard's view of "the decline of narrative."[2] According to Lyotard, the postmodern, by projecting its perspective into a "future anterior mode," whereby it seeks to "formulate the rules of what will have been done," has the effect not of denying or eliminating the modern, but of undermining the assumptions of progress and meaning upon which the modern is based.³ Or, as Terry Eagleton points out in what seems like an effort to salvage the modern and with it the value of meaning through a transformed and "political" rationality, even "meaninglessnesses" are not equal: "There is a difference . . . between the 'meaninglessness' fostered by some postmodernism, and the 'meaninglessness' deliberately injected by some trends of avant-garde culture into bourgeois morality."⁴ In this sense, the "fragmentary or schizoid self" of the modern, while fraught with contradictions, points to the passion with which modernism seeks to "deconstruct the unified subject of bourgeois humanism." Indeed, for Eagleton, "the fact that modernism continues to struggle for meaning is exactly what makes it so interesting." Postmodernism, on the other hand, while "inheriting" the schizoid self from modernism, "eradicates all critical distance from it."⁵

The stupefying eclecticism of the postmodern juxtaposes the most outrageous things. But, unlike radical avant-gardes of high modernism, the shock value intended for the complacent bourgeois is now itself distanced, muted, inconsequential, and above all paradoxically unself-conscious. How, for example, can we distinguish between the cataclysmic horrors of the twentieth century, from poison gas to Nazi death camps to the atomic bomb to the prospect of total nuclear annihilation? One might suggest that until the full impact of the nuclear threat became manifest, it was still possible to incorporate what Lyotard calls the "unpresentable" in a coherent narrative, an aesthetic context, and confer on it an aura of legitimacy. For example, A. Alvarez considered that even in the face of modern technological mass destruction, it was both possible and desirable, given our "awareness of ubiquitous, arbitrary death [so] central to our experience of the twentieth century," for the artist either to "forge a language which [would] somehow absolve or validate absurd death," or to find a language appropriate to this "dimension of unnatural, premature death."⁶ For Alvarez, this was to be "the language of mourning" that, in Kafka's words, "make[s] us feel as though we were on the verge of suicide."⁷ There is here a belief in the language and power of the artist, and in meaningful action directed toward overcoming this "Savage God" of death. There is also in the modern perspective the sense that no matter how inconceivable the horror, whether it be

Hiroshima or the Nazi death camps, these are the *willful* actions of human beings. There is evil in the world, but it is still contained, and hence presentable within the metanarrative of good and justice vs. evil and injustice.

The thoroughgoing eclecticism of the postmodern, however, collapses these horrors to pastiche. Hiroshima and Hitler both can be, and are, turned into consumer kitsch (T-shirt emblems, sex shop playthings, kamikaze headbands) and even retro, the nostalgia mode of consumption. The space of the postmodern places the inconceivable and unpresentable—total nuclear destruction—next to an advertisement for diapers, and the effect is one of indifference. The willful evil of the modern is transformed into contingent amorality. So a colloquium and issue of *Diacritics* devoted to "nuclear criticism" asks:

> To what extent do all the current versions of apocalypse now merely feed the vice of the hypocritical reader, the deep-seated boredom of an alienated public that dreams of debris, of swallowing the world with a yawn? To what degree do the stereotypes of nuclear destruction, like the proliferative figure of the mushroom cloud, aim to make us forget by their mechanical repetition the reality they are supposed to designate?[8]

Frances Ferguson, for one, answers that "the nuclear as unthinkable [is but] the most recent version of the notion of the sublime."[9] Ferguson's idea of the sublime leans toward the high culture mode of Kantian "irreplaceable subjectivity": "the notion of the sublime is continuous with the notion of nuclear holocaust: to think the sublime would be to think the unthinkable and to exist in one's own existence."[10] Following Kant, she defines the sublime as a "species of experience that explicitly does not ground itself in objects." Sublime objects are those that are "great beyond all measure" such that, unlike objects of beauty, they "elude [our] apprehension." The sublime experience is unique to the individual and nontransferable; furthermore, it eschews contingency and accident, as its goal is to ensure subjective control over an elusive environment. It is this quest for control that leads Ferguson to see a connection between the sublime and suicide.

The insistence in accounts of the sublime on the subject's determination of his own death comes to be a way of underscoring the sublime determination to remove itself from the world of objects subject to accidents. Thus when Schiller describes suicide, taking one's own death into one's own hands, as the inevitable outcome of the logic of the sublime, he is of course right: the outcome of the subject's search for self-determination is not the achievement of absolute freedom in positive form but rather the achievement of a freedom from the conditions of existence by means of one's nonexistence.[11]

Suicide also becomes the ultimate metaphor to suggest the impossibility of both being there and telling the tale. The very effort to diminish contingency has the effect of reducing the beholder of the sublime, the self-contained subjective consciousness, to the status of the *littératuricide* or the symbolic suicide, whose capacity to tell the tale, because it derives from the failure to join the sublime (die), can only result in a disenchantment (a sort of melancholic regret) with one's own waning creative/imaginative powers.[12] Thus does Ferguson show how Jonathan Schell, author of *The Fate of the Earth*, the bestseller on the nuclear issue, in his evocation of the nuclear sublime, ends up focusing on more mundane, more "calculable" matters which have the effect of diminishing the intensity that led to them.

The effort to think the nuclear sublime in terms of its absoluteness dwindles from the effort to imagine total annihilation to something very much like calculations of exactly how horrible daily life would be after a significant nuclear explosion.[13]

Ferguson identifies two aspects of the nuclear sublime which concern us in our effort to locate the possible specificity of Japanese postmodernism. First, she demonstrates how the inevitably anticlimactic rhetoric of the antinuclear movement focuses on the possibility of accident. Almost more horrible than nuclear holocaust itself is the idea that it might happen unintentionally, by mistake. This notion of accidentalism is precisely what the eighteenth-century sublime sought to repudiate. For the eighteenth-century individual subject intent on affirming individual identity by claiming a unique and irreplaceable subjectivity, it is the contemplation of suicide which comes to offer the only means of preempting the usurpation of control by contingency and accident.

Ferguson goes on to argue, on the basis of a suggestive parable she finds in the recent "rediscovery" of Mary Shelley's *Frankenstein*, that "the nuclear sublime operates much like most other versions of the sublime, in that it imagines freedom to be threatened by a power that is consistently mislocated."[14] From the eighteenth century to Jonathan Schell's *The Fate of the Earth*, the rhetoric of the sublime becomes that "nobler search for heroic encounter with the possibility of one's own death" which in fact masks the "world of generation": that is, "the world of society under the aegis of women and children" whose conditions (habit, custom, and familiarity) are so oppressive to the male subject. Ferguson sees the current interest in *Frankenstein* to be due to its "Gothic reversal of the sublime dream of self-affirmation, the fear that the presence of other people is totally invasive and erosive of self."[15] And this perception of a pervasive claustrophobia, which is what the aesthetics of sublimity is designed to counter, can be said to inform Schell's rhetoric of a "cramped, claustrophobic isolation of a doomed present."

> He's right, of course, to want to preserve the planet, the human species, and human culture, but what is particularly striking about his imagery is its portrayal of nuclear threat as a temporal version of claustrophobia that is ultimately less terrifying than the Gothic claustrophobia repeatedly brought on by the pressure of the thought of other minds acting to condition an individual and his dream of the uniqueness of his consciousness.[16]

Ferguson does not bring to bear on the issue of suicide her parallelism between the Kantian and the nuclear sublime. The connection is lurking there, however, and does emerge in another paper, from the same colloquium, by Dean MacCannell. In his discussion of the theory of nuclear deterrence, MacCannell notes that "the [nuclear] leader must exhibit an absolute *will* to use nuclear weapons even in the full knowledge that their use almost certainly means genocide and suicide." In the words of a nuclear analyst: "The enemy should be made aware that . . . danger may get out of hand. National suicide, then, is possible."[17]

A student of Japanese culture and history, familiar with that nation's wartime depiction as an irrational totalitarian monster bent on destruction, cannot help but be struck by the overtones here. That the logic of deterrence, like the logic of war, leads to the acceptance of the possibility of self-destruction is familiar. What is blatent in the nuclear analyst's remark, though, is the crassly strategic nature of the argument, which in effect posits not so much the specter of total annihilation as a postexistence which the leaders themselves have the best chance of attaining. The concept of national suicide, then, is not seen as a way of collectively preempting a nuclear holocaust, but rather of assuring survival and domination for the privileged elite.[18] Even in wartime Japan, most Kamikaze pilots, those literal embodiments of national suicide, were at best reluctant heros. Even so, the association of suicide with Japan has been linked in numerous instances with the motivations of an irrational leadership: the insinuation that the atom bomb was somehow just punishment for unacceptable behavior (as rape is ideologized) is an allusion to a presumed Japanese predilection for bringing death and destruction upon itself. Let us consider this manner of essentializing Japan in what has become one of the more infamous footnotes to history.

Alexandre Kojève (1902–1968), the Marxist philosopher and exegetist of Hegel, includes in a footnote to his second edition of *Introduction to the Reading of Hegel*, an extended meditation on the "disappearance of Man at the end of History." For Kojève in 1948, "the Hegelian-Marxist end of history was not yet to come, but was already present, here and now."[19] And in this "post-historical period," it appeared to him that the " 'American way of life' " was paradigmatic, "the actual presence of the United States in the World prefiguring the 'eternal present' future of all of humanity." Kojève viewed the United States at this point as, incredibly, a "classless society," one in which humans had become "post-historical animals" whose needs were satisfied, and, hence, who no longer had any need for a discursive "*understanding* of the World and of self."[20] But in 1959, after a visit to Japan, Kojève had what he called "a radical change of opinion on this point," leading him to write what may be one of the most startling accounts of Orientalism in the twentieth century.

> There I was able to observe a Society that is one of a kind, because it alone has for almost three centuries experienced life at the "end of History." . . . "Post-historical" Japanese civilization undertook ways diametrically opposed to the "American way." . . . *Snobbery* in its pure form created disciplines negating the "natural" or animal given which in effectiveness far surpassed those that arose, in Japan or elsewhere, from "historical" Action. . . . All Japanese without exception are currently in a position to live according to totally formalized values—that is, values completely empty of all "human" content in the "historical" sense. Thus, in the extreme, *every Japanese is in principle without exception capable of committing, from pure snobbery, a perfectly "gratuitous" suicide . . . which has nothing to do with the risk of life in a Fight waged for the sake of "historical" values that have social or political content. This seems to allow one to believe that the recently begun interaction between Japan and the Western world will finally lead not to a rebarbarization of the Japanese but to a "Japanization" of the Westerners* (including the Russians).[21]

In his final paragraph, Kojève extends his view of posthistorical humanity in a projection that seems to anticipate the postmodern and to relate his evocation of "gratuitous" suicide to a postmodern view of the shocking 1970 *seppuku* or ritual suicide of one of Japan's leading writers, Mishima Yukio.[22]

> Now, since no animal can be a snob, every "Japanized" posthistorical period would be specifically human. Hence there would be no "definitive annihilation" of Man properly so-called. . . . To remain human . . . post-historical Man must *oppose* himself as a pure "form" to himself and to others taken as a "content" of any sort.[23]

The insertion here of a correspondence between a posthistorical period and a postmodern style is emblematized by a view of Japanese suicide in which the subject, as both individual and nation, cancels itself out "gratuitously," as pure form, much in the same way suggested by sympathetic Western "readings" of Mishima's suicide as an exemplary instance of the "nobility of failure." [24]

Kojève's concept of gratuitous suicide, or suicide as pure form, prefigures Roland Barthes's view of Japan a mere twelve years later as an "empire of empty signs." Barthes's ability to view Japan as a series of empty signifiers was possible, as he himself acknowledged, because as an outsider he was unable or unwilling to glimpse the "inside" of oppression and struggle. In this way, like Kojève, he can present to us a reproduction of a photograph of the famous General Nogi Maresuke and his wife prior to their double suicide (in the wake of the Emperor Meiji's death) and tell us that "they knew" that they were going to take their lives. Barthes finds here an instance of a free-floating signifier, or, in Kojève's words, a case of pure form and formality opposed to itself. It is also an appeal to us as reader/voyeur to be complicitous in their knowledge of their own deaths, to accept the possibility that we too can see ourselves as already dead. [25]

What makes both Kojève's and Barthes's views of Japan "postmodern" is not only their fascination with a particular attitude toward death—that is, the possibility of complete control over one's self-destruction—but with its collective aspect: the implication is that all members of the Japanese empire are but empty signs able to erase themselves, an implication we may consider in the context of a specifically postmodern variety of suicide.

The case of Mishima Yukio (1925–1970) is suggestive. In the years since his death, he has come to be seen less as a hero or antihero of anti–modernism than as a pastiche of postmodernism. By the 1980s it is not uncommon for foreign writers to see the *seppuku* of Mishima as a parody of itself.

> His death was to be a warning . . . to the modern world, debased and degraded in the eyes of all those who believe they are alive although they do not know how to die. . . . But that world marked him in spite of himself, as his final act so complicitously testifies: a public/publicity exploit, the trivium of the century, immediately consumed by the society of the spectacle, duly spiced with that pornography of violence with which the media screens are

more and more avidly filled. A comparison of Mishima's boister-
ous death with that of a true soldier in the pure tradition like
Nogi reveals what it is that perturbs and unsettles. Kitsch and
retro: the tradition today is no more than a parody of itself.[26]

Where Maurice Pinguet sees parody, however, and still hopes for
that different truer past of a "pure tradition," we might prefer to see
Fredric Jameson's postmodern "pastiche," the successor to modernist
"parody."

> Pastiche is, like parody, the imitation of a peculiar mask, speech
> in a dead language: but it is a neutral practice of such mimicry,
> without any of parody's ulterior motives, amputated of the satiric
> impulse, devoid of laughter and of any conviction that alongside
> the abnormal tongue you have momentarily borrowed, some
> healthy linguistic normality still exists. Pastiche is thus blank
> parody, a statue with blind eyeballs.[27]

The recent Paul Schrader film *Mishima* provides us with a postmodern Mishima, a pastiche whose past, present, and literary imagination are integrated via multiple media to evoke a Japan of Kojèvian
posthistorical dimension. The use of multihued color on Ishioka
Eiko's futuristic stage sets creates the effect of people as pure form,
as literary cardboard figures living "according to totally formalized
values."[28] And the humorless appeal to psychoanalysis and aesthetics
as the universal keys to the Mishima mystery ("People will understand this film on any level. They'll love it. Paul has made this
literary figure internationally understandable"[29]) reinforces that lack
of conviction in the continued existence of "some healthy linguistic normality." For pretentiousness and lack of humor seem in this
film to be the natural concomitants of Japan's postmodern myth.
Where Mishima himself may be said to have magnified his problems
to a national scale, it was Schrader, according to Ian Buruma, "who
took them seriously enough to blow them up to international proportions."[30] Moreover, "Schrader cannot take his subject lightly, presenting us with a Mishima utterly without charm, a pompous bore" who
only occasionally "unbends" by cracking "some embarrassingly dumb
joke."[31]

If Mishima's own humorless words and writings undermined their

stated purpose of restoring the Japanese spirit to its pure and historical state, so does the context of the late twentieth century. In the
international space of the mass media, the Japanese male becomes the
plastified cartoon image of the samurai/businessman-employee, while
the Japanese woman is projected as the geisha/sacrificing eternal
housewife-mother, both enhancing a vision of life in which values are
"completely empty of all 'human' content in the 'historical' sense."[32]
In such a context, to say that Mishima is exceptional (as Schrader
does) is only to reassert the suspicion lurking in the cesspools of the
Western mind that Kojève's postulation of "gratuitous suicide" could
be true (although one wonders whether Lieutenant Colonel Oliver
North might not be a more worthy exemplar of empty human value
in a historical void): "Thus, in the extreme, every Japanese is in principle without exception capable of committing, from pure snobbery,
a perfectly 'gratuitous' suicide . . . which has nothing to do with the
risk of life in a Fight waged for the sake of 'historical' values that have
social or political content."

The preeminence of Japan as a most exemplary instance of the postmodern is very much a part of a political as well as an aesthetic
discourse which feeds into (and is generated by) two persisting metanarratives: of an unrepentant modernization paradigm, on the one
hand, and of a premodernist nativism with atavistic overtones, on
the other. In other words, inasmuch as the modernization story—in
spite of modernizationist disclaimer smoke screens—is still a vital
structuring reading device, it is clear that an opposition between
modernity and its repressed anti-modern ethos continues to "make a
difference" both in Japanese literature and thought as well as in the
way that the West "reads" Japan.

It has been argued that the construct of modernization has sig-
nificantly informed our understanding of the contemporary world,
including the way in which the first world (and Japan) and the third
world see themselves and each other.[33] In Lyotard's terms, we could
say that modernization theory gave legitimation to our queries about
the world in the "form of a narrative in a set of stories about the
growth of knowledge and culture." Suicide, as a narrative instance
within the metanarrative of modernization, may be seen to serve

as a marker of the "difference that continues to make a difference," whereby those who conceive of and present Japan to themselves or others as a self-contained subject have a stake in its being modern in a progressive (if alienated and nostalgic) mode. So the modern alienated writer may be opposed to the anti-modern regressive mode associated with Mishima. From a postmodern perspective, however, such clear-cut oppositions become a matter not only of "undecidability" but also of indifference as to which aesthetic is or should be dominant.

Unlike a modernist or romantic perspective, therefore, which would highlight the death of the author-creator-artist as a Christ-like sacrificial gesture to humanity (or to one's readership), the postmodern perspective appears to posit the death of both narrator-author *and* listener-reader. This move is implicit in the use of pastiche to characterize the postmodern. The collapsed critical distance implied by Jameson's pastiche (the "statue with blind eyeballs") projects not just the death of the artist but also the death of the audience. Barthes's seductive invitation of the Western reader to the Japanese "empire of empty signs" is part of the process of "Japanization of the Westerner" spoken of by Kojève. It involves the transformation of both author and audience by the image (newspaper and photo) into the "pure snobbery" of surface form and prescient death.[34] The juxtaposition of incongruities and paradoxes designed (or contextualized) to induce unemotional elegance, refined indifference, requires an imaginary voyage into Lyotard's future anterior mode. It requires, in other words, seeing oneself *with the world* as having died and still continuing to exist—as part, therefore, of a living dead. The zombie look is not only a style—it is the way the audience must see itself in order to respond to what it is viewing. How else, for example, can one relate to fashion designer Kawakubo Rei's evocation of rich elegant people in beggar's rags or atom bomb fashions? The postmodern, then, in its particular brand of materiality, which exploits its technological media capabilities to the utmost, pushes its audience to transcend its own fears by going beyond death, or indeed controlling its own death, by fantasizing life after death while still undead. In literary terms, the reader is being asked to narrate his or her own story after the story is over—hence, a postnarrative.

Suicide, always already the conditioning factor for all writing, now offers us the implicit paradigm of the postmodern nuclear suicide. And it does so because of the way in which it reveals the complicity between artist and audience (and not a few critics) to generate a postnarrative narrative. This "postmodern suicide" as a metaphor for writing differs from "modern suicide" in that it posits the death of the narrator *in tandem* with the annihilation of the world. It thus makes suicide a collective act instead of an individual subjective one. Its perception of the world, or of the present viewed as the past from a future time, differs from conventional utopian/dystopian narratives with their exhortation either to appreciate the present or change it. Note how Jimmy Stewart's suicidal ploy in *It's A Wonderful Life* generates a world in which an individual life does make a difference, as maudlin as that vision may be. The postmodern is better evoked by the pop horror of the *Return of the Living Dead* to that deadest of all worlds, the death-in-life of the American shopping mall, where the difference between the zombies and the shoppers is tentative at best.

It may be useful here to return for a moment to Ferguson's nuclear sublime, and to draw two distinctions between it and the postmodern. As noted earlier, Ferguson characterizes the sublime as a male subject's effort to achieve total control over his subjectivity, thus repudiating accidentalism and the claustrophobic presence of "the world of generation" (women and children). Ferguson's critique of Schell's *Fate of the Earth* rests above all on the perception that his postmodern future, like his "cramped, claustrophobic . . . doomed present," is represented as the impingement on the individual consciousness, which alone can aspire to its sublime. But the postmodern eliminates the tension between intention and accident, between isolation and claustrophobia. In the postmodern era, we have become the race of monsters that Frankenstein's creation wanted the doctor to help him to generate; we are the proliferating undead, living dead, vampires that Dracula spawned. The difference between the modern and the postmodern is the difference between Mary Shelley's *Frankenstein* and the pop horror figure we have come to know and love. We recognize not the tortured soul of Shelley's literary imagination, but the technicolor poster of Frankenstein's monster, Boris Karloff's face grinning and proposing to keep us in stitches while visiting Express Health Care at a local hospital, or a companion poster of

Count Dracula inviting us not to let a sore throat become a pain in the neck.

The "world of generation" which becomes so oppressive to the male subject in the eighteenth century is the result of that shift identified by Michel Foucault, whereby the ruler's legitimacy is no longer his power to decree death but rather his ability to manage the organization of life-sustaining potential.[35] If modern suicide offered escape to the modern monarch and modern male subject from his heavy responsibility to provide for the nation and the family—those obstacles to his hard-earned enjoyment of the golf-club sublime—then we can imagine how oppressive must be the postmodern world of generation in which not only are women and children asking for a share of the pie, but so also are all those blacks, Asians, Arabs, Chicanos, etc., not to mention the Europeans, Canadians, and Japanese.

The "Japan as Number One" syndrome is familiar throughout Japan and a good part of the American business community.[36] But it is a bivalent construct that points equally to American and Japanese insecurities, which return us to distinctive characteristics of the postmodern. One aspect of this construct is retro, as suggested by a mildly critical reading of Ezra Vogel's book, subtitled *Lessons for America*, which calls attention to a nostalgia for "lost" American values, now miraculously rediscovered in transmogrified form in postwar Japan. The second has to do with Kojève's posthistorical (nostalgia-free) Japan. Japan as a society with "values completely empty of all 'human' content in the 'historical' sense" is not unlike Frankenstein's monster: it emerges intact out of the atomic ashes of 1945—out of dead or empty life—as a nonhistorical being, a creature without a history. At the same time, this creature has great learning potential (note how Shelley's monster learns to speak, to read, etc.) and strength, but even more importantly is possessed of a sensitivity greater than its master's, in part because of its sense of difference and insecurity about its historical identity.

In the Japanese case, there is no less a sense of being a monster created by the machinations of a mad Western scientist. When Japan seeks to behave like the imperialist master, it is spurned, ostracized, beaten down. Behind the polite respect offered by the good Doctor to his creation is a fear of that creation running amok and overpowering the master, while for the sensitive monster there is the constant embarrassment of having to overcome its physical and cultural "differences."

No Japanese are more aware of this problem as part of the specificity of Japan's postmodern than literary and cultural critics, who, in addition to the social and political struggles that apply in the West, must deal with the dilemma of what has been called by one writer "the Great American Allergy," and by another "the Shadow of America."[37] The ultimate irony of the Japanese postmodern, which makes indifference its trademark, is that the Japanese critic finds it necessary to distinguish once again a uniquely different Japanese postmodern. In this sense, Japanese postmodernism may appear as an accidental event of culture over which Japanese have no control. The postmodern, difficult enough to locate in its own genetic context of late Western capitalism, is all the more elusive in its Japanese evocation. It is characterized by one of its enunciators, Karatani Kōjin, however, in a specifically non-Western locus.

> The Japanese postmodern has a different character [from its Western counterpart]. While it does involve a radical process just as in the West, the Japanese postmodern does not include that "resistance" so endemic to the Western world.[38]

In order for Karatani to define Japanese postmodernism this way, of course, he must have a distinctively "Western" version of the phenomenon in mind. He does, and it is a twist on the notion of a poststructuralism directed at the deconstruction of Western metaphysics. While it is the latter, too, it can "also be said that the postmodern is the generic term corresponding to the totality of anti-Western tendencies in the west."[39] Seeing Western postmodernism thus as a type of ultimate category of resistance, Karatani defines the Japanese postmodern as its opposite, a lack of resistance, which leads him ironically to adopt a perspective similar to Barthes's: unlike the supreme signifier God of Western thought, posited by Barthes, Japan's ultimate signifier is the "degree zero." For Karatani, "in Japan, there is no construction to deconstruct." The postmodern entered Japan without any resistance.

> A postmodern thought is but a consumable decor in a self-sufficient discursive space and functions ultimately only to further the development of consumer society. In Japanese society, where there was no "resistance" to this movement, concepts like absence of the subject or decentering do not have the intensity they might have in France. But precisely for this reason, Japanese consumer and information society accelerates its process of rotation without the slightest obstacle.[40]

Karatani's effort to identify a Japanese postmodern leads him to discover those elements of the Japanese "native tradition" which distinguish it from its Western counterpart, to erect a Japanese cultural generality which would account for this "difference." In what might appear to be quasi-neonativist fashion, Karatani turns this "lack of resistance" into its opposite, a distinctively Japanese, and hence anti-Western notion of modernity, an "empty structure of power." Such an effort to maintain a Japanese other from within, albeit in a mode which need not set itself against a native or foreign metaphysical tradition, reinforces a view of a Japan as collective subject. And inasmuch as the existence of such a subject depends on its capacity to act in a cohesive manner, it should not be surprising that it is associated with suicide as the metaphor of ultimate control. Suicide represents the capacity for the subject to resist without resisting, to undermine emptiness itself, to preempt death and destruction, or undo the end of history itself.

If the underside of the West's modernization narrative is romanticism (the obsessive, all-absorbing subjectivity and all-consuming presence from which the postmodern seeks to escape by positing an end/closure to consciousness), in Japan the underside of the imported modernization narrative is the myth of cyclical rebirth, of endless eternal desire and suffering. That this notion is tainted with "premodernity" by its Buddhist associations is secondary to the still vivid sense that Japanese modernity has been marked by a cycle of death and rebirth. Hence, the syndrome of Japan as Number One testifies not so much to a knockdown drag-out fight with the West as it does to the ability to stay, survive, be reborn: the ultimate symbol of that truth is the historical experience of the atomic bomb and the devastating destruction of Japan. For Japan, then, unlike for the West, postmodern means not nuclear sublime but postnuclear, and the issue is not whether survival is possible, but how to survive in what has always been recognized as a precarious existence.

To speak of Japan as postmodern in this nonresistant way calls to mind Roland Barthes's *Empire of Signs* and how difficult it is to evade the Orientalist, and hence modernizationist mode. It recalls to us, as with the modernization metanarrative, that Japan is not just postmodern: it is above all a part of the Western postmodern. In Vogel's *Japan as Number One*, Japan's success is not ultimately in achieving modernization or even in being different; it is in being a more successful version of the American past, able to achieve what America has "forgotten" how to do. In analogous fashion, Japan as postmodern is not so much a different but a purer version, this time of the future, promising (to borrow Lyotard's future anterior tense) "to have done" that which the West "will have forgotten how to do."

The Japan as Number One syndrome should mark the culminating point of Japan's modernization story. The story should be over, and indeed one can detect a desire, in certain Japanese writing, for this traumatic narrative of love/hate with the West to end. The unparalleled longevity of Emperor Hirohito in this connection, linked as it is with the official calendar, seems to be the cause of, or at least the catalyst for, the inability of historians and critics to declare the postwar period at an end. But beneath and beyond the periodization issue is the strong sense that the metanarrative has not ended, that the Japanese story will continue to be written by forces beyond any writer's control, by an accidentalism which impinges on a subjective Japanese sublime, and by the intrusive presence of that "world of generation" of women and children (not to mention the increasing number of foreign tourists and scholars) whose demands seem to be growing geometrically.

Yet all such advocative evocations of the postmodern—whether apocalyptic and Orientalist in a mystical Marxist manner like Kojève's, sublimely nuclear like the subjects of Ferguson's critique, or "resistant to non-resistance" like Karatani's—end up, for all of their collapsing of narrativities, as instances of a discursive, ideological process. In this discourse, they repress, preclude, elide, and marginalize both the undiminished vitality of advanced capitalist imperialism as well as the narrative possibilities for struggle and evolution. In this sense, postmodernism is very much an extension of modern alienation, of anomie, ennui, to that desultory attitude toward nuclear destruction and collective suicide: a cosmic "What's the difference?" And the Japanese postmodern, in Karatani's terms, is supremely indifferent to the possibility of an end. The semiotic overtones of both the Japanese and the Western postmodern convey to its advocates a claustrophobic sense that there is nowhere else to go except in circles, via performative language games or the replaying of the record of one's life or the endless circulation of increasingly unnecessary consumer goods and images. And all of these aspects of "crisis" appear to be déjà vu in the Japanese postmodern, where they have been a way of life for so long.

But for nations and peoples in daily struggle with Western and Japanese imperialism, it must come, if they hear about it, as a surprise to learn that the game or story "is over." For the third world, the idea that Japan or the first world has no system, no structure, no content, no signifieds does not induce apathy so much as vigilance; the view of the postmodern as a postnarrative, hence postpolitical stage is itself a dangerous narrative ploy designed to defuse the potential of political struggle. Is it then mere coincidence that the notion of the postmodern is a product of a European and American intelligentsia at a time when the socialist experiment seems at a particularly low ebb, in its apparent inability in Europe to distinguish itself from its capitalist nemesis? This leveling of systemic differences and dulling of expectations is surely part of the postmodern. But while it may be the case for Japan, whose postmodern condition may be no more than a passing vogue, is it so for Africa, Asia, and Latin America, where the struggle for survival continues to structure daily life, even without or in spite of the nuclear perspective?

In the final analysis, Japan, with or without its postmodernity, is an imperialist power striving to control increasingly large realms of the world's necessity. As with the United States' nuclear leadership and its plans for moving minorities to city centers, Japanese leaders are also concerned with manipulating populations, space, and capital both nationally and internationally (recall Tanaka Kakuei's plan for the Japanese Archipelago). The issue of the postmodern, for all of its straddling of nuclear suicide and the sublime, masks a social and political reality in which differences and struggles and narratives promise to persist at least until the end of historical time.

Notes

1   See Fredric Jameson, "Postmodernism, or the Cultural Logic of Late Capitalism," *New Left Review* 146 (July–August 1984): 53–92.
2   Jean-François Lyotard, *The Postmodern Condition: A Report on Knowledge*, trans. Geoff Bennington and Brian Massumi (Minneapolis, 1984), 37.
3   Ibid., 81.
4   Terry Eagleton, "Capitalism, Modernism, and Postmodernism," *New Left Review* 152 (July–August 1985): 70.
5   Ibid., 72.
6   A. Alvarez, *The Savage God: A Study of Suicide* (New York, 1973), 234–36.
7   Ibid., 236.
8   Preface to special issue on "Nuclear Criticism," *Diacritics* 14, no. 2 (Summer 1984): 3.
9   Frances Ferguson, "The Nuclear Sublime," *Diacritics* 14, no. 2 (Summer 1984): 5.
10   Ibid., 7.
11   Ibid., 6.
12   On *littératuricide*, see Alvarez, *Savage God*, 199.
13   Ferguson, "Nuclear Sublime," 7.
14   Ibid., 9.
15   Ibid., 8.
16   Ibid., 9.
17   Dean MacCannell, "Baltimore in the Morning . . . After: On the Forms of Post-Nuclear Leadership," *Diacritics* 14, no. 2 (Summer 1984): 41.
18   See Alvarez, "The Closed World of Suicide," in *Savage God*, 73–132, and Ivan Morris, "The Kamikaze Fighters," in *The Nobility of Failure: Tragic Heroes in the History of Japan* (New York, 1976).
19   Alexandre Kojève, *Introduction to the Reading of Hegel*, trans. James H. Nichols, Jr. (New York, 1969), 160.
20   Ibid., 161.
21   Ibid., 161–62; emphasis mine.
22   On Mishima's life and writing, see John Nathan, *Mishima: A Biography* (Boston, 1974); for a graphic account of Mishima's final moments, see the first chapter of Henry Scott-Stokes, *The Life and Death of Yukio Mishima* (New York, 1974).

23 Kojève, *Introduction*, 162.

24 Morris dedicates his *Nobility of Failure* to the memory of Mishima, "whose own last act . . . belongs squarely to the scenario of heros as described in these chapters" (xi).

25 Roland Barthes, *Empire of Signs*, trans. Richard Howard (New York, 1982), 91–94.

26 Maurice Pinguet, *La mort volontaire au Japon* (Paris, 1984), 314; my translation.

27 Jameson, "Postmodernism," 60.

28 Ishioka, whose set design for *Mishima* won a Cannes Festival prize in 1985, has been referred to as "Japan's ultimate designer." She is famous, among other things, for a magazine cover painting of Adolph Hitler and Che Guevara having their facial hair shaved off. See Robert S. Dye, "Japan's Designing Woman," *VIS à VIS* (March 1987): 88.

29 Mata Yamamoto, Japanese co-producer of *Mishima*, quoted in Don Morton, "The Mishima Miasma," *Tokyo Journal* 5, no. 2 (May 1985): 11.

30 Ian Buruma, "Rambo-san," *New York Review of Books*, 10 October 1985, 16.

31 Ibid., 15.

32 See Ian Buruma's *Behind the Mask: On Sexual Demons, Sacred Mothers, Transvestites, Gangsters and Other Japanese Cultural Heroes* (New York, 1984).

33 On modernization theory and Japan, see John Dower, "E. H. Norman, Japan, and the Uses of History," in *Origins of the Modern Japanese State*, ed. John Dower (New York, 1975), especially 65–90.

34 In addition to the photo of the Nogis, see Barthes's vision of himself as an object/subject of "Japanization" in *Empire of Signs*, 90.

35 Michel Foucault, *The History of Sexuality, Vol. 1: An Introduction*, trans. Robert Hurley (New York, 1980), 138.

36 Ezra Vogel's *Japan as Number One* (New York, 1980) is itself part of the phenomenon.

37 Nosaka Akiyuki, "American *Hijiki*," in *Contemporary Japanese Literature*, ed. Howard Hibbett (New York, 1977), 435–68; Katō Norihiro, *Amerika no kage* (*The Shadow of America*) (Tokyo, 1985).

38 Karatani Kōjin, "Généalogie de la culture Japonaise" in *Cahiers pour un temps* (Paris, 1986), 18; my translation.

39 Ibid.

40 Ibid.

Brett de Bary

Karatani Kōjin's *Origins of Modern Japanese Literature*

The brief afterword to Karatani Kōjin's *Origins of Modern Japanese Literature* (*Nihon kindai bungaku no kigen*, 1980) contains several disclaimers. "This book," he writes, "is not the type of 'history of literature' specified in the title. My use of what appear to be literary historical materials has been solely for the purpose of criticizing 'literary history.'" Coming at the end of the argument sustained through six chapters of the text, the disclaimer would appear superfluous. Yet it is necessary to explain an apparent inconsistency, for the title of the book consists entirely of words in which the text itself professes disbelief.

> Let me say a few words to clear up a misunderstanding that may easily arise. In my title, *The Origins of Modern Japanese Literature*, the words "Japanese," "modern," "literature," and especially "origins," should in fact be bracketed.[1]

Although these words appear in brackets throughout most of the text, Karatani does not explain why they are not bracketed in the title; it's likely that a title consisting entirely of bracketed words might unsettle or even alarm prospective readers. He simply closes the matter by raising the possibility that his book will, indeed, "be read as one more literary history," in which case the discourse of literary criticism will have demonstrated its ability to both "ignore" and "outlive" his text. He provides the additional information that he conceived of the book while attending a seminar in the literature of the Meiji period (that of Japan's initial "modernization," 1868–1912) at Yale in 1975; the actual writing was done in Japan over an unexpectedly long (five-year) period. After an acknowledgment of those in the Japanese literary world who were instrumental in bringing about the publication of his writings, Karatani's afterword ends. However much he may have wanted to explain an apparent inconsistency, Karatani's tone in the afterword, with its mixture of defiance and accommodating pessimism, resembles that of the text itself. The *bundan* (as the world of Japanese writers, critics, and publishers is known) study abroad, a gesture which throws the conventions of writing into relief while continuing to acquiesce in them—in other words, in and in spite of its very perfunctoriness, Karatani's afterword situates his writing in its social context, delineates his stance as a critic, and underscores the performative dimension of *Origins of Modern Japanese Literature*.

Published as a series of separate essays beginning in autumn 1978, *Origins of Modern Japanese Literature* preceded the coalescing of what is now known as the Japanese postmodern movement. But in its criticism of "literary history" and its attempt to radically redefine the phenomenon of modernity in Japanese literature, the book articulates major concerns of that movement. In the following pages I want to consider the ways in which the first two essays published by Karatani ("The Discovery of Landscape" or *Fūkei no hakken*, published in *Kikan geijutsu*, summer 1978, and "The Discovery of Interiority" or *Naimen no hakken*, fall 1978) deconstruct "modern Japanese literature" as a category of academic discourse, grounding it instead in a set of material practices and processes constitutive of Japanese modernity. It is in its attempt to find a position of critical distance from that modernity that Karatani's text may be characterized as postmodern.

The notion of an inversion (*tentō*) figures prominently in *Origins of Modern Japanese Literature*. As the designation of a radical rupture, or what Karatani sometimes defines as the "overturning of a semiotic constellation," inversion is a key factor in Karatani's analysis of Meiji literary history, those decades in the late nineteenth century which are typically described in terms of the gestation and birth of the modern. According to Karatani's multifaceted definition, Japanese modernity, as both a mode and an object of representation, is predicated upon inversion. The term "inversion" also aptly describes a rhetorical strategy deployed by Karatani on multiple levels. As he mentions in his afterword, the very words which comprise its title and designate its object of investigation appear in brackets in the body of the text. The use of brackets inverts the truth claims of "modern Japanese literature." This rhetorical calling into question of the existence of what modern Japanese literary criticism takes for granted as its object is one aspect of Karatani's attempt to defamiliarize and denaturalize it. In keeping with this attempt, the titles of six essays that comprise this series systematically invert categories which are assumed a priori in canonical accounts of modern Japanese literary development: "The Discovery of Landscape," "The Discovery of Interiority," "The Institution of Confession," "Sickness as Meaning," "The Discovery of the Child," and "On the Power of Structure." The origins of modern Japanese literature, in this account, lead us neither to self-evident essences nor to a self-evident starting point, but to a series of "discoveries" which are, in fact, "inversions."

Karatani's inversion is a double operation fraught with ambivalence. To suspend belief in modern Japanese literature is both to deny and affirm its existence. For the same theatrical gesture with which Karatani consigns "modern Japanese literature" to oblivion as a self-sufficient essence exposes its historical specificity as a concrete set of social practices. The apparent inconsistency he calls attention to in his afterword is in this sense merely an extension of a pattern of argument pursued throughout the text, where the theatrics of disbelief call attention to necessity, in this case accommodation to specific conventions of writing and the exigencies of "making sense" to one's contemporaries.

But the looping back on itself of Karatani's rhetoric does not stop here. To expose the historical conditions of the possibility of modern Japanese literature is also to suggest it might be otherwise: that is, not "modern." This brings the term "modern" to the center of Karatani's argument: it is modernity which includes and makes "modern Japanese literature" possible. But the use of the modern as a category both signifies and exemplifies Japan's marginal position in a discourse whose definitions emanate from a Western center of cultural power, which leads to another form of oscillation: as a "natural" phenomenon, modern Japanese literature can only be alienating; only insofar as it is defamiliarized can it be reclaimed and repossessed. As the dilemma of brackets has suggested, however, the very act of writing and the demands of intelligibility make ultimate transcendence of "modern Japanese literature" impossible. Karatani's text is thus imbued with the contradictory, "tragic" quality that Roland Barthes has described as characteristic of modern literature, in which "Writing as Freedom is . . . mere moment."

> . . . writing is an ambiguous reality: on the one hand it unquestionably arises from a confrontation of the writer with the society of his time; on the other hand, from this sort of social finality, it refers the writer back, by a sort of tragic reversal, to the sources, that is to say the instruments of creation. Failing to supply him with a freely consumed language, History suggests to him the demand for one freely produced.[2]

It is perhaps in just this sense that Karatani evokes and symbolically links himself with the celebrated Meiji author Natsume Sōseki (1867–1916) at the outset of his argument. Karatani rereads and reclaims the author so often taken as the ultimate index of Meiji modernity, casting the familiar ingredients of Sōseki's "tragedy" in a new light. What appeals to Karatani are Sōseki's insecurity as a scholar of English literature, his crisis of confidence as a theorist of literature, his despair over the possibility of understanding English literature:

> As a child I enjoyed studying the Chinese classics. Although the time I spent in this kind of study was not long, it was from the

Chinese classics that I learned, however vaguely and obscurely, what literature was. In my heart, I hoped it would be the same when I read English literature, and that I would not necessarily begrudge giving my whole life, if that were required, to its study. But what I resent is that despite my study I never mastered it. When I graduated I was plagued by the fear that somehow I had been cheated by English literature.[3]

It is Sōseki's sensitivity, as one whose life spanned a marked historical transition, to the unnaturalness of modern literature, his resentful suspicion of it, that Karatani admires, while in his inability to transcend modernity Sōseki prefigures Karatani. It is the Sōseki "standing in the vanguard of the Meiji government's students of the West, dogged by a desire to flee from their ranks" that Karatani implicitly names his predecessor.[4]

Sōseki, as Karatani reconstructs him, becomes both an object of inversion and an inverting strategy, a multivalent sign which subtly but immediately throws off the canonical narrative of modern Japanese literature. Karatani accomplishes this, first, by identifying Sōseki, not as the author of the "psychological novels" which have long been seen as the pinnacle of his achievement, but as author of the *Theory of Literature* (*Bungakuron*), an incomplete work deemed of lesser significance in most critical commentaries on the author, especially the few which have appeared in Western languages. By reclaiming Sōseki as theorist, Karatani reinterprets his notorious "loneliness"—it is no longer the "inevitable" price of progress toward modernity (and therefore, in the canonical account, a correlate of the emergence of Western-style individualism in Japan), but rather the loneliness of the odd, the contingent, and the discontinuous. It is in these terms that Karatani explicates Sōseki's preface to the *Theory of Literature*:

Sōseki's preface reveals an understanding that readers of his time would be unprepared for the appearance of his *Theory of Literature* and would find it somewhat odd. This has, indeed, proven to be the case, not only in Sōseki's time but in our own. Even if we posit that Sōseki as an individual was compelled by some necessity to produce such a work, there was nothing inevitable about its appearance in Japanese (or Western) literary history. *Theory of Literature* was a flower that bloomed out of season, leaving no seeds. . . . Sōseki himself must have been keenly aware of this. In either a Japanese or Western context, Sōseki's vision was an abrupt and solitary one which he himself must have found disorienting.[5]

Karatani dislodges Sōseki from his place as preeminent Meiji novelist while transforming him into a precursor of his revisionist critique. In selected passages from *Theory*, for example, Karatani finds Sōseki expressing skepticism toward precisely those categories which are the major target of his own criticism: "the modern" and "literature." In the following passage, Sōseki appears to refute quite directly what Karatani labels the "ethnocentric" and "historicist" bias inherent in the concept of a universal modernity in literature.

> Whether it be social mores, customs, or emotions, we must not acknowledge the existence only of those mores, customs, and emotions which have manifested themselves in the West. Nor should the attainments reached after many transitions by Western civilizations at this point in time set the standard, however much it may serve the standard for them. It is commonly said that Japanese literature is immature. Unfortunately I, too, hold this view. But to admit that one's literature is immature is quite a different thing from taking the West as a standard. If the immature Japanese literature of today develops, we cannot categorically declare it will become like the literature of contemporary Russia. Nor will it follow stages identical to those whereby modern French literature produced Hugo, Balzac, and Zola. Since no one can logically maintain that there is only a single path a developing literature can follow, or a single point it should attain, it is rash to assert that the trends of Western literature today will be those of Japanese literature tomorrow. We should not leap to the conclusion that the developments in Western literature are absolute.[6]

Karatani would see Sōseki as Foucauldian in his rejection of linear history as an inevitable succession of stages; indeed, linear history for Sōseki is the product of an arbitrary teleology: it is only if we assume that some standards are "absolute" that history appears to move forward. As he observes later in the same passage, "What we have been taught is history may be assembled in many different ways within our minds. . . ." Thus his theory can be made to demonstrate the contingency of his own opus; once the universality of the modern has been rejected, there is nothing inevitable about modern Japanese literature.

But Sōseki is of further significance in Karatani's argument, for the figure of the theorist unmasks a hierarchical opposition contained within the notion of the modern. As Masao Miyoshi has observed, "the signifier 'modern' should be regarded as a regional term peculiar only to the West," yet insofar as Western expansionism has affected nearly every culture in the world, native conceptions of history and culture have been fragmented.[7] Karatani's almost jarring description of Sōseki's theory as "odd" thus raises a provocative question: Why has Sōseki the novelist been privileged over Sōseki the theorist? In addition to being the result of a teleology which insists on the centrality of novelistic fiction in modern Japanese literature, is it because of the sheer oddness, from a "modern" perspective, of a Japanese writer claiming to put forth a theory of literature? Insofar as the West is the source, the authority, and the standard for modernity in literature, Sōseki as a theorist can never write from that center and cannot speak with authority. The term "modern" relies for its meaning on its opposition to the "premodern," yet in his Japan, as well as in our own, this opposition masks another, unequal one: West vs. non-West. As contingency, oddity, and theorist, Karatani's Sōseki defies the inevitability, the universality, and the unequal hierarchical opposition implicit in "modernity."

Perhaps the most radical dimension of Sōseki's *Theory*, however, is its implicit skepticism toward "literature." For Karatani, the very passion which drove Sōseki to attempt a theoretical explanation of the nature and existence of literature sprang from a fundamental doubt as to its validity. From the midst of the Meiji transition, Sōseki was doubly aware of the "newness" of "literature," not only for Japan but for the nineteenth-century West. It was his ability to perceive that, at some point in the mid-1890s, Japanese "literature" had become inseparable from and was a product of modernity, that impelled Sōseki to produce the *Theory of Literature.* To put it another way, *Theory* grew out of his sense of estrangement from "literature," articulated in the question "What is literature?"

> What I am saying is that there was no other mode of existence possible for Sōseki except as a theoretician—that is, as a person who maintained a certain distance between himself and "literature."[8]

Karatani sees Sōseki's question as "iconoclastic," one which made his obsession "private," as well as "difficult to share with others." *Origins of Modern Japanese Literature* would lay claim both to Sōseki's distance and his iconoclastic question.

—————

Sōseki's articulation of the poignant fear that he had been "cheated by English literature" is described by Karatani as the "anxiety of a man who suddenly finds himself in the midst of a landscape" and is thus linked to one of the major disruptive figures of the text. For it is with the figure of "discovering landscape" (surely enigmatic for most readers upon first encounter) that Karatani launches his inversion of the dominant paradigm of Meiji literary history. The linear sequence unfolded by canonical accounts is flattened out by Karatani into a horizon charged with a sense of loss. In the face of this horizon, such staples of Meiji literary history as the concepts of "enlightenment" (referring to the initial impact of Western thought on Meiji intellectuals) and "influence" lose their historicist explanatory force.

   With its absent subject, the image of "discovering landscape" is curiously, abstractly pastoral, yet it wields considerable subversive force in Karatani's argument. On the most ambitious and general level, Karatani uses it to challenge and invalidate the epistemological foundations of modern positivist history, the conditions under which modern Japanese literature is assumed to be "known." In this sense, Karatani's landscape self-consciously evokes the Foucauldian image of the "opening" which is also the "space" of discursive practice. Flat and all-encompassing, landscape rebuffs the search for origins, chronology's "logic," in the same way that Foucault's "opening" in

The Order of Things depicts man as "always already there," unable to move beyond his signifying practices to account for their origins:

> It is in him . . . that things find their beginning: rather than a cut, made at some given moment in duration, he is the opening from which time in general can be reconstituted, duration can flow, and things, at the appropriate moment, can make their appearance.[9]

It is in this sense that Karatani wishes to bracket and set aside the search for the "origins" of modern Japanese literature. Rather than chronicling the beginning and end of a "stage," Karatani will describe Japanese modernity as a discursive space, one which is limiting, all-enveloping, and cannot be seen beyond.

Yet Karatani does not wish to freeze time and render it motionless; with Foucault, he would simply "suspend the theme that succession is absolute" in order to bring into view the historically specific discursive formation which is modernity. It is such a landscape, or discursive space, which produces "modern Japanese literature." On this point, the image produces a hall of mirrors effect. For while landscape may stand for modernity writ large, as it were, as a totality of signifying practices, it is also a metaphor for the *object* (and objects) produced by these practices, each landscape mirroring back the other. Karatani achieves this effect by playing on an ambiguity of the modern Japanese word for landscape, *fūkei*. He imparts a bit of long-buried knowledge: the word "scenery" (or *fūkei*) had not been used in premodern Japanese to designate paintings of landscapes, but was incorporated for the first time in the Meiji period into a new term, *fūkei-ga* ("scene" or "landscape painting"), referring to landscape paintings in the *Western* style. Karatani's *fūkei* confuses the distinction between "natural" object and representation—what the contemporary reader takes as the designation of an "external" scene began as the designation of a representation. Furthermore, because it evokes the image of Western-style landscape painting characterized for the Japanese chiefly by its use of Western principles of perspective, *fūkei* mirrors itself on yet another level: "landscape" is a representation which represents/exposes the conventions of its own representation.

In a brilliantly compressed way, the image of landscape simultaneously problematizes the relationship of modern Japanese language to
representation, relativizes "nature" (by showing that our perceptions
of it are always mediated in historically specific ways), and alludes
to a pervasive convention of modern representation, the principles of
perspective. In a final mirroring effect, the principles of perspective
in their turn are made to stand as a metaphor for the subject-object
relations produced by, and included in, modernity as a totality of
signifying practices. We can now understand why the notion of "origins," although rejected as chronology, is maintained as a heuristic
device by Karatani as he deconstructs modern representation:

> Once a landscape has been established, its origin is repressed
> from memory. It takes on the appearance of an "object" which
> has been there, outside us, from the start. An "object," however,
> can only be constituted within a landscape. The same may be
> said of the "subject" or self. The philosophical standpoint which
> distinguishes between subject and object came into existence
> within what I refer to as "landscape." Rather than existing prior
> to landscape, they are products of it.[10]

Set within this context, the political nature of Karatani's rhetorical moves emerges in relief. For if Karatani's landscape is charged
with a sense of loss, it is the result of a tension whereby the text,
by pointing toward (but never attaining) alterity attempts to resist
modernity, or at least to relativize it and expose it as tragically limiting. Thus he proposes *fūkei* as a model of the logic everywhere produced by modern language and representation, in which reality is
dichotomized into inner experience and outer world, and in which,
as Derrida puts it, "this spatial pair inside-outside . . . gives life to
the opposition of subject-object."[11] Karatani draws on the philosophical critique of modernity of Japanese thinkers like Nishida Kitaro
and Kobayashi Hideo and of Western post-Hegelian thought, pointing repeatedly to the parallel, indeed interdependence, between the
stationary Cartesian subject and the principles of perspective. As a
fixed, stationary subject, "the subject of Descartes' cogito ergo sum
is confined ineluctably within the schema" established by "the principles of perspective." Modern scientific thought, also a product of

the Cartesian age, reproduced the same dichotomy between subject and object; Karatani observes that in this same period "the 'object' of thought" came to be seen as a "homogeneous, scientifically measurable entity—in short, as an extension of the principles of perspective." This Cartesian model in which all certainty is locked in the ego "as 'predator of the Other'," is seen by Karatani as leading to a "cul de sac" of modern thought from which "I myself cannot break away."[12] While he avoids the essentialist pitfall which would identify modern representation as inherently Western (it is, rather, specifically modern), he attempts to repudiate and resist its hegemony as a product of Western cultural imperialism. On the conceptual level, he does this by evoking Japanese and Western philosophical debates which have analyzed the Cartesian subject and its representational schema as a source of modern "man's" alienation from himself, as a subject-in-language, and from the objects he would know. Alice Jardine has recently summarized these developments in Western thought:

> Representation is the condition that confirms the possibility of an imitation (mimesis) based on the dichotomy of presence and absence and, more generally, on the dichotomies of dialectical thinking (negativity). Representation, mimesis, and the dialectic are inseparable; they designate together a way of thinking as old as the West, a way of thinking which French thought, through German philosophy, has been attempting to rethink since the turn of the century.[13]

On the linguistic level, Karatani attempts to create moments of resistance to the system of representation within which his own text is inscribed by inverting and manipulating it. "Discovering landscape" must finally be seen as one such moment. For Karatani takes a central theme from the master narrative of Western expansion, that of "discovery," and destabilizes the subject-object dichotomy on which it depends. By using two nouns linked by a possessive to signify "discovery," he replaces the conventional transitive grammatical construction ("Columbus discovered America") for one which places the two terms in a position of parity, while rendering the causal and chronological relation between them ambiguous. In the grammatical order of the Japanese text—*fūkei no hakken*—landscape, or *fūkei*, *precedes* discovery, or *hakken*, making it impossible in a literal sense to differentiate either temporally or on the basis of an active/passive opposition between the two terms. Was it "landscape's discovery" or "the discovery of landscape"? Meiji literature as "landscape" would render irrelevant the cause-effect logic inherent in the question of the West's "influence" on Japan or Japan's "discovery" of the West. It is only in such a destabilized space that the "history of modern Japanese literature" can be contested.

≡≡≡≡

While I have associated "landscape" with such terms as "discursive space," "representation," and "signifying practice," Karatani himself has consistently refused to define it or equate it to these or any other terms. Infrequently, in *Origins of Modern Japanese Literature*, Karatani offers the Japanese *kigōronteki na fuchi* as an alternative to "landscape," for which he has suggested the English translation "semiotic constellation." His repeated use of the far less easily assimilable "landscape" at key points in the text is a strategic one. While his argument is informed by a knowledge of contemporary Western theory as well as of Meiji literature, "landscape" acts to foil those who would read the book as another application of Western methodologies to the Japanese case, or to see in it the subjugation of "Japan" to the hegemony of a new, postmodern Western discourse.

Because of its strong association with "nature," moreover, "landscape" leads us toward, rather than away from, the specificity of Japanese modernity, opening directly onto a more fine-grained version of "the history of modern Japanese literature." In Karatani's essays, "The Discovery of Landscape" and "The Discovery of the Interior," "landscape" (as exteriority) and "interiority" are linked, not only as the interdependent poles of an opposition, but in terms of an ideology and a representational system which would posit that opposition as necessary and "natural." Karatani proceeds through "landscape" to "interiority," and to the problems of nature, naturalism, and naturalization in modern Japanese literature.

His observation that the canonical history of Japanese literature is "biased toward the novel" may be illustrated (in much abbreviated form) by the analysis set forth in the introduction to Nakamura Mitsuo's *Japanese Fiction in the Meiji Era* (1966). This was the first book of literary criticism selected by the Japanese government-sponsored Society for International Cultural Relations (*Kokusai bunka shinko-kai*) for inclusion in a series of English translations "to be used as introductions to various aspects of Japanese life and culture." The choice was indicative of the prestige Nakamura, a scholar of French literature at Tokyo's Meiji University, commanded in the Japanese *bundan* of the period, as well as of the fact that his approach to Japanese modern literature, as one well-trained in the study of European literature, must have been deemed particularly appropriate for Western consumption. Nakamura's well-known comparison of the modern Japanese novel to a "mirror," in the introduction to this book, appears and reappears in different guises throughout the critical writing on the subject. Nakamura introduces the image of the mirror to explain why "the study of the novel has occupied the chief position in the history of Japanese literature" of the modern period. "This is not," he claims, "a tendency which literary historians themselves have created," but should rather be attributed to "something in Meiji-Taisho literature itself which led to . . . this fiction-centered view." Nakamura explains this "something":

> Let us put it this way. Concisely, the novel is the least deceptive and the most reliable mirror of the spirit and the lives of Meiji and post-Meiji Japanese. The naturalistic movement in Japanese literature which came into existence toward the end of the Meiji period regarded the depiction of truth as the purpose of the novel.[14]

The logic of this linear narrative leads to a decisive "triumph" of the naturalist movement about 1912; although he acknowledges that this movement quickly went into decline, even the "various anti-naturalist schools which succeeded it . . . inherited unchanged all the basic features . . . of naturalism."[15] Nakamura's evaluation of Japanese naturalist novels and novelists is layered. On the one hand, both achieve only second-class stature in a geopolitical context in which Nakamura, contradictorily, posits the universality of the novel, yet finds its "pure" and "original" form only in the West. In the Japanese context, however, he depicts Meiji novelists as a heroic elite. While he states that because of the formation of the *bundan*, or society of literati, in the Meiji period, Japanese writers lived "in a laboratory-like environment" which was "divorced from real life," he also characterizes the *bundan* positively as a "scene of life-or-death struggles."

> For them the novel was not merely an artistic representation of human life. Rather, it was the means of searching for a new, true way of living. At the same time, it was the record of this search.[16]

Nakamura's logic, in fact, binds him to such a two-tiered analysis, for by affirming the "struggle" of the Westernized elite of Meiji Japan, he endorses a modernizationist ideology which can only represent Japan as several steps behind the center and source of modernity, which is the West.

Two recent American studies analyze at some length the complex ramifications of the paradigm of modern Japanese literature presented in the work of Nakamura and many others. Edward Fowler, for example, suggests that the discourse of modern Japanese literature draws distinctions between "fiction," "fabrication," and "the real," which differ from those of "classical western narrative"; Alan Wolfe has analyzed the novel-centered (and thus individual-centered) view of modern Japanese literature as the offshoot of a modernizationist metanarrative which, in the postwar period particularly, has legitimated American global dominance.[17] For the purposes of this article, I wish primarily to point to the way in which Nakamura's novel-centered view, with its mimetic theory of representation and emphasis on language as truth, ends up relegating Japanese literary practice to marginality in the same breath that it chronicles its accession to the universal realm of the modern. As a result, Nakamura finally faults the modern Japanese novel for "developing only weakly and insufficiently as an expression of the Zeitgeist," observing that "as an art form it probably became trapped in the cul de sac which it entered." To Japanese modernity he offers only the consolation of knowing that "nevertheless it [the modern novel] was a conscientious, honest voice."

> This is the minimal condition for the modern novel to be valid fiction, and the Japanese novelists succeeded in fulfilling this condition in their own way.[18]

This self-abnegating, self-alienating rhetoric finds its most extreme expression in Nakamura's citation of the remark of a character in a Nagai Kafū (1879–1959) novel:

> The success of naturalism signified the triumph, both in style and in contents, of literary concepts transplanted from the West over traditional Japanese "art." In his novel *Shinkichōsha no nikki* (*Diary of a Person Recently Returned from Abroad*), Nagai Kafū has one of the characters remark: "Purely Japanese literature died out completely around the year 1897. The literature written after then is not Japanese literature.[19]

It is the essentialism involved in Nakamura's story of modern Japanese literature's attainment of "something" that Karatani makes the focus of his critique. Any attempt to redress the cultural balance between "Japanese" and "Western" culture which does not reject essentialist categories will simply lead back to Nakamura's doubles —superior/inferior, original/copy, universality/marginality. Karatani attempts, rather, to deconstruct the language within which the "history of modern Japanese literature" is inscribed, the same language which produced and reproduces "modern Japanese literature."

In his inverted schema of Japanese modernity, then, Karatani puts symbolic cart before horse, denying the ontological status of whatever Japanese literature has been seen as "attaining" and "expressing" in the wake of the Meiji restoration and positing these rather as categories produced by language. Thus he places primary emphasis on the Meiji language reform movement (usually referred to as the *genbun-itchi* or movement for the "unification of the spoken and written languages"), which he sees as a central element in the organization of the modern Japanese state; the proliferation of Meiji reform movements in fiction, poetry, drama, and so forth, are for him subsumed *within genbun-itchi*. This reverses the order of the canonical narrative which places Tsubouchi Shōyō (1859–1935), author of a critical treatise promoting "a new kind of fiction, realistic in nature and satisfying Western literary criteria," in the position of "founder of modern Japanese literature," and assigns the language reforms largely instrumental status.[20] Rather than tracing modern Japanese literature's quest for "interiority" (as in *The Search for Authenticity in Mod-*

ern Japanese Literature and other titles too numerous to mention), Karatani sees modern language as producing the modern self.[21]

> The modern self came into existence through a certain materiality or system. Therefore, I do not propose to examine *genbun-itchi* from the standpoint of "interiority." On the contrary, I am attempting to understand the "discovery of interiority" as premised on the establishment of *genbun-itchi* as a system.

Or, as Karatani puts it elsewhere, it is not interiority which is inside us but "we who are inside it."[22] Lest he appear, at this point, to be arguing for what some have termed "linguistic determinism," I should note that, by linking *genbun-itchi* to the organization of the modern state and the production of its subject, he specifies that his concern is with the ideological function of language.

Karatani makes a crucial reformulation of the role and purpose of the *genbun-itchi* movement. The term *itchi*, or unification, is generally taken to connote an effort to make written Japanese, highly codified in the premodern period, closer to the spoken language, and thus accessible to a much larger readership. In the canonical history of modern Japanese literature, the movement is discussed almost entirely in terms of early modern writers' search for a "neutral" verb-ending which would avoid the question of the hierarchical relationship between speakers which is necessarily expressed in the spoken language. Karatani cites linguist Tokieda Motoki's observation that "the use of honorifics is inherent to the Japanese langauge" to counter this argument. Japanese can never be "neutral"; Meiji writers adopted verb-endings which expressed "same status or superior to inferior relationships" and simply tried to use them as if they were neutral.[23] For Karatani, the emphasis on verb-endings is ideologically determined, displacing the more important question of the impact of *genbun-itchi* on the status of writing itself. Motivating *genbun-itchi* was an impulse to "modernize" written Japanese by making it "more economic, direct, and democratic," an impulse which in its most radical form would abolish the use of Chinese ideographs and institute a purely phonetic writing system. Karatani attempts to illustrate the intertwined nature of this impulse toward phoneticization and the organization of the modern state by quoting a memorial submitted to the Tokugawa shogunate in the mid-nineteenth century by Maejima Hisoka, an official who had studied with American missionaries in Nagasaki. In his "Reasons for Abolishing Kanji," Maejima declared that Chinese characters, "which could be read in so many different ways and gave rise to numerous errors," were an obstacle to "creating the educated population which was essential to the nation."[24]

The Meiji reforms did not, in fact, purge Japanese writing of Chinese ideographs (they remain in use today, albeit in steadily decreasing proportion to phonetic script); but for Karatani the literal presence or absence of ideographs is not an issue in the face of dramatic indications that, during the decade of the 1890s, the status of writing in Japan was profoundly altered. The Chinese ideograph, which may have numerous pronunciations and meanings, and which produces a *graphic* meaning quite autonomous from the flow of phonetic symbols, gradually declined in significance as a site of heterogeneity in the text. As efforts were made to bring the Japanese writing system into greater conformity with that of "advanced" Western languages where a cipher could be equated with only one sound, the written language became more and more derivative in relation to the voice, as an instrument of vocalization. "Once Chinese characters had come to be seen as serving vocalization, whether to use an ideograph or a *kana* from the phonetic syllabary became a simple matter of choice."[25] The text was now seen as producing meaning in a more purely linear fashion, while the Chinese ideograph as *figure*, as productive of a graphic meaning independent from and at times even in conflict with phonetic meaning, was slowly suppressed.[26]

To take the problems of language and representation as crucial to the analysis of Japanese modernity is to effect a deconstruction of the terms of the dominant discourse on Japanese modern literature from the late nineteenth century on. Karatani, by insisting on the importance of the institution of a phonocentric writing system in the formation of the modern state, and by redefining the nature of the *genbun-itchi* movement, exposes the accepted "objects" of modern Japanese literary studies as categories assumed in, and imposed by, the language of late Meiji Japan, as well as of our own day.

In linking modern Japan's phonocentric conception of writing to an attendant metaphysics of presence (interiority), Karatani draws explicitly on the work of Jacques Derrida in ways that need not be elaborated here. More germane to my discussion is the startling revision of modern Japanese literary history that Karatani achieves in this manner. A linear narrative of progress (however halting) is replaced everywhere by the observation of reversals. For the narrative of the triumph of naturalism (the novelist's heroic struggle to capture the modern self and commit it to the transparency of language) he substitutes a broad metaphor of background and foreground (landscape and interiority) changing places as modern representation emerges. Familiar benchmarks of Meiji literary and cultural history—whereby the Japanese arts are seen as attaining a progressively greater degree of "realism"—are thus redefined in terms of an "inversion of semiotic design." If Karatani would see *genbun-itchi* as subsuming all other reform movements intended to make the Japanese arts more "modern" and "realistic" it is because this adoption of a phonocentric conception of language signified a profound rupture in all aspects of premodern signifying practice: the suppression of the ideograph in writing parallels the suppression of rhythm and figure (as productive of nonlinear meaning) in narrative, drama, and poetry. For example, Karatani points out that Tsubouchi Shōyō, the "founder of modern literature," was criticized by contemporary writers as "insufficiently realistic" in his own fictional writings, since they preserved the 5-7-5 rhythm of narration in the Edo puppet theater.[27] Similarly, he suggests that the emergence of "psychological realism" in the *kabuki* theater was premised on the replacement of "masking" makeup with the actor's "naked face." Karatani follows Lévi-Strauss's observation that in many premodern societies "it is the mask which is the face, or rather creates the face," to pinpoint the reversal here, whereby "the plain face, once seen as insignificant, is endowed with meaning." In premodern societies the face *as figure* is endowed with meaning. Insofar as there is an "inner" or "hidden" meaning which the naked face must now "express," Karatani sees the plain face of Meiji *kabuki* as parallel to the cipher which, in a phonetic writing system, is subordinated to the vocalized sound which it "expresses."[28]

> Itō Sei has written that Ichikawa Danjūrō "labored to convey a psychological impression to the spectator," but what was in fact happening in *kabuki* was that the ordinary ("realistic") face now

appeared as an entity which conveyed meaning, and that "meaning" was "interiority." "Interiority" was not always there. It was what came to be expressed as the result of the inversion of a semiotic constellation. But once "interiority" existed, the naked face was seen as "expressing" it. The meaning of performance is here inverted.[29]

This is one of Karatani's diverse examples, in texts and performances of the 1890s, of the background (the plain or the ordinary) becoming foreground, and simultaneously becoming invested with a type of depth or "hidden" meaning which the Edo arts were seen to have lacked.

One of Karatani's most radical reinterpretations is of the contribution of the haiku poet Masaoka Shiki (1867–1902), usually credited with achieving the "modernization" of haiku. Impelled by a sense that the haiku form was on the verge of extinction in the late nineteenth century, Shiki advocated a practice of "sketching from life" (or *shasei*). Rather than composing haiku on a set topic, as was customary at the time, Shiki and his students took pencils and notebooks into fields, woods, and city neighborhoods, taking the materials for their poems from whatever they found there. Thus, as Janine Beichmann has written, "Shiki made the observation of reality into a strict discipline, the most fundamental exercise in a poet's training."[30] She recounts that Shiki adopted the term *shasei* after discussions with a close friend, Nakamura Fūsetsu, who studied with the Italian landscape painter, Antonio Fontanesi.

> Asai Chū told the story of how he and his classmates had been assigned by Fontanesi to make sketches of the Marunouchi district [of Tokyo]. Dutifully arriving there, they all looked around, but could find nothing suitable to sketch. When they confessed their failure in class the next day, Fontanesi scolded them, saying that there was nothing wrong with the place, but with them, and that if they would only look around them there was enough there to keep them busy drawing for two generations. Such an emphasis on observation cannot help but remind one of Shiki's advice to the young poet . . . "Take your materials from what is around you."[31]

So influential was Shiki's conception of the "sketch from life" that the practice was taken over by the so-called Japanese romantic poets, including Shimazaki Tōson (1872–1943), who subsequently became a pioneer of realistic (the late Meiji term *shajitsuteki*, or "realistic," is related to *shasei*) writing in the naturalist school. Karatani, however, dissolves the notion of "observation of reality" so crucial to the canonical narrative of progress into a problem of language and representation. The "modernity" of Shiki, by contrast to Edo haiku poets, was his conception of language "as a kind of transparent sign"; from this derives his emphasis on objectivity of description. Furthermore, as is vividly illustrated in the Fontanesi anecdote, nature and scenery as they emerged in Shiki's time were unknown to premodern signifying practice. "Description, as practiced by these writers, was something more than simply portraying the external world," Karatani observes. "First, the external world itself had to be discovered."[32]

Kunikida Doppo (1871–1908) stands in relation to Karatani's discussion of interiority as Natsume Sōseki does to landscape. Two "giants" of Meiji literature, Mori Ōgai (1862–1922) and Natsume Sōseki, are displaced by Karatani to the borderlines of the "modern" because both could at least conceive of the possibility of alterity. Thus Sōseki, in the last decade of his life, wrote "psychological" novels in the morning, but spent his afternoons immersed in brush-painting and the composition of Chinese poetry (*kanshi*). It is the unlikely figure of Kunikida Doppo, primarily a writer of short stories, who died at the age of thirty-seven and has always been seen as falling somehow "between" the Japanese romantic and naturalist movements, that Karatani describes as "a man standing for the first time on a new horizon." By Kunikida's time, the *genbun-itchi* movement had lost its urgency; writing was no longer problematic and the "question of spoken versus written language no longer presented itself to writers."[33] Kunikida had lost the sense of "distance" between himself and writing experienced by earlier writers; rather, his sense of familiarity with the new writing made it possible for him to "express" an "interior." For Karatani, this is the first time that interiority constituted itself in a direct and present way in Japanese literature, and it did so necessarily in opposition to an objectified, alienated nature. Kunikida's depictions of landscape are routinely included in high school textbooks, for example, because he broke with literary precedent in describing, not the "famous sites" (*meisho*) celebrated in traditional literature, but the then unsettled Musashino Plain to the west of Tokyo, including trees and plants whose names were unknown in the vocabulary of classical literature. For Karatani, the significance of this development is twofold: first, in Kunikida's work, writing no longer produces "famous sites," as it did in traditional poetry and prose, and second, the writer's innovative "landscapes" coexist, seemingly paradoxically, with brooding, unusually introverted narrators. This constitution of and contradistinction between inner subject and outer object, the acceptance of such a distinction as a natural one which is nowhere subjected to doubt, appears for the first time in Japanese literature in the work of Kunikida.

Karatani compares Kunikida, as Japan's first modern writer, to Rousseau, as the latter has been analyzed by Jean Starobinski.[34] For Starobinski, it is in Rousseau's work that writing is relegated to secondary status vis-à-vis speech for the first time in European history. Simultaneously, a new "inner man" is constituted, *as inner speech*. Rousseau maintained that only self-consciousness, only what was directly present to the self, was clear. This was not spoken language, but the voice one heard in one's mind, an inner voice. Whereas linguistic activity had been seen up to that point as a mediating instrument, for Rousseau it became a site of direct experience. The literary work, accordingly, no longer functioned as a go-between for the writer and reader. Rather, a writer "expresses" his or her self by means of a literary work, seeking confirmation of the truth of individual experience. "For Rousseau," Starobinski writes, "subject and speech are no longer external to each other. . . . Subject, speech, and feeling can no longer be distinguished."[35] Here, certainty, as Karatani has observed earlier of the Cartesian cogito, is locked "inside." Thus Karatani would locate Japanese literature's first representations of this interiority and its finitude in Kunikida's work, in a story like "Shi" ("On Death") whose narrator, while trying to come to terms with the death of a friend, senses himself sealed off by a figurative "membrane" from all that is "outside":

As I was thinking all this, I had the sense that I was enclosed in a kind of membrane, and that my perceptions of all existence were somehow distanced by that single layer of skin. My anguished self believes, even now, that if I cannot confront facts and phenomena directly, face to face, then neither god nor truth nor beauty exists, they are simply an empty game. This is all that I can believe.[36]

Notes

1   Karatani Kōjin, *Nihon kindai bungaku no kigen* (*Origins of Modern Japanese Literature*) (Tokyo, 1980), 218. All translations from Karatani's book are my own.
2   Roland Barthes, *Writing Degree Zero*, trans. Annette Lavers and Colin Smith (New York, 1976), 16–17.
3   Natsume Sōseki, *Bungakuron* (*A Theory of Literature*), in *Natsume Sōseki zenshū* (*The Complete Works of Natsume Sōseki*), ed. Ito Sei and Yoshida Seiichi (Tokyo, 1960), vol. 16, 8–9. All translations of Sōseki's *Theory of Literature* are my own.
4   Karatani, *Origins*, 41.
5   Ibid., 7–8.
6   Sōseki, *Natsume Sōseki zenshū*, vol. 5, 334–35.
7   Masao Miyoshi, "Against the Native Grain: Reading the Japanese Novel in America," in *Critical Issues in East Asian Literature: Report on International Conference on East Asian Literature*, 13–20 June 1983 (Seoul, 1983), 225.
8   Karatani, *Origins*, 15.
9   Michel Foucault, *The Order of Things: An Archaeology of the Human Sciences* (New York, 1973), 69.
10 Karatani, *Origins*, 30.
11 Jacques Derrida, *Writing and Difference*, trans. Alan Bass (Chicago, 1978), 79.
12 Karatani, *Origins*, 36–37.
13 Alice Jardine, *Gynesis: Configurations of Woman and Modernity* (Ithaca, 1985), 119.
14 Nakamura Mitsuo, *Japanese Fiction in the Meiji Era*, trans. Donald Philippi (Tokyo, 1966), 1.
15 Ibid., 6.
16 Ibid., 7.
17 See Edward Fowler, "Shishōsetsu in Modern Japanese Literature," in *Working Papers in Asian Pacific Studies* (Durham, 1985) and Alan Wolfe, "Suicidal Deconstruction: Dazai Osamu and the Dilemma of Modern Japanese Literature" (Ph.D. diss., Cornell University, 1984).
18 Nakamura Mitsuo, *Meiji bungakushi* (*A History of Meiji Literature*) (Tokyo, 1964), 8.

19 Ibid., 6.

20 Donald Keene, *Dawn to the West: Japanese Literature in the Modern Era* (New York, 1984), 97–99.

21 See Yamanouchi Hisaaki, *The Search for Authenticity in Modern Japanese Literature* (Cambridge, 1978).

22 Karatani, *Origins*, 67, 81.

23 Ibid., 51.

24 Ibid., 47.

25 Ibid., 49.

26 Ibid., 55–56.

27 Ibid., 64.

28 Ibid., 58–62.

29 Ibid., 60–61.

30 Janine Beichmann, *Masaoka Shiki* (Boston, 1982), 46.

31 Ibid., 55.

32 Karatani, *Origins*, 26.

33 Ibid., 78.

34 Jean Starobinski, *Jean Jacques Rousseau: Le transparence et l'obstacle* (*Jean Jacques Rousseau: Transparency and Obstacle*) (Paris, 1954).

35 Starobinski, cited in Karatani, *Origins*, 78.

36 Kunikida Doppo, cited in Karatani, *Origins*, 78.

Karatani Kōjin

One Spirit, Two Nineteenth Centuries

The Japanese nineteenth century belongs unequivocally to the age of Edo (1600–1867). Notwithstanding the rapid economic and political transformations brought about by the Meiji restoration of 1868, Japanese tastes and ways of life did not change radically. Today's "modern literature" emerged only during the last decade of the nineteenth century. Whereas in Europe at this time literature and philosophy were seeking to deny the very idea of a nineteenth century—and looking to other alternatives—Japanese literature was barely beginning to conceive of its own nineteenth century.

To be sure, this problem can be eluded by recourse to a "modernization" perspective and its concomitant notion of underdevelopment, which is premised on a vision of the world as a homogeneous entity, a vision that derives from the industrial revolution and the rise of the world market in the nineteenth century. What the term "modern" in fact refers to is the nineteenth century of the West, that century which has managed to extend Western culture all over the world and to reorganize world history on a Eurocentric basis. The encyclopedists of the eighteenth century, for all of their resourcefulness in identifying even Confucianism as an Enlightenment paradigm, did not yet possess the quantitative criteria of "modernity" they were to require in order to rewrite universal history. The Eurocentrism of that era, in other words, was only too typical of the egocentricism characteristic of all nations.

In Hegelian thought, then, world history is narrated within a fundamental identity, and successive, heterogeneous "worlds" are appropriated into this as "stages." Exteriority or difference gestates and is sublated within interiority, as contradiction. Hegel's spirit is in this sense the unification within a centralized, linear perspective of what had been a network of communication with multiple centers and directions. What made this development possible was the nineteenth century of the West. No matter how far back in history Western thinkers take their criticism of the West, they end up targeting the nineteenth century, to which they feel irrevocably linked. And regardless of how negative their criticism might be, it invariably and conspicuously privileges the nineteenth century.

≡≡≡

Postmodernism had been defined by Jean-François Lyotard as the death of the great metanarratives. This does not mean that history has literally come to an end; the death of "history as narrative" is really the death of that "spirit" which surveys history in terms of its end or goal. This is not the dawn of yet another historical stage. It is precisely the modern consciousness which seeks to delineate such beginnings. The postmodern, on the other hand, is what Husserl has called a "transcendental" consciousness that attempts to bracket trancendent consciousness which would organize history within the unitary perspective of subjectivity.

In Japan, eras are named after reigning emperors and differentiated on that basis. It is in this sense that "Meiji literature" and "Taisho literature" can be said to exist. This method of periodization provides us with beginnings and ends. We have here a form of narrative which organizes a self-regulating discursive space in which exteriority is either suppressed or internalized in an arbitrary fashion.

By contrast, the Western calendar may appear to be "universal." But the Western calendar was initially organized around a Christian narrative in which the one-hundred-year period was invested with ritual significance, as marking the "death" and "rebirth" of an era. The concept of "fin de siècle," for example, has served both to interpret events and to produce them. The same could be said of the differentiation between "nineteenth" and "twentieth" centuries. When I use the term "nineteenth century," I am not simply making use of an ordinal number; I am giving tacit recognition to the universality of a Western narrative/history.

It is not my intention here to deny all forms of historical periodization. Narratives inevitably confer beginnings and ends on events as a means of rendering them intelligible. To reject one form of periodization is to participate in another, and we must not be naive about this. I am here constructing a narrative about Japan's nineteenth century. Thus, on the one hand, I have temporarily bracketed Japanese imperial era names as a means of demarcating time and giving it meaning in the Japanese context. On the other hand, I wish to bracket the narrative/history which universalizes the West's nineteenth century.

It is in this sense, and this sense only, that the Japanese nineteenth century differs fundamentally from the nineteenth century of the West: it can in no way be characterized as "premodern." If twentieth-century Japanese generally feel an aversion to this era, it is not that they reject the feudal regime of Edo in toto: on the contrary, they have always appreciated the philosophy and literature of the eighteenth century. But in the nineteenth century, "man"—or rather, "meaning"—is absent from Japan. This absence is not linked to any premodern character of the period, but is rather the culminating point of a maturation process. If the West can be said to remain dependent on its nineteenth century, it may also be supposed—from the very fact that they did not truly experience a nineteenth century —that the Japanese should be relatively free of all restraints with regard to nineteenth-century ideas and sensibilities. And yet these same restraints weigh heavily upon the Japanese of today.

To be sure, modern thinkers actually failed in their attempts to repudiate the nineteenth century. It was rather Westerners who noted that era's specificity: Europeans of the mid-century, especially the

Impressionists, were captivated by "things Japanese." Van Gogh writes in several letters that he wishes to see reality "as the Japanese do." These "Japanese," it would appear, are those of the nineteenth century, from the end of the Edo era. The Europeans found in "Japanism" a way out of their own century: they discovered a world without a point of view (a subject), one indifferent to all meaning. This type of analysis, moreover, could have been applied to literature, had literature been at all accessible to them, for Japanese literature was without either interiority or objectivity: it offered a pure play of language. To be sure, these were characteristics of nineteenth-century literature, and were in no way true of the eighteenth century, which in turn explains why Japanese literature textbooks dwell at some length on the latter while making practically no mention of the former. But the fact that Japan's modern literature has disavowed its nineteenth-century literature—and in a way endeavored to suppress it—is at the same time proof of that literature's tenacity.

It was during the last decade of the nineteenth century that modern literature made its appearance in Japan: while it did not derive from an epistemological model specific to the nineteenth century, it was made possible only by the breach and overthrow of this model. This phenomenon cannot be explained as a consequence of the introduction of Western ideas; it must be examined at the level of writing.

In the 1880s there arose a movement for the "Unification of the Written and Spoken Languages," whose ostensible goal was to make the written language conform to the spoken, but whose real aim was to create a new written language in place of the existing one. It was not a matter of writing as people spoke, because writers of the popular literary genre known as *gesaku* had already instituted a mode of writing based on nonliterary and vernacular speech. It was rather a question of making language transparent in order to subordinate it to meaning (interiority), and hence to suppress its exteriority. In this regard, we may note that this movement did not originate with literature, but was conducted in tandem with the policy of Westernization initiated even prior to the Meiji restoration. That policy had sought to eliminate Chinese characters from written Japanese on the assumption that they were responsible for the difficulty involved in the learning of the writing system, and consequently constituted the cause of Japan's cultural underdevelopment. Chinese characters do not play the same role in Japanese as they do in Chinese, insofar as each character corresponds to several different sound values. While this feature allows for a broad range of possible plays on words, it does make considerable demands upon the learner. The movement, in any event, never achieved its goals. Still, its fundamental tenet was the elimination of Chinese characters, which suggests to what extent they symbolized the exteriority of language with regard to the subject, and how their elimination might reinforce the perception of a univocal relationship between language and meaning. Ultimately these observations had nothing to do with the actual usage of Chinese characters, since the issue at hand was to change the relationship between language and the thinking subject, between language and the world of objects.

Jean Starobinski says of Rousseau that he was the first to establish a delicate link between the self and language. As he noted in *Le transparence et l'obstacle* (1954), "Rousseau was the first to realize, in a prototypical manner, that dangerous liaison between the self and speech, that new fusion whereby 'Man' took himself to be language." It was just such an identification between language and subject that was sought by the movement for the "Unification of the Written and Spoken Languages." And clearly the "first" in Japan to do as Rousseau did was Kunikida Doppo, who in the 1880s engineered this delicate link between self and language. We may add that this new link also engendered the discovery of an exterior mode known as "landscape."

Kunikida was a minor writer whose originality lay in his discovery of a space in which interiority, language, and objects could mix. He was the first writer to introduce "landscape." Edo literature (or, more generally, classical literature) is known for the privileging of landscape and its description. Still, landscape was language. For example, when the seventeenth-century poet Basho traveled through the Japanese provinces, he was drawn less to actual landscapes than he was to the ancient poetry which had evoked them. Literature prior to the nineteenth century was interested in landscape only as a weave of language.

It is a paradox that the new "landscape" should have been discovered by a man so introverted that he was almost perverse in his failure to recognize the external world, just as Rousseau discovered the beauty of the Alps which had until then been no more than a geographical obstacle. Realism was made possible not by the observation of objects, but by a delicate link between language, interiority, and object. Naturally, the delicate nature of this operation was immediately forgotten, although it was evident to writers who came after Kunikida. In other words, Japanese literature was severed from the epistemological mechanism of the nineteenth century, at which point it became possible to speak of the birth of modern literature. Needless to say, this birth was but the implementation of "literature" as the same type of system that had been operative in the West of the nineteenth century. What is of significance, however, is the fact that this process, which evolved over several centuries in the West, was concentrated here within a period of approximately ten years.

To put it differently, Japanese literature attempted to use the nineteenth century of the West to suppress its own Japanese nineteenth century. At the very moment when the avant-garde of the West was challenging the epistémè of its nineteenth century and looking to the non-West (especially to Japan) for a way out of its impasse, Japanese literature found itself inscribed within the framework of the nineteenth century, or rather (to go back even further) within a logocentric system. But it is not all that simple. Japanese writers were entirely lacking in the ability to construct, to create a world in its totality, as appeared in Western nineteenth-century novels. The only Japanese to succeed at this were Marxists or "postwar" writers who had been Marxist before the war. The mainstream of Japanese fiction turned against the "logos" in its preference for what was called the "I-novel" (*shi-shōsetsu*). To be sure, Japanese writers considered themselves at the conscious level to be part of the structure of modern literature in general, although they did not hide their dislike of Western nineteenth-century literature. They were especially contemptuous of the idea of controlling a work with a single theme (meaning). This attitude ostensibly reminds one of Western self-criticism directed against the nineteenth century, although once again we should perhaps see here evidence of the tenacity of that nineteenth century.

To the extent Western painters were aware of the distinctiveness of the Japanese nineteenth century, what they perceived therein was not a perspective, but rather the deliberate negation of all perspective. Today, a century later, this perception does not seem to have changed. For example, the elements of Japanese life evoked in Roland Barthes's *Empire of Signs* are almost all products of this nineteenth century. What Barthes praises is the absence of "man," of the thinking subject. What he discovers, as did the Impressionists, is the "exteriority" of the Western world within the Japanese nineteenth century. I am not accusing Barthes of "Orientalism" (to use Edward Said's designation) by saying to him: "Look at the reality of Japan." Barthes was himself only too aware of this dilemma. He sought to discover a "Japan" situated outside the life and thought of the West, a "Japan" which was other than that life and thought and which was, of course, nonexistent. Barthes would have written the same thing had he seen the Japan of today, sliding, without any resistance, into postindustrial society. The Japanese nineteenth century may have been an impediment to "modernization," but it promises to be an accelerating factor for a postmodern society.

In *The Way to the Word*, Heidegger makes mention of the concept of *iki* as spoken of by the Japanese philosopher, Kuki Shūzō, whom he knew before the war. Notwithstanding Heidegger's desire to see in *iki* a possibility for going beyond Western thought, he is in total ignorance of what *iki* is. It is not, as he imagines, a Buddhistic, abyssal idea, but simply a designation for a sensibility which developed in the nineteenth-century Edo period (and remained exclusive to Edo). In his *Structure of Iki*, Kuki seeks to give a philosophical meaning to *iki* by means of a structural analysis of the different life-styles that developed in and around the pleasure quarters.[1]

Edo literature and fashion developed as part of the consumer society which grew around the world of the pleasure quarters, which offered a space free of class and sex discrimination (although money was a prerequisite), a space—albeit imaginary—where the feudal system could be transcended. The merchant bourgeoisie of the seventeenth and eighteenth centuries had created, by means of this zone of "deviance," a literature suggestive of its class potency. This process had begun in seventeenth-century Osaka, and by the time the cultural and economic center shifted to Edo at the end of the eighteenth century, the pleasure quarters had already been divested of their transcendental character.

Iki involves keeping a certain distance from the woman one loves in order to avoid passion and folly. According to Kuki, it is a matter of playing ad infinitum on this perilous distance. Or, in Heideggerean terms, it involves playing with the *Abgrund* (the "abyssal depth," in Gilbert Kahn's translation). It is at this level that Heidegger was attracted to Kuki's *iki*. And, in a sense, the Japanese nineteenth century may be understood as a "structure of *iki*."

Kuki was without doubt the only philosopher to seek the philosophical meaning of the nineteenth century in the "modernization" of Japan. In this respect, he differed from those who preached anti-Western Japanocentrism or the superiority of the "Japanese spirit." Kuki also differed from Nishida Kitarō, who looked to Zen for a means of overcoming the dualism of Western philosophy. Notwithstanding his discriminating intellect, Kuki was a willing participant in the "overcoming the modern" movement of the prewar fascist period.

For Kuki, *iki* had three components—seduction, renunciation, and valor—which, he argued, yielded a synthesis of Japanese naturalism, Indian nihilism, and Chinese (Confucian) idealism. Not only is this most plausible; it also suggests why Heidegger may have seen in *iki* the essence of Far Eastern philosophy. Nonetheless Kuki, in another context, applies this same argument to the "Three Divine Regalia" which are taken as symbolic of the imperial system:

> If the Japanese character may be seen as a fusion of three fundamental components of Japanese culture—nature, valor, and resignation—may we not regard the "Three Divine Regalia" as symbolic of this fusion? It must be for this reason that the jewel is said to express benevolence, the mirror wisdom, and the sword manliness. And is it not for this reason that the jewel is also seen as a symbol of refinement, the mirror of civilization, and the

sword of sovereignty over the world? Among nature, valor, and resignation, is it not fitting to see nature as represented by the jewel, valor by the sword, and resignation by the mirror?

It is surprising to see how *iki* imperceptibly shifts toward the idea of *kokutai* ("national body"). Even as Kuki searched for the forgotten "being" of the modern world in the aesthetic way of life of the nineteenth century, he was transforming himself into a typical ideologue of nineteenth-century imperialism. The same may be said of Heidegger, who, during the same period, declared: "Spirit is neither sagacity operating in a vacuum, nor is it the irresponsible play of wit; it does not consist in endless intellectual dissection, and even less is it universal reason. Spirit is, as disposed by origin and fully conscious, the definite opening to the Being [*Wesen*] of the individual." Following this declaration, Heidegger speaks of the "historical mission of the German people, situated at the center of the West." It is in this context that Kuki's *iki* and Heidegger's *spirit* resonate with each other. And each in its own way arrives, respectively, at the "Great East Asian Coprosperity Sphere" and the "Third Reich."

It is foolish of Heidegger, ten years after the war, to speak of *iki* as if it were something that goes beyond the limits of Western thought. He finds that spirit in the nineteenth century is dissolved by the dualism of subject and object, and by industrial society, but it is precisely in the nineteenth century that spirit comes to be attached to "community." In Japan, too, moreover, it is in the nineteenth century that one begins to speak of "Japanese spirit."

≡

Those who critique nineteenth-century thought always look back to Descartes. But for Descartes "spirit" was not the same as thought, nor was it a psychological subject. "I think, therefore I am" was but a formula repeated since St. Augustine. Descartes as traveler and foreigner is a doubter: he asks if what we think is not merely a custom peculiar to each community, and if, rather than thinking, we are not just conforming to a prescribed system. Descartes thus doubts, wondering whether or not he is dreaming, and it is this doubt which constitutes spirit and makes it clear that spirit is exteriority. As Husserl has observed, the Cartesian cogito is a transcendental ego through which the psychological ego is bracketed. But to be trancendental is to be exterior—I exist in exteriority and can exist only there. The Cartesian cogito is alien to interior certainty, consisting rather in the doubting of such an interior presence. For such a presence to exist, proof of the cogito would have to be guaranteed by God (the Other), which is not the God believed in by the community or by individual conscience.

When the Cartesian cogito was interiorized as a thinking subject, Spinoza criticized Descartes in order to remain faithful to him. For Spinoza, the psychological ego, or free will, was purely imaginary. Subjectivity (spontaneity) was imaginary in the sense that, although it is regulated by a multiplicity of systems, we are not aware of this. Nevertheless, Spinoza recognized the existence of a kind of will which is knowledge. Subjectivity, therefore, is that which strains to discern the ways in which unconscious structures and the system of the community constrain it—subjectivity, in this sense, is transcendental. It is the cogito as exteriority. Spirit is never reduced, as with Heidegger, to a "historical mission of the nation." It is a will (to power, as Nietzsche says) which seeks to distinguish itself; it is an identity which differentiates itself. Spirit is a will that externalizes itself, a position that nullifies all positions.

In the following passage from Alan Bass's translation of *Positions*, Derrida speaks in different terms about this "spirit":

> To "deconstruct" philosophy . . . would be to think—in the most faithful, interior way—the structured genealogy of philosophy's concepts, but at the same time to determine—from a certain exterior that is unqualifiable or unnameable by philosophy—what this history has been able to dissimulate or forbid, making itself into a history by means of this somewhere motivated repression.

But this "certain exterior" is nowhere to be found in a positive form. It is a purely transcendental exterior; if it were not so, it could only be a transcendent, imaginary subject. For example, the "Japan" of the *Empire of Signs* is a place of absence. Barthes's project was to reexamine Western thought in terms of an exteriority free of the sovereignty of the thinking subject which would be called "Japan." It is in this sense that Barthes's "spirit" exists: as a critique of the Western nineteenth century, seen as an autarchy devoid of exteriority. But the "Japan" discovered by Barthes—that is, the Japanese nineteenth century—is also a despotic system. The structure of *iki*, defined by Kuki as "Japanese spirit," is a mode of thought which has lost all exteriority by wrapping itself in its identity. At the same time, moreover, and for the first time in Japanese history, the "Japanese spirit" has found an advocate.

Until the eighteenth century, Japanese thought operated in accordance with Confucian and Buddhist texts, which is to say that Japanese people were conscious of exteriority. It was neo-Confucianism, a synthesis of Buddhist philosophy and Confucianism, which dominated the Edo period and had been introduced from China, functioning exactly like a scholastic philosophy. At the end of the seventeenth century, Itō Jinsai, a scholar with origins in the merchant class, undertook an interpretation of Confucian texts in order to criticize the rationalism (or logocentrism) of neo-Confucianism. Itō had no nationalistic pretentions; his goal was rather to affirm the universality of the texts of Confucius. He focused his critique on Zen-like thought emanating from individual awareness. What Itō emphasized was the exteriority of language. Thus, in the eighteenth century, Japanese thought took the form of a critique of philosophy, that is, a hermeneutics. This critique of *ri* (reason, principle, etc.) was then taken up in the second half of the eighteenth century by Motoori Norinaga, who became the first to reject Buddhist, Confucian, and Taoist texts in favor of a critique of rationalism based on an interpretation of ancient Japanese texts like the *Tale of Genji* and the *Records of Ancient Matters* (*Kojiki*). Motoori Norinaga writes in *Tamakatsuma*:

> By Chinese spirit [*karagokoro*], I do not mean only the veneration of China and its ways, but all the influence engendered by these Chinese books, which have led so many people to seek to judge good and evil as components of all actions, and to define the principles [*ri*] inherent in all things. This is not only the doing of those who have read Chinese texts, but is true even of those

who have not read a single Chinese book. Those who do not read Chinese books should not be tempted in this way, but, insofar as China has been considered superior in all domains for over a thousand years, and insofar as Chinese studies have not declined, it is not surprising that this spirit has spread and penetrated our hearts in such a powerful way. While we may believe that we are free of this Chinese spirit, or that certain observations are entirely natural and not derivative from it, the fact is that we are irrevocably tied to this Chinese spirit.

Motoori Norinaga adopts an ambiguous style here, and it is true that this tone and approach are to become the basis for a nationalistic movement called "National Studies." Motoori extends his notion of Chinese spirit to include even Japanese Shinto; he does not, however, put forward a substantive conception of a "Japanese spirit" (*yamato-gokoro*). The latter term may simply be called spirit. What Motoori Norinaga calls "Chinese spirit" and "Buddhist spirit" has nothing to do with Kuki's "Confucianist idealism" and "Buddhist nihilism." Motoori is referring to a system in which we believe we think spontaneously when in fact it is the system which is making us think. That which Husserl might have termed "naturalism" corresponds precisely to the "Chinese spirit" of Motoori Norinaga, for whom true spirit is an act of phenomenological reduction of a consciousness which has been morally and intellectually deformed.

Motoori Norinaga as a textual scholar thus clearly locates his "Japanese spirit" in the Ancient period, much as Nietzsche found his "beyond good and evil" in the age of Greek tragedy. He takes Itō Jinsai's critique of *ri* a step further, refusing to discern any sign of *ri* (meaning) in the language of the *Kojiki*. Motoori was a thoroughgoing materialist, declaring that all men, good and bad, end up beneath the ground. This position was, without doubt, untenable for his successors. In the nineteenth century, Hirata Atsutane introduced Christian notions in his interpretation of the *Kojiki*, and went on to develop it into a fanatical theory of Shintoism which eventually became the ideological basis for the Meiji restoration.

Nonetheless, at the end of the eighteenth century, the thought of Motoori Norinaga may be said to have constituted an epistemological zenith. At that point, there was only one alternative remaining: to push further the idea that all is language, an idea leading to a world of pure surface, one devoid of all meaning and interiority. The structure of *iki* enters into this category. At the same time, it was also necessary to rediscover "meaning," a process which was to lead to nationalistic fanaticism.

The Japanese nineteenth century is distinguished, then, by the fact that, as it begins, the deconstruction of *ri* is already accomplished. It is therefore impossible to consider the nineteenth century simply as a premodern era. What stubbornly resisted the "modernization" of Japanese thought and literature in the twentieth century was not simply a premodern sensibility but a mode of thought which in some senses had already transcended the modern. This naturally took the form of a citation of the anti-Western elements of Western thought. Its grand finale was the wartime ideology of "overcoming the modern."

A similar situation prevails in the Japan of the 1980s. Japan has become a highly developed information-consumption society, in which meaning is information and desire is the desire of the Other, because the "subject" of the nineteenth-century West has never existed in Japan, nor has there been any resistance to the modern. In 1980s Japan (a Japan "liberated" from its obsession with modernism), parody, pastiche, and collage have become dominant trends. But in the Japanese context, this amounts to a rehabilitation of the nineteenth century. It is a revival of that mood within which late Edo society saw itself as a "paradise of fools." There is an almost pathological play with language, with the reign of the superficial on the one hand, and the regeneration of ultranationalistic ideology on the other. The "overcoming of the modern" is once again being touted, but in a different context. This historical stage should not be called postmodernity. For the postmodern, as I have emphasized earlier, designates that which is transcendental in contradistinction to a mode of thought which lacks exteriority and perceives history in terms of stages and ends.

No matter what form the West's evaluation of Japan may take, Japan will remain for the West a place of exteriority rather than being what in fact it is: a discursive space filled with complacency and almost totally lacking in exteriority. Can there be a way out of this situation? The only word that comes to mind is "spirit," not, to be sure, interior or community spirit, but rather spirit as exteriority.

Translated by Alan Wolfe

Notes

1   *The Structure of Iki* by Kuki Shūzō (1888–1941) was analyzed in detail in an article by Hosoi Atsuko and Jacqueline Pigeot in *Critique* 308 (1973): 39–52; it is also partially translated in a chapter entitled "Structure compréhensive de l'iki," in Nakamura Ryoji and Rene de Ceccatty, *Mille ans de littérature Japonaise* (Paris, 1982). See also the complete French translation by Maeno Toshikuni, *Structure de l'iki* (Paris, 1984).

Asada Akira

Infantile Capitalism and Japan's Postmodernism: A Fairy Tale

Allow me to talk semi-extemporaneously —because I am not familiar with the academic customs of American Japanology, and because above all else, I am not only the analyst but the object of analysis. Yes, I happen to be Japanese; I am not a Japan scholar. It is not that I have never been aware of my deep involvement with Japan's postmodernism; even so, it was quite a surprise to discover through Marilyn Ivy's article that I was such a central figure.

Naturally I am aware that Japan's postindustrial capitalism has attempted to use my work; I, too, have attempted to analyze the mechanism of that very capitalism. Here, I would like to present very schematically and somewhat parodically a rough sketch of an aspect of that analysis. The parodic nature of my remarks, it will be fine for you to think, derives from the ambivalence of my position as narrator, as I have described it above.

When Marilyn Ivy discussed Nakasone Yasuhiro's transhistorical delirium, I recalled an almost equally delirious discussion I had with Félix Guattari during his visit to Japan. We talked about capitalism's global trajectory and the three stages along that trajectory: elderly capitalism, adult capitalism, and infantile capitalism.

Elderly capitalism is found in countries like Italy and France which developed an early mercantile capitalism, countries where a transcendental value system like Catholicism still remains. Such a value system is a vertically centralized system, supported by the Subject, with a capital S. Only in relationship with this Subject can each individual find the position of his own self, and identify himself as the subject. The position of this capitalized Subject is occupied by God, the King, the father, or, in economics, gold. But for now it is fine to call it more abstractly "transcendental signifier." In any case, those who believe in such external values—in other words, those who hoard gold—are the "elderly" people I am talking about here. Now, needless to say, capitalism starts to operate by striking off the head in the center and by decoding the system; in other words, by decimating the system and putting the separate elements into a current. It is not a system of static differences but a process of dynamic differentiation in which differences are constantly created and consumed. Therefore, at this point vestiges of a static system are nothing but impediments. From here stems the relative inactivity of elderly capitalism.

In contrast, industrial "adult" capitalism is far more dynamic: it is found where capitalism's trajectory has crossed Europe and gone across the sea, for example in England and the United States. There, leading roles are no longer played by the possessors of transcendental values embodied by gold, but by entrepreneurs who will invest values into the endless process of growth. Through their activities, the entire system is decimated and thrown into a dynamic current. In other words, the process of relative competition replaces a system of positions and roles. Through this new stage of mutual competition in which everyone competes with his neighbor as the model/ rival, a strange kind of subject emerges. This is the subject which, having internalized the model/rival, has begun to compete with himself. To describe it after Foucault, it is the subject as an odd duality which is both empirical and transcendental, *étrange doublet empirico-transcendental* that has learned to supervise and motivate itself through discipline and training. Or, to describe it after Deleuze and Guattari, it is the subject which, internalizing paternal instance through "Oedipalization," has come to make itself its own colony. Whichever it is, this subject which has internalized the structure of vertical control within itself is precisely what Max Weber analyzed and what modernists like Ōtsuka Hisao and Maruyama Masao use as their model: subject (*shutai*) as the bearer of classical industrial capitalism, the individual that bears responsibility for himself. To them, the formation of such an individual subject is the indispensable condition for Japan's modernization. If we call this subject the adult, modernization is precisely the process of maturation.

In reality, however, Japan did not at all mature. Far from it. It seems to be growing progressively more infantile. Yet Japanese capitalism appears to be functioning all the more smoothly and effectively. Is the formation of the adult subject in fact really necessary and indispensable to capitalism, if not to modernization? The answer, I think, is "no." What is indispensable is, rather, the process of relative competition; it does not matter whether the relationship becomes internalized or remains external. Clearly, the latter is the case with Japan. Thus, in Japan, there are neither tradition-oriented old people adhering to transcendental values nor inner-oriented adults who have internalized their values; instead, the nearly purely relative (or relativistic) competition exhibited by other-oriented children provides the powerful driving force for capitalism. Let's call this infantile capitalism. This is a remarkable spectacle, and, in many senses, deeply interesting. In the manufacturing sector, for example, we may be able to say that Japanese engineers are cleverly maneuvered into displaying a childlike passion whereby they are easily obsessed with machines. Further, in such a postindustrial area as advertising, people become carried away by word play, parody, and all the other childlike games of differentiation. Even my book which analyzes that process has been consumed precisely in that process. The situation created in this way is indeed anarchic at first glance, and I almost feel like calling it children's frenzied capitalism, "*capitalisme énergumène*," to borrow the title of Lyotard's book review of *L'Anti-Oedipe*.

Is this utopian capitalism?—is this the goal of the global trajectory of capitalism that broke down territorial boundaries as it stretched from the Mediterranean Sea up north across Europe out to the ocean, crossed the Atlantic, crossed the United States, and finally traversed the Pacific? Is this the goal of capitalism's history as a process of infantilization which might as well be called a parody of Hegelian world history? Of course, it can never be anything like that: but this very negation must be uttered with a burst of laughter. And, we might add, after laughing, that it is a playful utopia and at the same time a terrible "dystopia."

In fact, children can play "freely" only when there is some kind of protection. They always play within a certain protected area. And this protected area is precisely the core of the Japanese ideological mechanism—however thinly diffused a core. It is not a "hard" ruling structure which is vertically centralized (whether transcendental or internalized), but "soft" subsumption by a seemingly horizontal, centerless "place." Here we can recall, as ideological expressions of the Japanese ideology, various stereotyped theories about the Japanese people. Despite frequent argument about Confucian patriarchy, the Japanese family is an essentially maternal arena of "*amae*," indulgence, and both the father and the children are softly wrapped in it (in other words, the mother is forced to provide that kind of care). In Japanese companies, the clever management, rather than mobilizing the entire company around its positive leadership, functions as an apparently passive medium which prompts agreement to be spontaneously formed from the bottom up. To begin with, the emperor is exactly that kind of passive medium, and this is reflected in the city structure which has an empty center. Whether this results in praise of the harmony and efficiency in Japanese institutions (revisionist modernism) or praise of the aesthetic of empty "relationality (postmodernism)," the ideological nature of these stereotypes is undeniable: that is, an aspect of Japan's ideological mechanism—a description which is ideological, yet, as such, adequate to a certain extent.

One of the most abstract and powerful expressions of this Japanese ideology is Nishida Kitaro's philosophy—his theory of "*mu no basho*," place of nothingness—which became the tacitly understood foundation of the postmodernism of the 1930s, or the so-called theory of "*kindai no chōkoku*": "overcoming the modern." "*Mu*," nothingness, is the principle of his philosophy, but we should not make it into an entity as a transcendental center. Rather, it negates itself and becomes an empty place, embracing seemingly contradictory elements. There, instead of being *aufheben*-ed toward the higher, contradiction is dissolved, so to speak, toward the lower. The dialectic of contradiction and strife, which is supposed to evolve into history, is replaced by the topology of subsumption which is atemporal and peaceful. Of course, all I am doing here is describing an aspect of Nishida's philosophy in a burlesque and simplified way; in order really to criticize it, it is necessary to examine in detail why his philosophy with its rich potential had to end up as such a theory of unification—or, rather, "zerofication." Yet we cannot deny that this was the point Nishida arrived at. Even more troubling, a text like *The Problems of Japanese Culture*, which played up to the dominant forces of the time, narrates the essence of his philosophy even better than any of his other writings. In this text, which consists of a series of his wartime lectures, Nishida regards the imperial household as the ultimate "place of nothingness." While European kings and nations, based on the principle of "*yu*," presence, contain conflict between individuals and the whole, and have no other choice but to repeat collision through striving to expand the self in space, the imperial household as the place of nothingness contains Japan like an empty cylinder which pierces time; and inside of this, on the basis of *zettai mujunteki jiko doitsu* (absolute contradictory self-identity) which exists between atomism and holism, individuals will each find a place and participate in "holonic," as opposed to holistic, harmony. When this spontaneously spreads, the "Great East Asian Coprosperity Sphere" —is this the absolute contradictory self-identity between liberation from European imperialism and aggression by Japanese imperialism?—will be formed.

This ideology is peaceful at first glance. All the more so because it has been exposed to no fundamental criticism; it still exists latently today. In fact, even when the simpleminded totalitarianism supported by the army had to be thoroughly criticized after the war, no such thorough criticism was directed against Nishida and his disciples, or against the Kyoto school. Naturally, hidden behind the shadow of modernism which held that everyone had to exit the protected area to become independent as an adult, it was long neglected. However, as the value of becoming an adult declined throughout the 1970s while Japan's infantile capitalism swept over Asia, it started to lift its head again. The tie between Nakasone Yasuhiro, formerly of the navy, and the so-called neo-Kyoto school can be seen as a symbol of this revival. If it is further refined, it may tie up with what was already recognized by the Ōhira regime: the "holonic paradigm" (the techno-capitalistic mandala based on the so-called soft science: mother technology which embraces the children?). It may then be advertised as postmodernism, which transcends the contradictions of modern times, and as transnationalism, which transcends the limitations of nationalism. If, however, that postmodernism/transnationalism is nothing but a repetition of the postmodernism/transnationalism of the 1930s, this is truly a farce.

Thus we can once again return to the delirious parody of Hegelian world history and polish it even further. Children are running around, each one as fast as possible, at the front lines of the history of capitalism as infantilization proceeds. They are enveloped by a "place" whose age is hardly known—the "place" that is transhistorical in the sense that Nishida demonstrated, or, if you like, posthistorical in Kojève's sense; the "place" which, moreover, is now electronic. Can this be the absolute contradictory self-identity between the "old" and the "infantile" which is achieved at the end of world history? Naturally, of course, such a vision is nothing but an extreme form of idealist perversion. At this point, the idiocy of it all is already evident. Or rather I should say, so that this vision will collapse by itself, I have purposely continued to engage in a grotesque parody. What remains to be done is to dismantle this perversion thoroughly, and from there to produce a realistic analysis. That work, however, is something I would like to undertake together with you, who know Japan better than I do, in future discussions.

Can you hear me laughing?

Translated by Kyoko Selden

Stephen Melville

Picturing Japan: Reflections
on the Workshop

My involvement with questions about post-modernity began some seven or eight years ago in the context of claims being advanced on behalf of certain visual works and practices in the New York art world that seemed to be emerging in crucial relationship with photography. These claims appeared to connect with both my direct interest in the work of Jacques Derrida and associated figures, and with the frame I was developing out of the writings of Stanley Cavell and Michael Fried in order to explicate the nature of Derrida's claim on philosophic and critical interests. I have continued to write in this area, and it is presumably because of this work that I was invited to participate in the workshop.

I came into it, then, with little more than a headful of images of Japan and a few half-formed questions. Because of difficulties in receiving papers ahead of time, I had little to go on in preparing my initial response on Sunday morning, so I took the only route open and plunged on into my own naiveté and stockpile of clichés. In particular, I brought with me a sense—shared by many of my colleagues at Syracuse and, I imagine, many other Americans—that "Japan just *is* the postmodern," and I glossed this by suggesting that the Western discourse on postmodernism is haunted by a certain "Japan" that is the simultaneous site of capitalism and Godzilla, of the microchip as an achievement of capitalism and of that same chip as the promise of something "beyond capitalism." "Japan": land not only of the cassette player, the VCR, and the DAT, but the land where these things multiply internally into high-speed dubbing decks, and start opening the imagination of *Bladerunner* or William Gibson's technopunk science fiction. I also suggested that at a presumably more sophisticated level, "Japan" promised a kind of heaven of theory where there are no choices to be made among Jameson, Lyotard, Baudrillard, Debord. . . .

I offered this explicitly as an imagination of Japan, and went on to ask how far one could take the simplicity of this genitive, its apparent objectivity, for granted, and how far it was reversible. Whose imagination *of* whom is finally at issue? How far does Japan—and now I don't know whether or not to put quotation marks around this name —matter in the context of the postmodern precisely because it displays this "of" as radically unreadable? Was our issue, interestingly elided in the workshop's title, the ways in which postmodernity was never quite "in" Japan but never simply exterior to it either?[1]

The other bit of ignorance I offered up for discussion was a dim awareness, which again I share with many of my colleagues, of the vast Japanese literature on Heidegger. I wondered why this literature has had no Western reception, and posed this as a problem of translation (with this I wandered, all unwitting, into the whole bundle of issues that I came to learn surround Kuki Shūzō, Nishida, and the Kyoto School). My interest here lay in exploring the differences between two meditations on translation raised within my own intellectual tradition and in the context of Japan: Heidegger's revision of his conversations with Professor Tezuka, and Derrida's letter to Professor Izutsu about translating the term "deconstruction."[2]

One can lay out quickly a striking array of differences between the two texts: Heidegger's is apparently a face-to-face dialogue held in Germany in the context of relations between teacher and student;[3]

Derrida's is a letter sent to Japan, isolated from both its occasion and its response, and addressed to "a friend." I hoped to make these differences count in a certain way as a difference between the modern and the postmodern.

On the face of it, Heidegger's essay is serious and "thoughtful" in a way Derrida's "merely technical" remarks are not. Heidegger explicitly aims at overcoming the difference between the two apparently separate "houses of Being" that are the languages of Japan and the West. His evident success in doing so is registered in the suites of ellipses that punctuate the text, marking not failures of sense or communication but their continuity, each speaker picking up the other's thread and spinning it to its conclusion. I also remarked that, reading this "success" now, it was hard not to see it as anything more than an Orientalist "folie à deux," a sort of ventriloquism betrayed at numerous levels by Heidegger's clear authority over and authorship of the "conversation." In contrast, Derrida would seem to write merely as himself and for another's reading. Rather than attempt to solve the problem of translation, Derrida attempts to dissolve it in two directions: on the one hand, he refuses to pose any special problem of translation (as if "deconstruction" had some authoritative origin beyond or prior to translation—Derrida cites Littré and refuses the credit of coinage); on the other hand, he refuses "deconstruction" any exemption from translation—whether into "the American university" or into "Japanese." Here the fact of language is the fact of translation and equally the fact of deconstruction. There is no room for Heidegger's question about whether or not "language" "thinks the same" as the phrase "koto ba" offered by Professor Tezuka as the Japanese word for "language." To make such room would be, for Derrida, to pose a site that is in itself already deconstructed, and that would be to fall back into Heidegger's ventriloquized mastery of dialogue and difference. I suggested that this would amount to a fall into the current fantasy or imagination of Japan as the heaven of postmodernism, and I posed this chiasmatic crux, turning postmodern into modern and modern into postmodern, in particular relation to what I took to be the position of Professor Karatani (a position I take to be shared in important respects by Professors Asada and Mitani). With this I understood myself to have returned to the first question about the ambiguous status of a certain "imagination of Japan" within postmodernism.

During the course of the workshop I learned how right I was to consider these remarks naive, and I am still writing as someone who knows not more but only more about how little he knows; however, the course of the workshop worked primarily to tighten the hold of these questions and to demand of me a fuller formulation of them. I am not sure how far I can go toward this fuller formulation, but I want to take at least a few steps along this line before returning to the conclusion of my initial response.

———

It seems to me that the emergence of what I have been calling "Japan" within the Western discourse of postmodernity reflects and makes explicit the peculiar grammatical complexity of the terms "modern" and "postmodern." As Naoki Sakai put it in his paper: "This series premodern-modern-postmodern may suggest an order of chronology. However, it must be remembered that this order has never been dissociated from the geopolitical configuration of the world." One might say that a distinctive feature of the discourse of postmodernity is that it forbids us to forget this fact, as against a systematic interest in such forgetting that one might see animating the modern. In some sense, or multitude of senses, modernism meant to escape history and to lay some more direct claim to presence; in so doing it simultaneously took the non-Western as premodern and reached out to it as the already modern; in either case, it used the geopolitical relay to constitute itself in a space that was neither explicitly historical nor explicitly political. What we see in the Heidegger dialogue is a strong version of this—"Japan" is constituted in a conversation ignorant of its own immediate historical situation and in close proximity to the already modern premodernity of the pre-Socratics: "Japan," like Parmenides or Anaximander, figures forth the truth of presence; it is the place where the still distant possibility of a radical *kehre* (turn) in the tradition is directly lived and where language speaks in a way it does not yet (or no longer) speak to or for the Western "us." Against this view it would be tempting to imagine that one would then enter the postmodern through the dissolution of this Western "us" and a concomitant dissolution of the non-Western Other: "we" would then be men and women speaking as and to other men and women. One would then want to say that the geopolitical mark of postmodernity is Japan's coming to speak for itself.

But this too is a dream of presence and deliverance from history, another version of the modernist project (Habermasian rather than Heideggerean). The crucial point—and again it is made forcefully by Naoki Sakai—is that "Japan" has never been outside of quotation marks: "even in its particularism, Japan is already implicated in the ubiquitous West, so that neither historically nor geopolitically can Japan be seen as *outside* of the West. This means that, in order to criticize the West in relation to Japan, one has necessarily to begin with a critique of Japan. . . . [I]t seems to me that, insofar as one tries to speak from the position of *us*, the putative unity of either the West or Japan, one would never be able to escape the dominion of the universalism-particularism pair, that is, one would never be effective in criticism no matter how radical a posture one might put on."

"Japan" is in this sense an imaginary country (this was discussed by a number of the participants as "a closed discursive space" and figured frequently in more informal conversation as "a black hole"). It is as such that it both figures for and enters into the discourse of postmodernity; and yet it is also an actual country, a modern nation that is a considerable force in the world. It is this doubleness that allows it its peculiar status as the place where Jameson and Baudrillard coincide. One can read into this "imaginary" the full force of Lacan's exposition of the Imaginary, and one will be tempted to participate in that Imaginary through its theoretical extension and generalization in figures like Deleuze, Guattari, and Baudrillard. Two paths of resistance will seem immediately open here: the first, akin to certain Western feminist strategies, would lie in a refusal of all representation in favor of a presumably radical but finally empty and self-defeating empiricism.[4] The object here would be to find oneself apart from all quotation marks—which would be to gain a voice at the expense of language. The second would be to attempt to find oneself within quotation marks—and here the risk is that of losing one's voice to its own radical ironization (the risk run, for example, by

Asada Akira's paper "Infantile Capitalism" or, differently, by *Nanton-aku, kurisutaru* on Norma Field's account). Here too certain Western feminist strategies come to mind, particularly those that turn on the visual practice of photographic appropriation.

Without rehearsing the discussions surrounding this work,[5] it seems fair to say that photography can raise issues simultaneously about the framing of the world and the world as frame to our representations. There is in this transgressive and duplicitous play of frames[6] the possibility of a sublime apprehended not as the name or place of self-possession or mastery but as the acknowledgment of its failure, of a finitude we can call only uneasily and in different languages "ours." I would want to separate this sublime of dispossession from Alan Wolfe's "suicidal sublime," which I can read only as a late modernist revision of the "alienated suicide" from which Wolfe would distinguish it (the logic here would be parallel to that which makes of the claim to be the truth of postmodernism itself a modernist claim).[7]

The difficult line certain artists seem to be trying to steer by means of the photograph between appropriation understood as loss or denial and appropriation understood as recognition or acknowledgment may well be exemplary here. I want to comment briefly on two aspects of this effort.

The first is its linkage to feminist concerns. Both of the responses I have outlined to what I am calling "the imagination of Japan" have strong feminist analogues, and this seems to me not accidental: both "Japan" and "woman" are sites in which that which has been imagined now seeks to imagine itself. In this light the lack of reference to feminism within the workshop seems to be a striking feature of it.[8] Julia Kristeva's essay "Women's Time" sketches out the stakes for feminism in a way that may be useful. The stakes of traditional politics have always seemed clear enough: those who do not have power work to gain it. Beginning with the turn toward black power in the United States and becoming permanently explicit with the women's movement, a new uncertainty about the value of such stakes has become central to imagining the situation of politics. With reference to European feminism, Kristeva glosses this development in three stages: an initial desire to have what men have; an essentialist reaction toward defining what women have that is excluded by the very forms of masculine power and possession; and a third moment that would put an end to this oscillation. This third moment is particularly worrisome for traditional political practice insofar as it urges the dissolution of feminism itself as "but a moment in the thought of that anthropomorphic identity which currently blocks the horizon of the discursive and scientific adventure of our species."[9] This politics —or ethics, as Kristeva would have it—is unimaginable apart from a thought of time that is, in Kristeva's view, itself a product of the feminist impulse as it finds itself in time (thus the multiple resonances of her title). We thus return through a complex detour to the questions of chronology, periodization, and spatialization that underlie any attempt to enter the logic of postmodernism into our accounts of ourselves—questions that the powerful undercurrent of modernism always offers to reduce to matters of presence, self-presence, and localizable truth (even if that truth turns out to be absence and emptiness).

If we pick up a different thread of Kristeva's argument, we begin to move toward the second feature of photographic appropriation that I want to stress here. Kristeva glosses her third moment in the following terms:

This process could be summarized as an *interiorization of the founding separation of the socio-symbolic contract,* as an introduction of its cutting edge into the very interior of every identity whether subjective, sexual, ideological, or so forth. This in such a way that the habitual and increasingly explicit attempt to fabricate a scapegoat victim as the foundress of a society or counter-society may be replaced by the analysis of the potentialities of *victim/executioner* which characterize each identity, each subject, each sex. . . .

At this level of interiorization with its social as well as individual stakes, what I have called "aesthetic practices" are undoubtedly nothing other than the modern reply to the eternal question of morality. At least, this is how we might understand an ethics which, conscious of the fact that its order is sacrificial, reserves part of the burden for each of its adherents, therefore declaring them guilty while immediately affording them the possibility for *jouissance*, for various productions, for a life made up of both challenges and differences.[10]

What I want to focus on is the prominence of the notion of sacrifice—which arises not as a figure of suicide but as one of survival: a means to living on in submission to finitude within the permanent and intimate dispersion of truth and knowledge, being and knowing. The notion derives of course from Bataille; what catches my interest is the way in which Bataille has been found as a powerful resource in thinking about contemporary photographic practice. One might, at least emblematically, think of photography as a certain revelation of the duplicity of light—think of it, that is, as "solarization," the self-sacrifice of the sun on the photographic surface. And one might similarly think of, for example, Cindy Sherman's veiled self-portraits as a kind of sacrifice, a way of finding (and so also losing) her self outside her self, playing on the edges of composition and decomposition. In speaking of these images one will need to speak of both appropriation and disappropriation, construction and deconstruction, finding no final rest in either term. It is in something like these terms that I have tried to approach the question of picturing Japan.

"Our" chance would then be to know ourselves as living within quotation marks and not thereby ceasing to live. It seems that this is in a sense also "Japan's" chance—and risk. It is asked to live between itself—refusing to find itself in the embrace of the postmodern even as it poses the possibility of a movement beyond modernism. The chance missed (by whom?) in Heidegger's "Dialogue on Language" might lie just in that moment at which Heidegger and Tezuka face a certain picture of Japan (the picture is *Rashomon*) and, through it, fail to face each other.[11] What it would take to read this moment fully is unclear to me; what strikes me in the exchange is that it turns upon an interest shared by "the Japanese" and "the Inquirer" in refusing the application of any notion of frame—and any concomitant attribution of "objectness"—to the world of Japan. What "deconstruction" could mean in such a context—what could translate it—can hardly be clear in advance of its doing, but it seems possible that it will lie more nearly in an admission of history, context, and construction than in a will to become or have been the truth of deconstruction or of postmodernism.

I have no notion whether these remarks have any interest or utility for a Japanese audience. Deconstruction, at least in America, has always been exposed to a political critique that fails to find anything serious in the ghostly logics of temporal reversal and (dis)possession it reads in its objects; one lesson of the workshop for me was a newly explicit awareness of the way deconstruction finds some of its stakes in reimagining the world, and in understanding that imagination as both submitted to and informing of what we have to learn to recognize as politics. If I have managed here to bring out something of this, I am content.

Notes

1 In view of this formulation of the question, it was interesting to me that while Professor Mitani spoke in Japanese I was able to hear a few words obviously derived from English—"discourse," "postmodern," "perspective," "focal," "interior," and "exterior." This represents a crucial nexus of terms for getting the Western project of deconstruction off the ground. What does it mean that these words in Japanese are borrowed?

2 Martin Heidegger, "A Dialogue on Language between a Japanese and an Inquirer," in *On the Way to Language*, trans. Peter D. Hertz (New York, 1971), and Jacques Derrida, "Letter to a Japanese Friend," in *Derrida and Difference*, ed. David Wood and Robert Bernasconi (Coventry, England, 1985).

3 This context cuts deep enough that Heidegger, in a rare gesture, refers to Husserl as "the master."

4 See, for example, Craig Owens, "The Discourse of Others: Feminists and Postmodernism," in *The Anti-Aesthetic: Essays on Postmodern Culture*, ed. Hal Foster (Port Townsend, 1983).

5 See the journal *October*, especially from no. 10 (1979) on.

6 Heidegger and his interlocutor are briefly and interestingly trapped in this play at a moment to which I will refer in my conclusion. It should be noted that this topic of the frame is intimately connected in Heidegger with the political or quasi-political analyses of the "world as picture" and the dominance of technology.

7 I am in general reluctant to offer any hard-and-fast distinctions between the modern and the postmodern, but the shift from a rhetoric of suicide to one of survival does seem to me an important feature of much recent art and criticism.

8 I believe Jonathan Arac also raised this question during the course of the discussions and found no response.

9 Julia Kristeva, "Women's Time," in *The Kristeva Reader*, ed. Toril Moi (New York, 1986), 211.
10 Ibid., 210–11.
11 In the West this movie is usually taken, or at least remembered, as posing epistemological riddles. This seems to me a misreading of the film, and I wonder if it is so understood in Japan.

Glossary

Japanese names are given in the Japanese order—that is, the surname precedes the personal (given) name.

Abe Kōbō (1924–   ). Writer, whose novels have emphasized a reworking of science fiction themes and life in the future. Abe is best known for his early novel translated into English and called *Woman in the Dunes.*

Dōgen (1200–1253). Buddhist monk and founder of Sōtō Zen School in Japan. Famous for one of the most philosophically sophisticated elaborations of Buddhist teaching in his work, *Shōbōgenzō* (*The Treasury of the Eye of the True Teaching*).

Doi Takeo (1920–   ). Psychoanalyst. Studied and taught at Tokyo University. One of the leading theorists of *Nihonjinron* (discourse on Japanese uniqueness). Major works in translation: *The Anatomy of Dependence* and *The Anatomy of Self.*

Edo Period. The historical period, 1600–1868, when Japan was organized according to the feudalistic *Bakuhan* system with the Tokugawa clan as the central authority (shogunate). Also called the Tokugawa period.

Etō Jun (1933–   ). Literary critic. Studied English literature at Keiō and teaches at Tokyo National Institute of Technology. One of the leading literary and political critics today, concerned about the problems of Japanese literature and U.S.-Japan relations.

Fukuzawa Yukichi (1834–1901). The leading enlightenment writer of the Meiji period and the founder of Keiō University. Introduced Western knowledge into Meiji Japan and argued consistently for Japan's need to Westernize. Major works in translation: *An Encouragement of Learning* and *An Outline of a Theory of Civilization.*

Hakone Conference. An international conference on Japan's modernization, held in Hakone outside Tokyo in 1960. Mainly two different views of Japan's modernization were presented. American participants, many of whom based their argument on "modernization theory," put forth a positive vision of modern Japan against Japanese participants who tended to regard modernization as a process of historical praxis involving many social conflicts.

Hamaguchi Ryūichi (1916–). Architect and critic. Editor of *Hyumanizumu no kenchiku* (*Humanist Architecture*), which advocated functionalism presumably mediated by a version of humanism. Wrote *A Cross Section of Contemporary Architecture*.

Haniya Yutaka (1910–). Novelist, critic, and former member of the Japan Communist party in the 1930s who recanted. His most represented work is titled *Shiryo* (*Departed Spirits*).

Hara Tamiki (1905–51). Novelist injured in the atomic destruction of Hiroshima who wrote about this experience in a work titled *Natsu no hana* (*Flowers of Summer*). The work ranks with Ibuse Masuji's more familiar and translated novel *Black Rain*. Hara committed suicide in 1951.

Hotta Yoshie (1918–). Prize-winning novelist for *Hiroba no kodoku* (*Isolation in a Public Place*) and critic and scholar of medieval Japanese literature.

Ishida Takeshi (1923–). Studied and taught political science at Tokyo. His analysis of modern Japanese politics is well-known.

Kamei Katsuichirō (1907–1966). Literary critic and historian. Studied aesthetics at Tokyo and was involved in Marxism. Changed his political stance in the early 1930s and joined *Nihon romanha* (Japanese Romantics School). After the war, as a critic of Marxist historiography, wrote extensively on Japanese aesthetics and tradition.

Katō Hiroyuki (1836–1916). Originally a scholar of Western studies working for the Tokugawa shogunate. After the Meiji restoration (1868), he worked for the government as one of the leading enlightenment intellectuals. Contributed much to the establishment of the modern educational system. The first president of Tokyo Imperial University (today's Tokyo University). Major works include *A New Treatise on Human Rights*, which is based on social Darwinism.

Kim Chi Ha. Korean poet who was active in the student movement of the 1960s in Korea and played an important role in the democratic movement.

Kimura Bin (1931–). Psychopathologist. Studied and teaches at

Kyoto. His psychopathological and existential analysis of the
Japanese "ego" is famous. A leading theorist of *Nihonjinron* (discourse on Japanese uniqueness).

Kitamura Tōkoku (1868–1894). Writer, essayist, and poet of the
Menji period. Admirer of romanticism and writers like Hugo and
Emerson. Committed suicide at the age of twenty-five, despairing
Japan's turn away from political liberalism and considerations of
the spirit for authoritarianism and material development.

Kobayashi Hideo (1905–1983). Probably the most important literary critic in modern Japan. Studied French literature at Tokyo.
Adopting much from his reading of French symbolism, established a new literary genre of "criticism" and attempted to place
Japanese literature within a wide intellectual perspective. His
reading includes: Valéry, Dostoyevski, Marx, Bergson, quantum
mechanics, Western and Japanese visual arts, and Japanese classics.

Kōsaka Masaaki (1900–1969). Philosopher and political commentator. Studied under Nishida Kitarō and taught at Kyoto. A core
member of the prewar Kyoto School and theorist for the "Great
East Asian Coprosperity Sphere." After the war, argued for the
U.S.-Japan security treaty and worked closely with the ministry
of education.

Kōyama Iwao (1905–   ). Philosopher and political commentator.
Studied under Nishida Kitarō and taught at Kyoto. A core
member of the prewar Kyoto School and theorist for the "Great
East Asian Coprosperity Sphere." After the war, he attempted to
construct the metaphysical grounds for the U.S.-Japan security
treaty. Active in education.

Kuki Shūzō (1888–1941). Studied at Tokyo, Heidelberg, Marburg,
and Sorbonne, and taught with Nishida Kitarō and Tanabe Hajime (1882–1962) at Kyoto. Adopting certain aspects of Heideggerean existential analysis, conducted the philosophical analysis
of Japanese aesthetics (the structure of *iki*) and temporality.

Kyoto School. During the 1920s and 1930s, Kyoto University's philosophy department attracted many young intellectuals from all over
the country mostly because of the theoretical achievement of
Nishida Kitarō. Those intellectuals who studied at Kyoto around

that time formed a vaguely defined group which was called the Kyoto School. Recently, some intellectuals who are in one way or another affiliated with Kyoto University are active in the current policies of internationalizing Japan. They are sometimes called the New Kyoto School.

Lu Xun or Lu Hsun (1881–1936). Chinese novelist, literary critic, and scholar. Studied medicine in Japan, and switched to literature. It is often claimed that he is the most important literary figure of modern China. Wrote critically about Chinese society, Western and Japanese imperialism. Introduced literature by East European minority groups to China. Many of his works available in translation.

Maekawa Kunio (1905–1986). Architect. Studied under Le Corbusier. One of the earliest promoters of Japan's modern architectural movement. Designed the Tokyo Cultural Hall and the Tokyo Hall.

Maruyama Masao (1914–   ). Political scientist. The leading writer of postwar Japan. Studied and taught at Tokyo. Wrote about Tokugawa intellectual history (*Studies in the Intellectual History of Tokugawa Japan*), Japanese fascism (*Thought and Behaviour in Modern Japanese Politics*), and the possibilities of democracy in Japan. Strongly opposed to the U.S.-Japan security treaty in 1960.

Meiji Period. The period of the Emperor Meiji's reign (1868–1912) when Japan was transformed into a modern industrialized nation-state.

Mishima Yukio (1925–1970). Novelist. Studied law at Tokyo. A leading novelist and playwright in postwar Japan. Because of his literary talent, chauvinism, and reversed Orientalism, became the best known Japanese writer outside Japan. Committed a ritualistic suicide in 1970. *Confessions of a Mask*, *The Temple of the Golden Pavilion*, and many other works available in translation.

Miyazawa Kenji (1896–1933). One of Japan's foremost poets of the prewar years whose imagery and themes often revealed Buddhist sentiments.

Murakami Haruki (1949–   ). Writer, concerned with the spirit of contemporary Japanese youth, whose *Forests of Norway* was a runaway best-seller.

Murakami Yasusuke (1931–   ). Economist. Studied and teaches at

Tokyo. Participates in the making of social and political policies based on the notion of *ie* as a member of the advisory board to the prime minister.

Murano Tōgō (1891–1985). Western-Japan (*kansai*) architect. Remaining outside the modernist main currents, he is known for craftsmanlike details and energetic originality.

Nakamura Yūjirō (1925–). Philosopher. Studied at Tokyo and teaches at Meiji. Argues for the importance of emotion and pathos in terms of common sense and *isshokuta* (synthesis of many into one).

Nakane Chie (1926–). Social anthropologist. Studied at Tokyo and London and taught at Tokyo. Summarizing the works of prewar Japanese ethnographers, projected a vision of Japanese society that is free of social conflicts (*Japanese Society*) and contributed to the *Nihonjinron* (discourse on Japanese uniqueness). Participates in the making of social and cultural policies as a member of the advisory committee to the prime minister.

Natsume Sōseki (1867–1916). The leading novelist of modern Japan. Studied and taught English literature at Tokyo. Resigned from the professorship and became professional writer. Depicted the dark sides of modern Japanese society. *I Am a Cat, Light and Darkness*, and other works available in translation.

Nishida Kitarō (1870–1945). The leading philosopher of modern Japan. Studied at Tokyo and taught at Kyoto. Based on his critical reading of Bergson, James, Kant, Leibniz, neo-Kantians, Husserl, Aristotle, Hegel, and Marx, attempted to criticize the concept of consciousness, put forth theories of subjectivity and knowledge, and established a new philosophical logic of *basho* (place or Platonic *chora*) in order to question the relationship between knowing and action. Some of his followers formed the Kyoto School. *A Study of Good* and other works available in translation.

Nishiyama Uzo (1911–). Scholar of architectural design. He analyzed the relations between social forms and architectural designs and criticized both modernism and traditionalism.

Nogi Maresuke (1849–1912). Army general. Famous for his role during the Russo-Japanese war (1904–1905). Committed suicide, following the death of the Emperor Meiji.

Noguchi Takehiko (1937–). Literary critic and historian. Studied at Waseda and Tokyo and teaches at Kobe. Writes extensively about Japanese literature and Tokugawa Confucianism.

Noma Hiroshi (1915–). Postwar novelist and critic known for his account of the war, *Shinkuchitai* (*Zone of Emptiness*).

Ōkawa Shūmei (1886–1957). Nationalist activist and writer. Studied Indian civilization and British colonialism. Attempted to formulate theories for the emancipation of Asian peoples in national socialist terms. Arrested as a war criminal for his collaboration with Japanese colonialism in China, but released on the grounds of insanity.

Ōoka Shōhei (1909–1988). Postwar Japan's most celebrated antiwar novelist whose novel *Nobi* (*Fires on the Plain*) has been translated into several languages, including English, and made into an enduring film.

Sei Shōnagon (ca. 966–ca. 1027). A classic, *Makura no sōshi* (*The Pillow Book*), an anthology of short poetic essays, is attributed to this female writer of the Heian period (794–1185).

Shiina Rinzō (1917–1973). Writer and former member of the Communist party. Best-known works are *Shinya no shuen* (*Banquet in the Dead of Night*) and *Jiyū no kanatade* (*Beyond Freedom*).

Shimao Toshio (1917–1986). Writer of novels who also recorded his wartime experience in a special assault force.

Shutai. Japanese term for "subject." In modern Japanese intellectual discourse, the term "subject" is translated into: "shugo" for grammatical or propositional subject; "shukan" for epistemological subject; "shudai" for thematic subject; and "shutai" for the subject of acting, sometimes implying the body that initiates or leads the action. These differentiations, however, are not stable and, to define the interrelations among those four "subjects," leads to the not linguistically but philosophically complicated problems about subjectivity. It may be no accident that modern Japanese intellectuals have been very much concerned about the problems of subjectivity.

Suzuki Shigetaka (1907–). Historian. A core member of the prewar Kyoto School. Studied European history at Kyoto. Ideologue for the "Great East Asian Coprosperity Sphere."

Takeda Taijun (1912–1976). Writer and active participant during the student movement.

Takegoshi Kenzo (1888–1981). Western-Japan (*kansai*) architect who enjoyed the patronage of the Osaka financial world.

Takeuchi Yoshimi (1910–1977). Critic and sinologist. Studied Chinese literature at Tokyo. During the war (1930–1945), organized the *Chūgoku bungaku kenkyūkai* (Chinese Literature Study Group) with Takeda Taijun (1912–1976), a leading novelist in postwar Japan, and others, and resisted the state's war effort and the idea of the "Great East Asian Coprosperity Sphere." Also during the war, came across the works of Chinese writer Lu Xun. After the war, continued to study and translate his works and write about the war responsibility of Japanese intellectuals. Strongly opposed to the U.S.-Japan security treaty in 1960.

Tanaka Kakuei (1918–). Politician. Active as the most financially influencial member of the Liberal Democratic party until a few years ago. Prime minister (1972–1974). Arrested for his involvement in a bribery case (Lockheed scandal).

Tange Kenzō (1913–). Postwar Japan's premier architect who is best known for his work on the Tokyo Olympics (1964) and the International Exposition of Osaka (1970). The most representative and influential of the modernist architects of Japan, he also designed the new offices of the metropolitan government of Tokyo, scheduled to be completed in 1990.

Tanizaki Jun'ichirō (1886–1965). Novelist who has possibly been most widely studied outside Japan. Studied at Tokyo and led a very prolific literary career. Many of his works available in translation: *The Makioka Sisters, The Key,* and others.

Tokieda Motoki (1900–1967). Linguist. Studied and taught at Tokyo. Criticizing the ethnocentric bias of nineteenth-century European linguistics, tried to construct a theory of language (language process theory) based on phenomenology and premodern language studies of Japan.

Tokugawa. The name of the clan or domainal family that held the shogunate and ruled over other domains during the Edo period (1600–1868). Hence, the Edo period is also called the Tokugawa period.

Tōyama Shigeki (1914–). Historian. Studied at Tokyo and inherited from the 1930s the incomplete project of writing the history of Japan in Marxist terms. His study of the Meiji restoration is well-known.

Tsubouchi Shōyō (1859–1934). One of the founders of the modern novel in Japan who wrote the first study of literary criticism.

Uchimura Kanzō (1861–1930). Christian writer and activist. Studied Christian theology in the United States (Amherst and Hartford). Criticizing the colonialist attitude of Christian missionaries, founded a rather nationalistic Christianity for and by the Japanese, and organized *Mu-kyōkai* (churchless church), which criticized hierarchical order both in churches and the Japanese state. Wrote extensively both in Japanese and English, including *How I Became a Christian* and *Japan and the Japanese*.

Umezaki Haruo (1915–1965). Writer who recorded the experience of the war. Best known for his novel *Sakurajima* (*Cherryblossom Island*).

Watanabe Setsu (1884–1962). Influential architect of western-Japan (*kansai*) who enjoyed the financial backing of the Osaka business world.

Watsuji Tetsurō (1889–1960). Philosopher. Studied at Tokyo and taught at Kyoto and Tokyo. Applied Heideggerean hermeneutics to the typological study of Japanese culture and tried to build a philosophical theory of ethics in terms of *aida*, human relationality. Has been quoted by many of the *Nihonjinron* writers. His studies range from Kierkegaard, Italian Renaissance, and Buddhism to theatrical arts.

Yamaguchi Masao (1931–). Symbolic anthropologist who has been responsible for introducing structuralist and post-structuralist strategies into contemporary Japan. Most of his work still remains in Japanese and has concentrated on showing the function of the outsider in Japanese society.

Yasui Takeo (1884–1955). Architect who established the leading style for office buildings. A member of Osaka Club.

Yoshimoto Takaaki (1924–). Poet and leading literary critic. Studied chemistry at Tokyo National Institute of Technology. Attempted to construct Marxist theory to deal with the relationship between the collective imaginary and literary language. Criticized those intellectuals who collaborated with the state during the war. Tends to be rather communalistic.

Notes on Contributors

Japanese names are given in the Japanese order—that is, the surname precedes the personal (given) name. The names of Japanese Americans, however, follow the usual American practice.

ASADA AKIRA is an Assistant Professor at the Research Institute for Economics, Kyoto University, and the author of *Kozo to chikara* (*Structure and Power*) (1983).

BRETT DE BARY is Associate Professor of Japanese Literature in the Department of Asian Studies at Cornell University. Her criticism and translations in the area of modern Japanese studies, particularly postwar fiction, include *Three Works by Nakano Shigeharu* (1979).

NORMA FIELD is Associate Professor in the Department of East Asian Languages and Civilizations at the University of Chicago, where she teaches courses on Japanese literature. Her publications include *The Splendor of Longing in the Tale of Genji* (1987) and a translation of Natsume Sōseki's novel *Sorekara* (*And Then*, 1978).

H. D. HAROOTUNIAN teaches in the Departments of History and East Asian Languages and Civilizations at the University of Chicago. His most current research on Japanese nativism has been published by the University of Chicago Press, 1988, and is called *Things Seen and Unseen*.

ISOZAKI ARATA is an architect among whose best known buildings are the Museum of Contemporary Art in Los Angeles as well as the Tsukuba Center Building. He is currently at work on an art museum in Nice, France, a museum of Egyptian culture in Cairo, and a stadium for the 1992 Olympics in Barcelona.

MARILYN IVY, recently a postdoctoral fellow at the Reischauer Institute at Harvard University, is currently an Assistant Professor of Anthropology at the University of Chicago.

KARATANI KŌJIN is a Professor of Literature at Hosei University and the author of *Marukusu sono kanosei no chushin* (*The Center of the Possibilities for Marxism*), *Nihon kindai bungaku no kigen* (*The Origins of Japanese Modern Literature*) (1980), among numerous other publications.

J. VICTOR KOSCHMANN is Associate Professor of Japanese History at Cornell University, specializing in modern Japanese intellectual history. He is the author of *The Mito Ideology: Discourse, Reform and Insurrection in Late Tokugawa Japan, 1790–1864* (1987).

STEPHEN MELVILLE is Associate Professor of English at Syracuse University and author of *Philosophy beside Itself: On Deconstruction and Modernism.*

MASAO MIYOSHI is Hajime Mori Professor of Japanese, English, and Comparative Literature at the University of California, San Diego, and is currently at work on a book, *Colonialism and the Shape of the Novel.*

TETSUO NAJITA is Robert S. Ingersoll Distinguished Service Professor of Japanese Studies at the University of Chicago. He is the author of *Visions of Virtue in Tokugawa Japan* (1987).

ŌE KENZABURŌ is a novelist and critic. Among his works already translated into English and other languages are *A Personal Matter, The Silent Cry,* and *Hiroshima Notes.* His most recent novels, *Wakai hitoyo mezameyo* and *Natsukashii toshi eno tegami* are being translated into English.

NAOKI SAKAI, Assistant Professor in the Department of Asian Studies at Cornell University, has written about philosophy, Japanese intellectual history, and Japanese linguistics. He is currently working on a book on the problems of verbal and visual texts.

ALAN WOLFE is Assistant Professor of Japanese and teaches in the Comparative Literature Program at the University of Oregon. He is working on a book, *Suicidal Deconstruction: Dazai Osamu and the Dilemma of Modern Japanese Literature.*

Index

Library of Congress
Cataloging-in-Publication Data

Postmodernism and Japan / edited by Masao
  Miyoshi and H.D. Harootunian.
      p.   cm. — (Post-contemporary
  interventions)
    ISBN 0-8223-0779-0. — ISBN 0-8223-0896-7
  (pbk.)
    1. Japan—Civilization—1945– . 2. Post-
  modernism—Japan. I. Miyoshi, Masao.
  II. Harootunian, Harry D., 1929– .
  DS822.5.P62 1989
  952.04—dc 19   89-7709
                                            CIP